Catholic Social Thought

This series focuses on Catholic social thought and its application to current social, political, economic, and cultural issues. The titles in this series are written and edited by members of the Society of Catholic Social Scientists. They survey and analyze Catholic approaches to politics, sociology, law, economics, history, and other disciplines. Within these broad themes, authors explore the Church's role and influence in contemporary society.

The Society of Catholic Social Scientists was formed in 1992 to rejuvenate a distinctively Catholic scholarship in the social sciences.

1. *The Public Order and the Sacred Order*, by Stephen M. Krason, 2009.
2. *Bioethics, Law, and Human Life Issues*, by D. Brian Scarnecchia, 2010.
3. *Pope Pius XII on the Economic Order*, by Rupert J. Ederer, 2011.
4. *Economics As If God Matters*, by Rupert J. Ederer, 2011.

Economics As If God Matters

More Than a Century of Papal Teaching

Expanded and Revised Edition

Rupert J. Ederer

Catholic Social Thought, No. 4

THE SCARECROW PRESS, INC.
Lanham • Toronto • Plymouth, UK
2011

Published by Scarecrow Press, Inc.
A wholly owned subsidiary of The Rowman & Littlefield Publishing Group, Inc.
4501 Forbes Boulevard, Suite 200, Lanham, Maryland 20706
http://www.scarecrowpress.com

Estover Road, Plymouth PL6 7PY, United Kingdom

British Library Cataloguing in Publication Information Available

Library of Congress Cataloging-in-Publication Data

Ederer, Rupert J.
Economics as if God matters : more than a century of papal teaching / Rupert J. Ederer. — Expanded and rev. ed.
p. cm. — (Catholic social thought ; no. 4)
Includes bibliographical (p.) references and index.
ISBN 978-0-8108-7798-6 (hardcover : alk. paper)
1. Economics—Religious aspects—Catholic Church—History of doctrines. 2. Encyclicals, Papal—History and criticism. I. Title.
BX1795.E27E33 2011
261.8'5088282—dc22 2010052903

™ The paper used in this publication meets the minimum requirements of American National Standard for Information Sciences—Permanence of Paper for Printed Library Materials, ANSI/NISO Z39.48-1992.

Printed in the United States of America

*This work is dedicated to Blessed John Paul II, the Pope of Solidarity,
with gratitude for his courageous service to the Catholic Church
in a time of great tribulation*

For too long has the name of God been either totally excluded from scientific discussion, or it has at best been mentioned with a certain reticence or with tongue-in-cheek. Actually, this most holy name should be professed before the whole world, so that at least where God's dominion is acknowledged and where divine moral law is regarded with reverence, the true common good of nations can find a secure safeguard and a powerful affirmation. The practical application of a divine moral law whose norms are unchangeable does not deprive morality, as science today understands it, of a firm basis. On the contrary, it reaffirms respect for what tradition has provided thus far, and for what has already been accomplished in our science. In addition, it alone secures for the highest social norms the stability, the constancy, and the universal validity, which a merely historical and human tradition would never be able to provide.

Heinrich Pesch, S J. (1854-1926)
Lehrbuch der Nationalökonomie
Volume I, 1924

Contents

Citation and Documentation for Papal Encyclicals

Papal encyclicals are published with numbered paragraphs so as to standardize references to content even in differing editions or translations. Consequently, documentation of text references in critical analyses of encyclicals takes the form of paragraph numbers in parentheses after the quote or paraphrase of a text passage. Numbers in parentheses in the text—with no further elaboration—refer to paragraphs in the texts of the encyclical that is the subject of each chapter.

Foreword

Dr. Rupert J. Ederer has for decades been one of America's premier Catholic economists. Since the inception of the Society of Catholic Social Scientists (SCCS), he has served as a trusted member of the Board of Advisors and we were privileged in 1977 to bestow on him our annual Pope Pius XI Award for Contributions toward the Building Up of a True Catholic Social Science. His long-time work in making the social teachings of the Church better known and understood in the U. S—where they have perhaps been the best-kept secret—and in translating and promulgating the work of such pioneers in developing modern Catholic social thought on economics as Bishop Wilhelm Emmanuel von Ketteler and Father Heinrich Pesch, S. J. has been remarkable and admirable. He has been distinguished for all aspects of the Church's social teaching; he has faithfully represented all that the popes have put forth in their many social encyclicals. More impressively, he has strongly and consistently defended the entirety of that teaching, without downplaying or dismissing parts of it for ideological reasons. In that sense, his work has been clearly in the spirit of the SCSS: to present and uphold the Church's social teaching fully and without compromise.

What Dr. Ederer has done in this book reflects this latter spirit and is an extension of his career-long effort. He examines in detail each of the major encyclicals of the Church that have dealt with economic questions (it is a one-hundred-twenty year corpus of teaching beginning with Pope Leo XIII's *Rerum Novarum*). There is a chapter devoted to each one, with citations to the pertinent section of the encyclical covering the points under discussion. He considers the teaching and major points of each encyclical, and how the respective pope builds on the teachings of his predecessors and addresses new socio-economic questions that have emerged. An earlier version of this book was published in 1995. He has revised and expanded that and included a discussion and analysis of Pope Benedict XVI's first social encyclical, *Caritas in Veritate*. There is probably no other book like this in print. Unlike so many books that summarize the various encyclicals, Dr. Ederer provides detailed but manageable explications. As such, this book is at the same time useful as: a classroom text for college use; a secondary source for students, scholars, and writers to turn to for information about the content of the various social encyclicals (indeed, it so carefully presents the content, part by part of each encyclical, that it is almost a translation of the document); and a book to be used by parish and other study groups on the social encyclical. The focus of the book, of course, is on the efforts by the popes to bring the Church's teaching to bear on economic questions; this has been the major focus of the social encyclicals. As an economist, Dr. Ederer is able to explain well certain economic principles, and ideas that come up or stand behind different points raised in the texts of the documents, and this enables the reader to gain a better and fuller understanding. He also gives useful historical information about the encyclicals and their historical context and influences, and also occasional commentary that helps to show the contrasts between Catholic moral principles regarding economics and the way that economic affairs are often carried out in modern life. He explains the points in the encyclicals that are moral imperatives (i.e., which are interpretations/applications of natural law and that no one is free to reject) and those that are simply recommendations and proposals. He also provides a helpful index.

The Church embraces no one school of economic thought or socio-politico-economic perspective. As Pope John Paul II said, she provides no programs and her social teaching belongs to the realm of moral theology, not ideology (*Sollicitudo Rei Socialis* #41). It is evident from Dr. Ederer's presentation of the teachings of the encyclicals that many perspectives are compatible with her social teaching, some are only partly so, and others are hardly or not at all. Throughout the history of the modern social teachings of the Church we have seen that many people—regrettably, even many Catholics—ignore or remain oblivious to the Church's social teachings. Some even claim that it addresses matters outside her competence, or else try to twist the teachings to fit them into a pre-determined ideological framework. While economics certainly concerns the here-and-now, it is hardly disconnected from man's ultimate end, the hereafter. That is seen vividly when one considers that among the sins that cry to heaven for vengeance are the oppression of the poor and defrauding the worker of his just wages. Unlike so many modern economic thinkers and the philosophers who provide the basis for their thought, Dr. Ederer and the Church hold squarely that economics is fundamentally a moral science. Catholicism is not an overly spiritualized religion. While man's highest end is a spiritual one, he is rightly body and soul and the two are complementary. The often mundane-seeming matters of economics can have a profound effect on man's spiritual good. The Church realizes that something as basic as the question of the possession of material goods has a direct effect on man morally and hence spiritually (e.g., men are often driven away from their focus on God, for different reasons, if they have either an overabundance of material wherewithal or an extreme insufficiency). She also understands how men are led to many moral evils in other realms (e.g., revolutions and upheavals in politics, various kinds of crime) if the moral ordering of their economic lives is deficient. At bottom, while wealth creation, profit, economic growth, etc. are appropriate objectives for economic activity, economics is for man and not man for economics. Thus, the various types of justice and social charity must shape it and always guide it, so that preserving and furthering human dignity is the prime objective. That has been the essence of the Church's social teaching about economic matters. Pope John Paul II explained that the Church teaches about how man should act in his economic affairs because, while she has no technical solutions, she is "an expert in humanity" (*Sollicitudo Rei Socialis* #7). As an expert in humanity she knows human nature and realizes—from Revelation that has been entrusted to her and sound philosophical principles fully in conformity with it—the kind of conduct and way of life that is necessary to perfect it. That is why Pope John Paul II insisted, "It is necessary that Christians…conform their behaviour in economic and social affairs to the teachings of the Church."

Hence, Dr. Ederer has aptly entitled his book, *Economics As If God Matters.* The fact is that God *does* matter—in the final analysis, more centrally than anything else in economic life—and so man needs to know what it is that God expects of him. That is what the social encyclical tradition—and the entire history of Catholic social teaching rooted in the Gospels—has sought to convey to man. Christ, the Savior of mankind, bequeathed to the Church's Magisterium the authority to teach the moral principles and practices that man must follow in economic affairs and other human endeavors to insure that he goes through the door of eternal life that Christ opened for him.

To the extent that Dr. Ederer has worked to make the social encyclicals—the main vehicle for promulgating the Church's social teaching in the modern world—more accessible and comprehensible for Christians and other men of good will in this book, he has done an invaluable service. The Society of Catholic Social Scientists is honored to cooperate with him in this effort and to have this book included among the hopefully many volumes that will follow in the SCSS/Scarecrow Press Catholic Social Thought series.

Stephen M. Krason, J.D., Ph.D.
President, Society of Catholic Social Scientists
July 22, 2010 (Feast of St. Mary Magdalen)

Preface

Among many of the Catholic Church's faithful in the United States, what are known as Catholic social teachings unfortunately appear to have receded in importance, especially in the years since the Second Vatican Council. Amid the whirlwind of controversies which followed that Council, regarding ecclesiastical matters ranging from liturgical changes to serious disciplinary issues, and even to crucial doctrinal interpretations and misinterpretations, the century-old efforts by the Church to address the so-called "social question" have been somehow downgraded as being of lesser urgency, in the minds of even stalwart Catholics who take their Faith seriously.

The magisterial Church, on the other hand, has never ceased to continue adding to and developing further its body of modern social teachings. For the Roman Catholic Church, all of its doctrines represent a "seamless garment" which is not to be treated as if it were made up of separable segments. Indeed, it is the opinion of the author that no part of Catholicism is more relevant to the present condition in American society and in the world than the social teachings as presented in papal encyclicals since those of Leo XIII, and among the documents of the Second Vatican Council. Those teachings are antidotal precisely at the present point in our history for dealing with a degenerate social philosophy which is leading our nation toward disaster—a disaster engulfing now not only the economy, but also the political order, and the mainstay of all of society—the family.

The dramatic disintegration of the Soviet Empire has deprived the long-time, rival, surviving liberal-capitalist social system of its foil. There is what may be unwelcome irony in the fact that the socialist thing was, in a certain sense, a voice of conscience for liberal capitalism as it has gradually metamorphosed to its present collapse. Many of the recent generation of social scientists were forced to concede, even if reluctantly, that Marxism, for all of its inconsistencies and malice, was correct in accentuating certain grave shortcomings of historical capitalism.

As for those parts of the modern world where socialism actually became a grim reality, the demise of the systems ensouled by it left its victims groping about as if in an ideological vacuum for something to replace it. While it is the business of the laity, not of popes and churchmen, to devise economic systems and ideologies, the latter are entitled to provide moral guidelines and principles on which such ideologies and systems may be based. That is especially so since the faithful are hurting so badly from the fallacies of failed and failing social ideologies and the systems which are more or less based on them. Indeed, at present there appears to be no limit to the extent of the outrageous injustice which those are willing to perpetrate against their fellow human beings, who triumphantly champion an economic philosophy that provided the fertile seedbed for Karl Marx and his disastrous, counter-proposed remedy in the first place.

It is the opinion of this writer that, far from being passé, now is a golden hour for social scientists, economists, and politicians to acquaint themselves with Catholic social teachings. They offer hope for replacing systems which have failed mankind miserably over the past several centuries. The great Pope John Paul II in his post-synodal Apostolic Exhortation *Ecclesia in America,* delivered in 1999, urged all "agents of evangelization to make their own this treasure which is the Church's social teaching." At the same time Stephen M. Krason, the President of the distinguished Society of Catholic Social Scientists, has characterized Catholic social teaching as "one of the best-kept secrets in America." In any case, it appears as though the Church's body of social teachings was never more timely and relevant than at the present. These need to be studied, and applied in reshaping the social order for this new millennium. In the light of the most recent social encyclical by Pope Benedict XVI, the urgency for such action is now more than ever before worldwide in scope.

This book is intended to generate some renewed interest in the study of those teachings as addressed specifically to the economic order, by pointing out their applicability to the concrete, historical circumstances amid which we are now living. A commentary on nine papal encyclicals, it is clearly not a substitute for studying the documents themselves. *Economics As If God Matters* is written instead with a prayer that it will inspire persons to read, or to reread, and to study the encyclicals. The author's observations are clearly not magisterial. They represent his own reflections and views developed over an academic lifetime of studying these materials. Some of the proposals made by the popes who wrote the encyclicals are prudential and advisory. However, when Roman Catholic popes, in addressing the entire Church, pronounce on matters of morality, e.g., justice and charity such pronouncements, in the opinion of this writer, constitute a part of the ordinary magisterium of that Church.

I esteem highly and am grateful to the popes who have been the great strength of the Catholic Church, especially over the past century. It is difficult to fault these men for falling short either in their conduct or in the exercise of their teaching authority during what has turned out to be one of the most turbulent eras in world history! I thank God for them and for the special legacy of their social teachings.

Acknowledgments

I am indebted to many persons who were helpful and instrumental in various ways for the inspiration and preparation of this work for publication. These include especially Dr. Stephen Krason, President and Founder of the Society of Catholic Social Scientists, for his careful editing of my manuscript, and many valuable suggestions. It was he who presented this work to Scarecrow Press as meriting publication.

My sincere thanks to Dr. E. Michael Jones for extending permission for the republication of this work in its revised and enlarged edition. As editor of Fidelity Press in South Bend, Indiana, he published the first edition of *Economics As If God Matters* in 1995.

Beyond that, special thanks are in order to persons spanning the generations from my parents, the late John and Frances Ederer, to my son, Dr. Martin F. Ederer.

It was my parents who aroused my early interest in the interplay—and often clashes—between rival social, economic and political ideals and visions. When I came of age, they told me stories about such struggles that had become all too common in my native Munich at the time I was born there in 1923. They also told of the perilous encounters Eugenio Pacelli, Papal Nuncio to Bavaria, and then to all of Germany, faced with both the Communists and the Nazis as they were vying for control of Bavaria, and ultimately, all of Germany during those troubled years. My family left Munich for America in 1926. Cardinal Eugenio Pacelli went on, of course, to become Pope Pius XII.

My son, Dr. Martin Ederer is already of the cybernetic generation. His computer skills far exceed those of his father who was never that good even with the old-fashioned typewriter or, for that matter, with pen and ink. His help during my very senior years was indispensable for getting my manuscripts publication-ready.

Introduction
Economics As If God Matters

1991 was hailed widely as the 100th anniversary of papal social teachings. Actually, it marked only the centenary of those teachings addressed specifically to the economic order. What appeared in 1891 was *Rerum Novarum,* the social encyclical which came to be perhaps the best known and most widely studied. It was preceded by several others which also came to grips with the "spirit of revolutionary change," the contextual translation of two Latin words, *rerum novarum.* Literally those words translate to "of new things." The English title for the encyclical is some variant of *On the Condition of Labor*, referring to the circumstances in which the working class found itself during the century following the Industrial Revolution.

The very first encyclical by the brilliant Pope Leo XIII, *Inscrutabili Dei Consilio*, was issued in the first year of his pontificate, 1878. Given its usual English title, *On the Evils of Society,* it may properly be regarded as launching modern papal social teachings. *Inscrutabili* was followed in the same year by *Quod Apostolici Muneris*, the first encyclical addressed to socialism which was then still just a theory.

The distinguished philosopher, Etienne Gilson, served as editor and commentator for a work entitled *The Church Speaks to the Modern World,* first published in 1954. It bore the subtitle *The Social Teachings of Leo XIII*, and it included twelve encyclicals by that pope addressed in varying ways to the "new things" which were reshaping Western culture.

It was appropriate that a philosopher provided the commentary for those encyclicals, since they were addressed basically to problems stemming from the direction in which philosophy moved during the period known as the Enlightenment. Given the way in which that philosophical orientation altered thought, it was responsible to a large degree for shaping the post-Christian culture emanating from the period of the French Revolution and beyond. Together, these revolutions—in thought and on the ramparts—restructured the social order of the modern world, specifically in its political and economic aspects.

It is the purpose of this book to now provide an economist's updated commentary on the papal social teachings addressed to the economic order over the period commencing with 1891. Inasmuch as the economic order reflects economic philosophies, which, in turn, mirror the basic philosophies, indeed also the theologies, that shape the thoughts and actions of human beings in given time frames, allusions to underlying philosophical aspects are inevitable. Also, as Gilson deemed it legitimate to consider a wide-ranging series of encyclicals (*On Socialism, On Christian Philosophy, On Human Liberty, On Civil Government, On Christian Democracy*) as a *corpus*—a body—of doctrine,[1] we consider that the papal documents on the economic order also comprise such a body of doctrine. Each builds on the previous ones, so that we have here indeed a kind of organic development of doctrine, in the sense that principles common to all social encyclicals, including the first, persist throughout; and they come to be explicated further and applied to the changing historical context.

The entire *corpus* now includes the following: *Rerum Novarum (On the Condition of Labor*), 1891 (Leo XIII); *Quadragesimo Anno* (*Reconstructing the Social Order*), 1931 (Pius XI); *Mater et Magistra* (*Christianity and Social Progress*), 1961 (Blessed John XXIII); *Populorum Progressio* (*The Development of Peoples*), 1967 (Paul VI); *Laborem Exercens* (*On Human Work*), 1981 (John Paul II); *Sollicitudo Rei Socialis* (*On Social Concern*), 1987 (John Paul II); *Centesimus Annus* (*The Hundredth Year*), 1991 (John Paul II). This new and revised edition now includes also *Caritas in Veritate* (*On Integral Human Development in Charity and Truth*), 2009 (Benedict XVI).

There are references to other papal and Church pronouncements on matters relating to the economic order only where these are pertinent and provide further elucidation of matter under discussion. Thus, while the encyclical *Divini Redemptoris* (*On Atheistic Communism*) issued by Pius XI in 1937 extends well beyond simply economic considerations, it does contain some significant references to matters addressed in other encyclicals discussed here. The same is true of *Octogesima Adveniens* (*The Coming Eightieth*) issued as an Apostolic Letter by Paul VI in 1971. Even though it specifically commemorates the 80th anniversary of *Rerum Novarum,* this document ranges over a broad spectrum of social issues like urbanization, youth, and the role of women. Yet there are significant insights dealing with the economic order.

Vatican Council II, which involved the bishops of the Roman Catholic Church worldwide, including the bishop of Rome who is also the visible head of that Church on earth, is not treated separately here. The *Pastoral Constitution on the Church in the Modern World* (*Gaudium et Spes*) which appeared in 1965 includes discussion of the economic order, but it also goes well beyond that to include also the family and the political order.[2] In this commentator's opinion it synopsizes in abbreviated form what popes have had to say previously on the economic order, without adding anything substantive to the contents of social encyclicals prior to the Council.

That all encyclicals addressed to the economic order, even the pioneer one, *Rerum Novarum,* are still relevant and not simply superceded by later ones becomes clear if we reflect that significant elements in that encyclical are even now not fully comprehended and accepted over a century later! For that reason, we shall begin with the first modern social encyclical addressed specifically to the economic order.

Social teachings by popes suffer from certain handicaps which limit their acceptance, or their being taken seriously even among members of the Catholic Church. Papal encyclicals addressed to the economic order have, from the start, always encountered the objection that a pope is beyond his proper jurisdiction, or even out of his depth, when he deals with such matters. What is more, that criticism has been leveled ever since *Rerum Novarum* appeared by various critics whose ideologies are opposed to each other as well as to the papal position. The proper sphere of operation for popes, bishops, and church councils is supposedly limited to purely dogmatic matters and, in the realm of morality, to specific issues like sexuality.

That theft is a moral issue, and that the moral virtues, justice and charity, which have a special urgent social dimension, are clearly within the jurisdiction of a teaching Church, should be immediately apparent. The great and popular John XXIII made this clear in *Mater et Magistra* where he stated that, "What the Catholic Church teaches and declares regarding the social life and relationships of men is beyond question for all time valid" (218). He added: "Above all, we affirm that the social teaching proclaimed by the Catholic Church cannot be separated from her traditional teaching regarding man's life" (222). Pope John Paul II corroborated that in *Sollicitudo Rei Socialis* where he declared that *"solidarity* is undoubtedly a *Christian virtue"* (40). Given that it is a Christian virtue, and that it is therefore, along with other virtues like social justice and social charity, crucial for a correct social order, the Pope felt justified in adding that the Church's social doctrine "belongs to the field, not of ideology, but of theology and particularly of moral theology." What is more, "The teaching and spreading of her social doctrine are part of the Church's evangelizing mission" (41). Therefore the Church has a right to expect that Catholics, at least, should be guided by its social teachings, so that they are not entitled simply to read the social encyclicals more or less courteously and then disregard them. This body of doctrine constitutes an integral part of their Church's moral teachings overall. For example, that horrendous manifestation of barbarism in our time, abortion, along with the entire anti-natalist cult from which it stems, may also one day be combated more effectively when the heads of families are again able to earn wages adequate to support the offspring once numbered among God's greatest blessings.

The very fact that the Roman Catholic Church, intended by its Founder to provide the means for mankind to achieve eternal salvation, got itself intensely involved in what appeared to be the most mundane of matters—the economic ones—gave rise to widespread criticism. What should have happened instead was the realization that the economic order by the late 19th century must have been in serious trouble if the Church, designed for seeing to the ultimate spiritual concerns of mankind, felt compelled to inject itself quite literally into the market place to deal with such terrestrial matters. Apologists often referred to the fact that Christianity's Founder took pity on and fed the multitude. Moreover, one of the central issues in *Rerum Novarum* is the just wage doctrine. The roots of that important doctrine are contained not only in the natural moral law, but also in the scriptural admonition that, "He slays his neighbor who deprives him of his living; he sheds blood who denies the laborer of his wages." (Sir. 34:22); also: "The worker deserves his wages." (1 Tim. 5:18)

Nevertheless, the reader should note that papal social encyclicals addressed to the economic order are strictly speaking not, as they are sometimes erroneously designated, economic encyclicals, or that they represent Catholic economics. Economics stands by itself as a distinct, legitimate science. However, economics includes not only theories but also policies. And since policies involve human actions that are subject to the moral law, the expression "Catholic economics" comes to be used at times in the same sense as the expression "Catholic philosophy." It indicates an approach to economic understanding and action that is in full conformity with Catholic moral teachings. Thus, in order to understand why the Roman Catholic Church has felt justified, especially over the past century, to address economic issues, it is necessary to set aside the orientation of much of modern social science, which is due to the influence of, among others, Auguste Comte who was himself a creature of Enlightenment philosophy. Much of the positivistic thrust in modern economics is traceable to its Enlightenment roots, with its founders seeking to emancipate it gradually from any moral considerations and to install it among the so-called positive sciences. The search was for natural "laws" according to which the economy would operate for the good of all, but only if people and their social institutions would not interfere with the operation of those "laws."[3] Thus *laissez faire*, sprung from 18th-century French soil, gave rise to the false notion of freedom that is implicit in economic liberalism. In the process, ethical considerations, or "value judgments" as they came to be labeled subsequently, were eventually ruled out as improper for scientific inquiry, since they were not quantifiable and measurable like physical phenomena. Therefore, they are widely regarded as irrelevant to the economic order.

Lost in the process was the time-honored and still valid distinction that Aristotle made between speculative and practical sciences. The latter have to do with human actions, and they are therefore subject to ethical principles, just as the physical human body is subject also to physiological ones. Thus, it may be true theoretically that a worker could, in abstract economic terms, turn out three times as much product in a 24-hour day as in eight hours. However, the facts of the physiological science also apply to man, the worker, so the economist cannot disregard them. Now those facts make us aware that people working a 24-hour day would break down and ultimately produce less than they would with the proper rest called for by their physical constitution. By the same token, economists cannot artificially abstract from the ethical norms which govern human actions. Individuals may indeed prosper, at least for a time, by immoral actions: for example, by theft or by drug-dealing. Eventually, they may be apprehended, and their prosperity would then come to an end. In any case, thieves and drug dealers too depend on the honest productive labor of others to make their nefarious actions requitable. In any case, an entire nation of people cannot survive for long by theft or drug-dealing. Therefore, while *economics is a distinct science of how people organize limited means at their disposal in order to satisfy numerous wants,* the actions which make this possible are subject to ethical considerations, i.e., to the moral law. We do not live in an exclusively economic world.

Indeed, much of the thrust of papal social encyclicals has to do with theft in the broadest sense, i.e., with justice, and also charity—the active concern for fellow human beings made in God's image—which makes justice more possible and likely. It is legitimate to say, therefore, that the social encyclicals addressed to the economic order approach economics—the practical science—as if God matters.

In 1973, E. F. Schumacher published a book entitled *Small is Beautiful*, with the subtitle: *Economics As If People Mattered.* It became and remained for some time a best-selling book—an uncommon destiny for a work written by an economist. Probably *Small is Beautiful* enjoyed such success at least to some extent because it was in tune with the rising tide of ecological concern. More importantly, it extolled the human element, in the face of the until then largely unchallenged gods of technology. It also questioned the inevitable predominance of large-scale enterprise, which had come to be accepted for the most part as a given in the present and in future economic development. In any case, few would deny Schumacher's implicit premise that people *do* in fact matter, even in the face of the unprecedented technological leaps into the space-nuclear age which emanated, for better or for worse, from World War II.

There was another, perhaps less well-developed and certainly less widely heralded, aspect of Schumacher's approach to the economic problems of our age. It was marked by a definite religious undercurrent that boldly defied the predominant positivistic orientation of the social sciences in general, and of economics specifically. Schumacher spoke unabashedly of "Buddhist economics." He cited the acknowledgment in a leading Buddhist state that, "The New Burma sees no conflict between religious values and economic progress."[4] Then we find in a thoughtful "Epilogue" a quotation which expresses the same idea in different words: "Seek ye *first* the kingdom of God, and all these things (the material things which you also need) shall be *added* unto you" (Schumacher's parentheses and italics).[5] The appeal to New Testament wisdom is followed by a forthright insertion of "the Four Cardinal Virtues: *prudentia, justitia, fortitudo, and temperantia"* into the context of economic policy. Finally, there is the literal, word-for-word quotation of "*The Principle of Subsidiarity* or *The Principle of Subsidiary Function*" as stated by Pius XI in his encyclical, *Quadragesimo Anno.*[6]

That was a remarkable beginning toward a new economics, treating it as a practical science according to the ancient wisdom of Aristotle. Thus it also marked a break from the old standard, if unspoken, assumption that popes and preachers ought to mind their own business, of which economics definitely is not a part.

Nevertheless, Schumacher was already following in the footsteps of another, largely unknown, economist who, a half century earlier, tried to reconcile the need to satisfy temporal human wants in the face of limited means, with the inherent religious need in human nature. That effort earned for the German economist, Heinrich Pesch, S.J. (1854-1926), criticism that he was trying to "theologize" economics—a venture considered not unlikely for a Jesuit economist.[7] Perhaps also predictably, the Catholic Church adopted significant elements of Pesch's thought, like the above-mentioned principle of subsidiarity; and it included these in its subsequent social teachings addressed to the economic order.

Pesch along with the popes who wrote encyclicals on the economic order went a significant step beyond Schumacher's "economics as if people mattered." They developed their economic thought, specifically in the area of economic policy, *as if God mattered.* In other words, they substituted for mere humanism, Christian humanism. Humanism of the secular stripe has been a dominant *leitmotif* in the modern world, which, ironically, was then nearing the end of one of the most savage, inhumane centuries in history. If people matter, as they do indeed, then God matters too, because He is their Creator who seeks to lead them to Himself as well as to their ultimate Destiny. Indeed, what is worthwhile in humanism is the afterglow of the Christian era which it reflects, but which has been so tragically adumbrated in the present moment in history. This thought was expressed by Pesch in his monumental economic textbook as follows:

> When the sun goes down in the evening, it consigns its light to the constellations, leaving behind its warmth without which all forms of life would perish. For too many souls, the night of unbelief has taken over. Yet, humanity still enjoys the rich heritage of Christianity. Indeed, we do not encounter one single truly great idea among modern reform endeavors in social policy and welfare which does not stem ultimately from the notion of justice and charity in the Christian sense. Now this warrants the joyous and serene hope that the night will again soon turn into day, that the sunlight of Christianity will return in its full brightness, enlightening all souls, warming all hearts, and extending full recognition, grateful honor, and humble supplication to the One whom the Christian Faith has so aptly designated as the *Sol iustitiae, Fons amoris, Vinculum caritatis.*[8]

Notes

1. Etienne Gilson, ed., *The Church Speaks to the Modern World: The Social Teachings of Leo XIII* (Garden City, NY: Doubleday Image Books, 1954), 29.

2. Cf. Rodger Charles, S. J., with Drostan MacLaren, O. P., *The Social Teachings of Vatican II* (San Francisco: Ignatius Press, 1982), for an excellent commentary on *Gaudium et Spes* and other Vatican II social teachings. The complete texts of the Council Documents may be found in Austin Flannery, O.P., ed., *Vatican Council II, Vol. I, The*

Conciliar and Post Conciliar Documents (Collegeville, MN: The Liturgical Press, 1975), 903-1002.

3. The architects of unimpeded freedom in economic life, who came to be known also as Physiocrats and also as *Les Économistes*, are regarded by some as responsible for first establishing economics as a science. They perceived economic progress as resulting from the unrestricted operation of physical, natural laws, e.g., self-interest governed solely by competition. Although not proceeding in a straight line since the Physiocrats' efforts to establish it as a natural science during the 18th century, the physical bias in economics has persisted until it reached its ultimate form among present-day economists who write their learned treatises predominantly in mathematical terms. For a brief and readable account of Physiocracy, see: John Kenneth Galbraith, *Economics in Perspective* (Boston: Houghton-Mifflin Co., 1987), 46-56.

4. E. F. Schumacher, *Small is Beautiful* (New York: Harper & Row, 1973), 50.

5. Ibid., 277ff.

6. Ibid., 230.

7. Heinrich Pesch, S. J., *Lehrbuch der Nationalökonomie*, 2nd and 3rd ed. (Freiburg: Herder & Co., 1925), vi. See also the English translation by Rupert J. Ederer, *Lehrbuch der Nationalökonomie/Teaching Guide to Economics* (Lewiston, NY: Edwin Mellen Press, 2002), vol. II, bk.1, ii. (fn. 7)

8. Ibid., vol. III (1926), 837-838. Also Pesch/ Ederer, vol. III, bk. 2, 394.

Chapter 1
Leo XIII
Rerum Novarum

This encyclical by Leo XIII is usually entitled *On the Condition of Labor*, and it originated the tradition of papal encyclicals that present modern Church teachings addressed to the economic order. Indeed, the encyclical on labor or, more specifically, on the conditions facing the working class, was already one in a series of pronouncements made in a new style. The immediate predecessors of Leo XIII in the papacy were still involved in attempting to salvage what was left of the old Christian order, in other words, Christendom, which had been upset by the social consequences of Enlightenment philosophy and the French Revolution. Their encyclicals therefore, like the earlier ones of Leo XIII, had more the tone of Cassandra-cries addressed to what the popes were still looking at as their own rebellious children in places such as Italy and France. In 1891 Leo XIII began putting the first massive building blocks in place for a restored social order that would conform to principles acceptable to Christians. Thus, the Catholic Church's earlier warnings and lamentations about the emerging post-Christian condition of society were now slowly but surely giving way to bold constructive proposals for developing a new Christian social order.

"New Things"—the first two words of *Rerum Novarum*—reflect the Pope's recognition that the "new things," translated as "the spirit of revolutionary change," with which he and his predecessors were faced, represented something that had spread "beyond the sphere of politics and made its influence felt in the cognate sphere of practical economics" (1). Those "new things" involved both positive and negative factors. They included "marvelous discoveries of science," and "the vast expansion of industrial pursuits," but also the "enormous fortunes of some few individuals, and the utter poverty of the masses" which was not unrelated to "the prevailing moral degeneracy." The so-called Industrial Revolution was in large measure the result of a providential, dramatic upsurge in technological knowledge, flowing from an unprecedented development of the natural sciences. From the introduction of steam power and some ingenious improvements in textile-producing machinery during the late 18th century, there followed a succession of technological advances unlike any the world had ever previously experienced in their frequency and significance. The state of the technical arts in the world had remained, for practical purposes, almost the same from Graeco-Roman times until the 18th century. What happened from then until the present may be described as an "explosion" in technology. As the new technology came to be adapted to industrial production, the world experienced what is referred to as the Industrial Revolution. In oversimplified terms, that "Revolution" involved the application of steam power to machines, along with the widespread introduction of the factory system where many machines and workers were gathered under one roof. With all of this came an inevitable increase in total production and in productivity, which made it possible to enhance the lives and living standards of even the most ordinary workers.

Regrettably, the new science of economics, burdened with Enlightenment philosophy and its distorted notion of liberty, also emerged in this same era. The origins of the science are traceable variously to the French Physiocrats, who gave the world the notion of *laissez faire,* and to Adam Smith who gave us the "invisible hand" to guide economic activity. Probably, it is fairer to say that these persons, along with others, all contributed to developing the science in its present form. Nevertheless, the Physiocrats and Smith did leave an indelible imprint on it until our time, giving it its mechanistic bias, its naive reliance on automatic market forces, including the facile assumption that simply supplying goods will magically conjure up the requisite effective demand for them—resurrected in our own time as "supply side economics."[1] Along with this naturalistic, mechanistic orientation of modern economics came its eventual declaration of independence from ethical considerations. Economic policy, we were informed, is distinct from "science" which is purely analytical and does not involve "value judgments."[2]

All in all, the enormous potential for economic growth and development, destined ultimately to serve the rapidly increasing populations of the modern era, brought with it instead a highly erratic, distorted pattern of economic life leaving many of the working class—which constitutes the majority of people in a modern-type national economy—to fall by the wayside. In the face of no-holds-barred "free competition," captains of industry sought to solve their problems by increasing the hours of work, by reducing wages to the bare minimum necessary to avoid starvation, and by hiring women and children who would work for even less than subsistence-level wages in a desperate endeavor to supplement the abysmally low wages of the fathers of families. That was the situation which Leo XIII was talking about when he stated in *Rerum Novarum,* "that a small number of very rich men have been able to lay upon the masses of the poor a yoke little better than slavery itself."

Aware that some very dubious remedies were already being proposed to the aggrieved working class, the Pope felt compelled to reaffirm certain truths which were being run roughshod over by both the socialists and the defenders of the capitalistic *status quo*—a *status quo* found convenient by its protagonists for maintaining their ascendancy and economic dominance.[3] These truths included the natural right to private property (paragraphs 4-7, also 19) involving also ownership of the means of production. They included also the right and duty of the state to interject itself in economic matters where the common good—the very reason for the state's existence—called for such intervention (28). Then there was the right of workers to a just wage (34), along with their right to associate, i.e., to organize themselves in order to assure just wages and to enforce other legitimate demands concerning their working lives (36-38).

Indeed, if one were to undertake the risky task of summarizing the whole of *Rerum Novarum,* those matters could be said to constitute its nucleus. Clearly, they are perennial issues that transcend the immediate exigencies of the time when the encyclical first appeared. What is more, all three relate, even cogently, to the conditions that were still far too prevalent when a successor, Pope John Paul II, saw fit to commemorate the 100th anniversary of the first encyclical addressed to the economic order. If that were not the case, the Church could be accused of merely exercising its magisterium for a sentimental echo of what had already been said clearly a century before—an unlikely prospect given the plethora at the present time of what may appear to some to be more urgent, specifically church-related, issues.

Although Leo XIII clearly entered into a reconstructive phase of delivery in *Rerum Novarum,* the "old fire," if we may call it that, was still present here. For example, he referred to the "rapacious usury, which, although more than once condemned by the Church, is nevertheless, under a different guise, but with like injustice, still practiced by covetous and grasping men" (3). And in the same paragraph, we find what could scarcely be a more cogent reference to how, "a small number of very rich men have been able to lay upon the teeming masses of the laboring poor a yoke little better than that of slavery itself." "Rapacious usury," and "slavery": these are awesome indictments!

Specifically, "rapacious usury" was condemned twice by the Church in the modern era in encyclicals. In 1745 Benedict XIV issued the encyclical *Vix Pervenit* (*On Usury and Other Dishonest Profit*), where we find an admonition against usury, along with the stipulation that, "...at times together with the loan contract certain other titles—which are not at all intrinsic to the contract—may run parallel with it (III)."[4] Thus: "From these other titles, entirely just and legitimate reasons arise to demand something over and above the amount due on the contract."[5] Later, in the encyclical *Caritate Christi* by Leo XII in 1825, we find: "Move zealously against the injustice of money lenders, who, as the Roman catechism says, plunder the people and kill them with usury, for this evil has grown strong in present times."[6]

It is not possible to determine for certain whether the Pope already had in mind the activity of modern-type commercial banks which were by then responsible for creating the bulk of the money supply used in national economies. Such money came into existence in the form of loans, which vastly expanded the deposits derived from actual savings by depositors. Thus, while usury in past ages often took the form of transgressions by individual lenders, it had by now become an institutionalized by-product of modern commercial banking systems. Given the interpretation by certain contemporary scholars of what happens in the commercial bank lending process, it is possible that Leo XIII had this in mind when he spoke of "rapacious usury...under a different form, but with the same guilt" in *Rerum Novarum*. In the broadest sense, usury refers to any price which the offender does not have a legitimate right to charge, or one which goes beyond the limits of fair pricing.

With regard to "a yoke little better than slavery itself" (2), one can appreciate how the defenders of the *status quo* were not pleased with a Roman Catholic pope who used language similar to that employed by socialist agitators. Yet, it is an unpleasant truth that Marx and his cohorts were not wrong in everything they had to say about capitalism. Otherwise they would scarcely have been able to seduce many millions for more than a century with their half-truths. Slaves, like serfs, enjoyed a certain security, albeit harsh, which the present-day worker typically no longer has. The latter was deluded into thinking that his political enfranchisement also emancipated him economically from the arbitrariness and capriciousness of his employers. Actually, more often than not, he finds the terms of his employment dictated to him unilaterally by employers. That was so in a bygone era, when emergent labor unions were embattled and hard pressed; and it is true now once again when those same unions, once militant and reasonably successful, are again being negated or reduced to relative impotence. All too many workers, even in our "enlightened" present era, feel the harshness of that total dependence on their employers when the latter dismiss them summarily, often later in life when it is virtually impossible to find suitable new employment. It is not unlikely, therefore, that embittered workers, thus victimized and humiliated as the 20th century draws to its close, may even now appreciate words written by Leo XIII near the end of the 19th century about "a yoke little better than slavery itself."

Words contained in the opening paragraphs of *Rerum Novarum* about "ancient workmen's Guilds...destroyed in the last century" (2) have been misinterpreted by some as a nostalgic bid to restore such structures in modern economic frameworks for which they are clearly no longer suited. The Pope's lament in *Rerum Novarum* was rather that, "no other organization took their place (2)." That is a theme to which Leo XIII returned in the encyclical when he dealt with "Workmen's Associations."[7] Accordingly, further comment will be made later.

The Right of Private Property

Directly after what appeared to some like a socialist indictment of modern industrial "slavery," the author of *Rerum Novarum* launched into a traditional treatment of private property including ownership of the means of production. It was traditional in the sense that it proceeded according to the Aristotelian-Thomistic defense of the ownership of private property. The Pope therefore opposed the rising socialist tide of criticism. The collapse of Communist society near the end of the last millennium suggests the prophetic quality of Leo XIII's statement about the socialist rejection of private property made a century ago. "But their proposals are so clearly futile for all practical purposes, that if they were carried out the working man himself would be among the first to suffer" (3). They have been carried out; they were futile; and the workingmen in socialist society were indeed "among the first to suffer." We may add that it was precisely the workingmen of modern Poland who led the way in rejecting and overthrowing the socialist solution!

The Leo XIII defense of private property is traditional inasmuch as it affirms "that private ownership is according to nature's law" (7). In other words, it is rooted in the natural law. The right is traced to a man's right to what his labor produces; i.e., property is an extension of a man's work. Also there is the reasonable demand for "not merely...temporary and momentary use, as other living beings have them, but...stable and permanent possession" (5). In other words, it is man's rational nature which calls for "a storehouse that will never fail" (6). That is a role which it is not up to the State to fulfill, because, among other things, "Man is older than the State and he holds the right of providing for the life of his body prior to the formation of any State" (6).

Lest the champions of the *status quo* in the late 19th century should take any comfort from this clear defense of private property, the other component of the traditional doctrine on private property follows a discussion of the proper relationship between employers and workers, and the rejection of class conflict. After stating that "these two classes should exist in harmony and agreement," the Pope said: "Each requires the other; capital cannot do without labor, nor labor without capital" (15). Only centuries of social disorder could reduce mankind to a level where the eminent, common-sense reasonableness of such a statement would actually be in doubt so as to require restatement! Undoubtedly the remarkable recovery and rise to the status of leading economic world power by the Japanese after World War II was due in part to their having grasped the essentially simple idea that there is a natural partnership between workers and their employers.[8]

The presentation of the Church's doctrine on private property follows in a discussion of how the wealthy ought to view and use their riches. Leo XIII referred to the "chief and most excellent rule for the right use of money" as one"which the heathen philosophers indicated, but which the Church has traced out clearly" (19). That the "heathen philosophers," notably Aristotle, already grasped the social dimension of private property suggests its natural law basis, i.e., its being rooted in good common sense.[9] What Aristotle had said was "baptized" by the great St. Thomas Aquinas and made a part of Christian social teaching for all time to come: "Man should not consider his outward possessions as his own, but as common to all, so as to share them without difficulty when others are in need."[10] A brief summarization of that doctrine would be simply: while the ownership of property is private, its use must always be social. The fact that I own an automobile does not entitle me to drive it in such a way that I endanger others. The same principle obviously applies if I happen to own a factory: I cannot operate it in such a way as to deny the rights and endanger the welfare of those whom I employ. In other words, as Leo XIII stated this: "...it is one thing to have a right to the possession of money, and another to have a right to use money as one pleases" (19). It was at this point that the Pope complemented the requirements of justice by the demands of charity. Sharing with others one's overabundance: "is a duty, not of justice (except in extreme cases), but of Christian Charity—duty which is not enforced by human law. That is so because "the laws and judgment of men must give place to the laws and judgment of Christ, the true God" (19).

What is rejected explicitly here is the assumption that what is mine is mine to do with as I please. That, of course, is actually a reversion to the pagan Roman, absolute notion of private property—a reversion that is not surprising, given the naturalistic bias of the 18th century philosophy of economic liberalism which ensouled 19th century capitalism.[11] Leo XIII was reintroducing the specifically Christian dimension which had been progressively obliterated by the Enlightenment with its false, deracinated view of liberty.[12] The conventional wisdom of the emerging liberal capitalism was able to accept strict (commutative) justice as called for implicitly or spelled out explicitly in contracts between individuals. However, it was not open to obligations imposed on behalf of the common good, not to mention the requirements of charity—the specific contribution of Christian teaching to what is requisite for good social order.

Here, once again, Leo XIII showed himself to be the pioneer papal social teacher in this important matter. It was he who first suggested the additional dimension to justice, *social justice,* which was to become the watchword of the next social encyclical, *Quadragesimo Anno.* While Leo XIII never used the term explicitly, he presented the essence of it in this statement: "But all citizens, without exception, can and ought to contribute to that common good in which individuals share so profitably to themselves" (27).[13] Unfortunately, the expression, *social justice*, became somewhat ambiguous in usage. It came to be used synonymously with good social order—the situation that applies when justice in all of its various applications becomes widely operational. At times it also degenerated into a combative slogan. Indeed, socialists, among others, used it, even though they were obsessed with their own exaggerated perception of distributive justice. *Distributive justice,* derived from Aristotelian ethics[14] and absorbed into Scholastic ethics by St. Thomas,[15] applies to persons in a position of authority, requiring them to give to all who are under their authority what is their due. Now for the socialists, although in their theory the state was to eventually wither away, in actual practice political authorities were instead entrusted with the total task of assigning obligations and dispensing rewards to subjects of the state. Needless to say, whatever role would have been left to charity was also swallowed up in this totalitarian enterprise. Leo XIII was remarkably prescient about where actual socialism would lead, even though he died 14 years before its blueprint first became reality. At the same time, he was also painfully aware of what had been wrought by fallacious liberal capitalism which virtually abolished any significant, active participation by the state in economic life. He therefore set about establishing the proper role of the state.

The Role of the State

Just as the position taken by the Church in its social teachings about private property pleased neither the emerging socialists nor the triumphant champions of liberal capitalism, neither would its pronouncement on the state's role in the national economy. The Pope ventured into this part of the encyclical after first insisting that the state not infringe on the charitable activity of the Church, because "Charity, as a virtue belongs to the Church" (24).

We find in this defense of the Church's charitable role the culmination of a discussion which declaws the perennial Marxian insinuation that, so far as the poor are concerned, the Church and religion "neglect their interests temporal and earthly" (23). What follows is a cataloging of the various ways in which the Church has intervened directly and indirectly, and continues to do so, on behalf of the poor. It does so indirectly by inciting virtuous and frugal living which helps all persons, including the poor, to stay "out of the reach of those vices which eat up not merely small incomes, but large fortunes, and dissipate many a goodly inheritance" (23). Direct intervention for the poor dates back to the voluntary communistic demeanor among the earliest Christians who "deprived themselves of their possessions in order to relieve their brethren" (24). A whole host of endeavors followed down through history, which were called "deposits of piety" in Tertullian's time, because they were employed "in feeding the needy, in burying them, in the support of boys and girls destitute of means and deprived of their parents, in the care of the aged, and in the relief of the shipwrecked." Scarcely any person in the modern era remains unaware of the updated versions of these charitable operations conducted by the Church down through the ages until the present time. Indeed, there have been times when secularistic governments sought to elbow the Church out of the operation of charitable enterprises, proposing that those are the responsibilities of the state.

That led Leo XIII into his discussion of how the state fits into the emerging Church schema for reconstructing the social order. He made it clear that the state was not to stand by indifferently, since "not only the Church, but all human means must conspire." Thus began what this commentator regards as the second major part of *Rerum Novarum,* the one dealing with the role of the state. Also, the Pope was introducing here what was to be designated in subsequent social teachings as "the preferential option for the poor." Leo XIII did not coin that expression, so he never himself used it. However, in his Church's social teachings, it was he who pioneered the doctrine itself. First of all, it is necessary to recall that this encyclical was addressed principally to the problems facing what was undeniably the poorer sector of society—the working class. Accordingly, the Pope assigned to the ruler of the state the task of seeing to their plight, since it was in his power "to benefit every order of the State, and amongst the rest to promote in the highest degree the interests of the poor." It is at this point in the encyclical that the state's reason for existence is mentioned: "…for it is the province of the commonwealth to consult for the common good" (26).

What follows is an interesting and important equation of the well-being of the working class with the well-being of the entire national economy. It is an equation which has unfortunately been lost sight of in much of economics dating back to the origin of the science in the 18th century, with its obsessive concern for the "individual" and his well-being. We have here a most significant statement contrasting with that rampant individualism. Leo XIII referred to the "labor of the poor—the exercise of their skill and the employment of their strength in the culture of the land and the workshops of trade" as "most efficacious and altogether indispensable." He went on to state a truth, which, to a degree, echoed something found *both* in Adam Smith's *Wealth of Nations* and in Karl Marx's *Das Kapital*. It was the notion that human labor is the primary source of national wealth. In the Pope's words, "Indeed, their cooperation in this respect is so important that it may be truly said that it is only by the labor of the working man that States grow rich" (27). Unfortunately, Smith and Marx did not follow through consistently in the policies and actions they advocated. Leo XIII did: "Let it not be feared that solicitude of this kind will injure any interest; on the contrary, it will be to the advantage of all; for it cannot but be good for the commonwealth to secure from misery those on whom it so largely depends." That was a powerful statement which refutes the arrogant supposition, rampant again in our own time, that wealth is designed to trickle down from the wealthy and powerful, to those who make up the vast majority of the population and whose efforts are, to repeat the Pope's words, "most efficacious and altogether indispensable" for national prosperity!

At this point, Leo XIII took the occasion to draw the line on how intensely the state ought to get involved in economic life. What we have here is the earliest statement in papal social teachings, albeit in rudimentary form, of what would be called in subsequent social encyclicals the *principle of subsidiarity*. "We have said that the State must not absorb the individual or the family; both should be allowed free and untrammeled action as far as is consistent with the common good and the interests of others" (28). This is reaffirmed also in the next paragraph, following a listing of some of the situations in which the state ought to intervene, with these words: "The limits (of state interference) must be determined by the nature of the occasion which calls for the law's interference—the principle being this, that the law must not undertake more, nor go further, than is required for the remedy of the evil or the removal of the danger" (29). While that is not a full and precise statement of the principle of subsidiarity, it clearly prepares the way for it.

That principle, of course, refutes socialist pretensions to totalitarian control over all facets of human life, including the economic ones. Unfortunately, it is often overlooked that the principle may also be violated by omission, when the state does not interpose its action where that would clearly be called for, as when the rights of various citizens and groups of citizens are rampantly violated. Less obviously, omissive violations of the principle may also result when individuals and lower social bodies do not live up to their responsibilities as required by justice in all of its various applications, so that the state is forced to intervene where that would not otherwise be necessary, or where it would at least not be the most efficient way of dealing with certain situations. Leo XIII enumerated some of the areas where the state would be justified in intervening, for example: "If by a strike, or other combination of workmen there should be imminent danger or disturbance to the public peace...; or if employers laid burdens upon the workmen which were unjust or degraded them with conditions that were repugnant to their dignity as human beings— finally, if health were endangered by excessive labor, or by work unsuited to sex or age..." (29).

The right to strike is implicitly upheld here, even while it is made clear that this is not an unconditional right. Thus, the state should intervene only "if the strike, or the way in which and the purpose for which workers combine, would present an "imminent danger of disturbance to the public peace." While most American labor unions were not revolutionary in intent,[16] elsewhere in the world labor organizations were often merely an arm of wider political movements, intent on eventually promoting revolution generally in the direction of socialism. That also serves to explain the Pope's qualification about the right to organize which appeared later in the encyclical.[17] Subsequently, the right to strike is also implied in the statement that: "When work-people have recourse to a strike, it is frequently because the hours of labor are too long, or the work too hard or because they consider their wages insufficient" (31). Leo XIII proposed that "this not uncommon occurrence should be obviated by public remedial measures." In other words, the reasons which prompt workers to strike should be eliminated beforehand because, "such paralysis of labor not only affects the masters and their work-people, but is extremely injurious to trade and to the general interests of the public: moreover, on such occasions, violence and disorder are generally not far off, and thus it frequently happens that the public peace is threatened" (31). Thus it appears that the justification of the strike is treated in the same way as the concept of the just war, because in relations between employers and workers the strike is in a certain real sense the counterpart of war in relations between states. As it is reasonable to do all in one's power to prevent this ultimate weapon from being used in political relations among nations, the same applies in the important everyday area of economic life where goods and services are produced for the benefit of all.

Among certain areas in the world of work mentioned in *Rerum Novarum,* where public authorities have the right and obligation to interpose themselves, as in the matter of Sunday rest and reasonable hours of work, there was also mentioned the problem of child labor—rampant in the 19th century, but which has resurfaced again to a disturbing extent in our own time.[18]

In addition, Leo XIII also addressed the matter of women in the workplace in a manner that clashes with what is widely championed in our society at present. What politician, or churchman for that matter, would have the courage to make this statement in our time: "Women, again, are not suited to certain trades; for a woman is by nature fitted for home-work, and it is that which is best adapted at once to preserve her modesty, and to promote the good bringing up of children and the well-being of the family"(33). That statement would be accepted as eminently sensible, except in times when outrageous nonsense is rampant. Although the expression, "home-work" represents awkward translation, what is meant here is clear from the context. Women are different not only in their physical attributes, but also in their psychological makeup which may be somewhat less obvious to some. That difference makes them less suited for working as, e.g., coal miners, steelworkers, firemen, or, for that matter, for serving as combat infantrymen, in other words, in kinds of work which make extreme physical and psychological demands for which their in some ways more sensitive natures are not suited. What their natural endowments suit them for instead is, first of all, physical maternity which no man can accomplish; but it also suits them for the delicate and all-important task of nurturing and raising young children, in other words, for "home-work,"—work in the home as mothers and homemakers. Making such a statement is likely to incite a storm of vitriolic controversy in the present atmosphere that is charged with all manner of misinterpretations of the true meaning of "equality of the sexes." Clearly, such "equality" has nothing to do with "alikeness," all of which previous generations, when the general mental and spiritual health of our people was better, never felt compelled to confuse.

Beyond the physical and psychological realities, there is also the demographic one, widely lost sight of in the frenzied discussions about "equal rights." It is an inevitable fact that if the vast majority of women do not agree to become mothers of children, no society can endure in the long run.[19]

Largely lost sight of in the preposterous "battle of the sexes" which has been engendered by radical agitators is the fact that the majority of married women who seek work outside the home are quite probably victims of the rampant socio-economic disorder. Just as is the case with child labor, we have experienced a turn of events not unlike conditions prevailing when Leo XIII felt the need to address an encyclical to the condition of labor. What the socialists proposed in their warped ideology, where the so-called "emancipation of women" was extolled vigorously, has been accomplished also by the free play of market forces in non-socialist societies.[20] In the Soviet Union Russian women worked because ideologically they were expected to, and also, incidentally, because economic conditions brought about by centrally planned socialism were so deplorable as to require their work outside the home.[21] Chinese women work for the same reasons. What is more, in that gigantic, surviving, Orwellian Communist colossus, couples are told how many children they may have; and they are severely punished, even physically, if they transgress the will of their "Big Brother" state. Subsequently, men and women alike are told where to work and at what occupations while the state raises the children in official day-care establishments and schools. Ironically those women in the free market economies of the West, who are taken in by the radical feminist call for their "emancipation" from home and motherhood, traverse substantially the same route into the labor market, voluntarily surrendering their traditional feminine regency in the home. Nevertheless, a show of hands among married working women would quite probably reveal that if their husbands were in a position to earn an adequate family wage, the majority of them would give up their often less than fulfilling jobs, in order to return home and take proper care of their children and their husbands. It is this "adequate family wage" which Leo XIII first proposed for the context of modern society, and which represents a major, pivotal contribution in the Church's social teachings.

The Just Wage

In its modern statement, the just wage doctrine was first introduced in *Rerum Novarum.* Unfortunately, it has also been treated at times like merely a pious, platitudinous statement. It is everything but that; and later popes made this clear in the way they reaffirmed and further explained it in subsequent social encyclicals.[22] Thus, in its premier appearance Leo XIII introduced the doctrine of the just wage as "a subject of very great importance and one about which, if extremes are to be avoided, right ideas are absolutely necessary" (34). Once again, the "extremes" come from opposite directions. One came in the form of the tempting fruit dangled before the workers by socialist theorists: since human labor was responsible for all marketable value, the worker was entitled to the full product—the so-called labor theory of value.[23] This is dealt with implicitly by Leo XIII in the prior discussion of private property rights. Since it is clear that land and other productive resources also contribute to the market value of products, those who own such resources could only be denied a fair return from their productivity if they were stripped of the right to own them privately.

The other extreme opposing the just wage doctrine as proposed in papal encyclicals beginning with *Rerum Novarum* stemmed from the then predominant liberal capitalist ideology. This ideology, conveniently supportive of the ruling capitalist class, assumed a mythical kind of freedom and equality between the employer and the lone, unorganized worker. Thus, those who were firmly in control of the market situation gratuitously proposed that the worker, standing by himself, and often without any scarce marketable skill, was their equal in wage bargaining. Accordingly, there was the sanctimonious suggestion that the wage agreed upon between such workers and employers was "freely" agreed upon, so that it was automatically just; and the workers had no right to complain about it.

Leo XIII took issue with this hypocrisy when he indicated that, "there is a dictate of nature more imperious and more ancient than any bargain between man and man." (34). He opposed it on the grounds that human labor is not only *personal,* but also *necessary.* On purely *personal* grounds a person could "accept any rate of wages whatever; for in the same way as he is free to work or not, so he is free to accept a small remuneration or even none at all" (34). That is to some degree the counterpart of the view of private property which regards such property as "mine to do with as I please." However, with the wage too, there is also, beyond the merely *personal* dimension, the *necessary* one: namely, the fact that "without the results of labor a man cannot live; and self-conservation is a law of nature which it is wrong to disobey" (34). Being "necessary" also implies that this is a *social* dimension, since the natural law of "self-conservation" which the Pope referred to here also extends from the worker to the support of "his wife and his children" (35). This means, in effect, the conservation of society or, more broadly, of the human race itself. Interpreted in the most restrictive terms then, a worker may not accept less than the just family wage for the simple reason that not only he, but also his wife and children, depend on it for a living. Nor may he be forced into that situation by the employer because the conditions in the market for his labor happen to make such exploitation possible. "If through necessity or fear of a worse evil, the workman accepts harder conditions because an employer or contractor will give him no better, he is the victim of force and injustice" (34). Beyond that, if the particular worker happens to be in a situation, e.g., by inheritance or for whatever other reason, so that he does not need the just wage to accomplish the self-conservation purpose of the wage for himself and his family, selling his labor for less than that amount would still have serious implications for other workers who must compete with him in the labor market. Thus, a man's work and what he asks for it in wages is not merely a personal consideration, but also a necessary, i.e., social one.

All talk of a just wage remains platitudinous if it does not eventually get down to the details of exactly how much such a wage is in specific time and place circumstances. Obviously, inasmuch as living standards have and will continue to vary in different times and places, the precise amount of the just wage will vary also. Furthermore, a wage which is just for the beginning, unskilled worker will not be the same for experienced and more skilled workers. Thus, it is clear that what Leo XIII proposed was the very minimum just wage owed to all full-time, adult workers even though they may be without special skills or long experience. It is also clear that the Pope was not talking about the minimum wage legislated in, for example, the United States during the years following *Rerum Novarum*. That minimum wage provides an irreducible minimal subsistence, if indeed it is adequate for that; and it was designed to ward off only the most horrendous abuses by establishing a lower limit to what the so-called "market forces" might reduce the wage which the employer may feel justified in paying his workers. The just wage as defined in the encyclical "must be enough to support the wage-earner in reasonable and frugal comfort" (34). What is more, given the express preferential option for the mother to remain in the home and see to "the good bringing up of children and the well-being of the family," the workman's wages should "be sufficient to enable him to maintain himself, his wife, and his children in reasonable comfort." That being the case, "he will not find it difficult, if he is a sensible man, to study economy; and he will not fail by cutting down expenses, to put by a little property: nature and reason would urge him to do this" (35). Allowing once again for a certain awkwardness in translation along with what is perhaps 19th century idiom, the just wage should make possible savings in order to, for example, make possible home ownership and perhaps other modest savings. "To study economy" obviously means simply prudent, thrifty management. Such savings would also be made possible by and by as the worker progresses, becoming more experienced and perhaps more skilled and valuable to his employer, so that he graduates beyond the minimum just wage.

This dimension of the just wage doctrine, enabling the worker to "put by a little property," afforded Leo XIII an opportunity to again defend the right of private ownership. He saw three specific benefits stemming from widespread property ownership also among the working classes: 1) it would help to bridge the gulf between vast wealth and deep poverty so that the "two orders will be brought nearer together." 2) It would increase workers' productivity since "Men always work harder and more readily when they work on that which is their own." 3) It would halt the flood of immigration going on at the time (and at present!) because "men would cling to the country in which they were born; for no one would exchange his country for a foreign land if his own afforded him the means of living a tolerable and happy life" (35).

Determining an actual amount of pay required by the just wage doctrine has become a stumbling block for some. Yet, if we are not prepared to eventually talk about a specific amount of money, this important doctrine could be reduced to merely a pious, platitudinous proclamation. The key appears to lie in the use of the word "reasonable" which appears twice in the translation. It is assumed that "reasonable" men will arrive at what is fair in given circumstances. Also, the word "comfort" is used, so we are definitely not talking about merely a bare subsistence.

There is, in fact, ample evidence that "reasonable" people are able to come up with a decent approximation to what such a just wage should be. For example, as early as 1920, the State of California established a committee to determine what an adequate level of pay would be for its civil servants. It came to be known as the Heller Committee, functioning out of the University of California at Berkeley. The resultant budget developed by this committee "attempted to describe the 'commonly accepted' standard of living as the sum of those goods and services that public opinion currently recognizes as necessary to health and reasonably comfortable living." The report went on to state that, "The term, 'necessary,' as used here includes far more than a minimum of physical needs. It represents what men commonly expect to enjoy, what is urgently desired and striven for, special gratification attending substantial success and substantial failure yielding bitter frustration."[24] While there is no evidence linking the efforts of the Heller Committee to the just wage doctrine contained in the encyclical *Rerum Novarum,* the intention as expressed in committee's statement is remarkably concordant.

The same is true also of the so-called *City Workers' Family Budget,* first published by the United States Department of Labor in 1947 and continued until 1983. This enterprise eventually provided carefully detailed budgets for three different levels of living, and adjusted for 40 metropolitan and 4 nonmetropolitan areas in the United States. Once again its announced intention paralleled what Leo XIII proposed in his just wage doctrine: "This is not a 'subsistence' budget, nor is it a 'luxury' budget; it is an attempt to describe and measure a modest but adequate standard of living."[25] Another remarkable fact about these two budgets is that in 1959, one of the last years when both were still being published, despite differing techniques used in arriving at the minimum budgets, the results differed by only a few dollars.[26] One may conclude that "reasonable" people are able to come up with specific amounts of money needed to enable workers and their families to live in "reasonable and frugal comfort."[27]

Indeed "reasonable" people the world over have since persisted in coming up with specific figures for what is now termed the "*living wage.*" The concept *living* rather than *just* is employed by certain parties who are promoting it at present perhaps to preserve the ongoing value-neutral approach in economic matters. Or there may be a perceived need to avoid the denominational implication, since the concept apparently dates back to its use and development by Msgr. John A. Ryan who promoted the just wage doctrine of Pope Leo XIII in his work, *A Living Wage, Its Ethical and Economic Aspects,* first published in 1906. Given that the federal government has apparently surrendered to the pressures of the free marketeers who see the correct wage as a function of the "free" actions of buyers and sellers of the "commodity" human labor, there are ongoing widespread endeavors and abroad to enact measures at the state and local levels to require payment of a "living wage." Frequently this entails specifically situations where local governments engage in business dealings with private contractors in cities like Baltimore, San Francisco, Santa Fe, Boston, and Buffalo; and abroad, living wage initiatives are present in places so far apart as Australia, England, Scotland, and Switzerland. Meanwhile, in the United States anyone with access to a computer can determine what the hourly rate and annual amount for a living wage amounts to in his locality for earners ranging from one adult, to two adults with two children. Such research stems from places like the University of the state of Washington, not from some Catholic university where such things should be promoted. It is worth noting also that when the Heller Committee and the U. S. Labor Department first presented their detailed budgets, they were operating without the benefit of computers.

Workmen's Associations

Most of the remainder of *Rerum Novarum* deals with the workers' right to organize themselves into "workmen's associations," so that they may themselves contribute to securing just wages and other working conditions befitting the dignity of labor. That is vital, among other things, "in order to supercede undue interference on the part of the State, especially as circumstances, times, and localities differ so widely." (34). In other words, what was later to be designated as the principle of subsidiarity makes it advisable for workers themselves to accomplish much of this vital task of securing their rights.

Rerum Novarum is often cited as the papal social encyclical that defended the right of workers to form labor unions. It did indeed do that. However, the use of the expression, "workmen's associations" (in Latin, *sodalitia artificum*), is not simply co-extensive with the modern term, "labor unions"; nor is it merely an anachronistic expression. It is clear from what follows here in the concluding portion of the encyclical that the term is deliberately broad, even while it does include the modern-type labor union. Nevertheless, it also embraces the guild-type organizations suggested the Leo XIII early in *Rerum Novarum* (2). Now the Pope was once again attesting to the "excellent results...affected by the Artificers' Guilds of a former day" (36). Although the Church is accused from time to time by the uninformed of seeking to restore the medieval guilds, it was made clear at the outset in *Rerum Novarum*, as well as in subsequent social encyclicals, that what was being proposed is an updated application of the guild *concept*, not the outdated *structure* itself which was suited to the age of the crafts prior to the Industrial Revolution. Accordingly, we find here that "such associations should be adapted to the requirements of the age in which we live—an age of greater instruction, of different customs, and of more numerous requirements in daily life" (36).

Referring to "workmen's associations" then, the Pope applauded the fact that there were already "not a few societies of this nature, consisting either of workmen alone, or of workmen and employers together." Clearly, this includes the modern labor union, which is made up of "workmen alone"; but it just as clearly expresses something more than mere nostalgia with regard to societies "of workmen and employers together." In other words, while upholding the right of workers to organize in order to secure their rights in organizations made up of "workmen alone," the Church in its social teachings was already clearly looking beyond these to organizations which would give expression to the solidarity among those who work in the same industry or occupation.[28] Regrettably, that is a concept of "workmen's associations" which has become almost totally alien to modern Western culture, especially in its Anglo-American sector.

Meanwhile, there is no doubt that conditions were certainly critical enough for the workers by the end of the 19th century, so that they were within their rights to establish, perhaps as a stopgap measure, the modern, militant, defensive labor union in order to assure just wages, reasonable hours of work, and generally humane treatment in their places of work. Their right to organize was affirmed here as stemming from the general right to form associations for any legitimate purpose. Indeed, no less than a Scriptural foundation is presented at this point in the encyclical (37) for man's right to organize and for the wisdom of doing so: "Two are better than one: they get a good wage for their labor. If the one falls, the other will lift up his companion. Woe to the solitary man! For if he should fall, he has no one to lift him up." (Eccles. 4:9-10.) Also: "A brother is a better defense than a strong city, and a friend is like the bars of a castle" (Proverbs 18:19).

For those who are, for one reason or another, not impressed with the ancient wisdom of Sacred Scripture, Leo XIII also indicated here that the right of man to organize into "lesser societies" than the state is a natural one, therefore prior to the state. These have a less general purpose than the state which "exists for the common good and, therefore, is concerned with the interests of all in general, and with the individual interests in their due place and proportion" (37). Nevertheless they "cannot be prohibited by the State absolutely and as such" (38).

That is because, "to enter into a 'society' of this kind is the natural right of man; and the State must protect natural rights, not destroy them; and if it forbids its citizens to form associations, it contradicts the very principle of its own existence: for both they and it exist in virtue of the same principle, viz., the natural propensity of man to live in society" (38). The language here is clear enough so that it scarcely requires any explanation. The right to form associations is a natural one, prior to the state; and the state has no right to deny that right except, "when men join together for purposes which are evidently bad, unjust, or dangerous to the State." The restriction is an obvious one, because the good of all, and also individual rights which conform to that good, are the business of the state.

It is a significant anomaly that in American society, where liberty and equality are so vigorously and ritually extolled as essential components of a democratic society, nearly another half century passed before the right of workers generally to organize was explicitly protected by a law.[29] As if attesting to the naturalness of the right to organize, American workers had been forming unions and attempting to do so since the nation began. These efforts were sometimes more, sometimes less successful. Court decisions favorable to employers time and again made the path to organization thorny and difficult, as did the inherently greater power of employers to intimidate workers and to outlast them in strikes. Thus the celebrated exercise of democracy proved to be an elusive goal in its application to the economic order, specifically, to the work place where most people spend most of their waking hours during their lifetimes (as contrasted with a brief moment at a polling place once a year in November). Indeed, given the turn of events even in most recent times, when labor unions are once again reduced both in numbers and in effectiveness, it continues to elude great masses of working people!

Finally, some comment is required on the final part of *Rerum Novarum* following the statement: "Associations of every kind, and especially those of workingmen, are now far more common than formerly" (40). The historical ambience at the time the encyclical appeared helps to explain what is involved here. Leo XIII noted that there was at large, "a good deal of evidence which goes to prove that many of these societies are in the hands of invisible leaders, and are managed on principles far from compatible with Christianity and the public well-being..." (40). Here the Pope proposed therefore that "Christian workmen must do one of two things: either join associations in which their religion will not be exposed to peril or form associations among themselves—unite their forces and courageously shake off the yoke of an unjust and intolerable oppression" (40).

In 1891 when the encyclical appeared, the emergent socialist forces were appealing to the workers to unite for the eventual overthrow of the capitalistic system. Even the more moderate socialists, like various exponents of so-called evolutionary socialism and the democratic socialists, were advocating the use of labor unions and eventually labor parties to install a socialistic society. Accordingly, labor unions in Europe, in particular, were not politically and religiously "neutral" in the same sense that most labor unions in the United States have been, where the "revolutionary union" was the exception and where so-called "business unionism" was prevalent. The *business union* had no specific ideological program. Its purpose was to improve the living conditions of workers within the given social system. One can appreciate the concern of Leo XIII about dangers to the workers' religious faith, if they got involved with the socialistically or otherwise ideologically biased labor unions "whose objects are at once hurtful to Religion and dangerous to the State" (39). On the other hand, workers in the United States would with rare exceptions be joining organizations "in which their religion will not be exposed to peril" (40).

To assure such a course, many Catholic dioceses in the United States established "labor schools" during the heyday of labor organization in the late 1930s and 1940s. These were clearly foreshadowed among projects alluded to in *Rerum Novarum*: "The Bishops, on their part, bestow their ready good-will and support; and with their approval and guidance many members of the clergy, both secular and regular, labor assiduously on behalf of the spiritual and mental interests of the members of Associations."[30] In such continuing education programs, workers were instructed in the social principles of their own Church to enable them to counteract the kinds of influences about which the Pope expressed his concern in the latter paragraphs of *Rerum Novarum.*

With regard to the precise structuring of workmen's associations, Leo XIII stated what his successors have steadfastly reaffirmed in subsequent social encyclicals: that the Church is not in a position to establish "definite details on the subject of organization." It confines itself to broad, general guidelines and bedrock principles. The specifics "must depend on national character, on practice and experience, on the nature and scope of the work to be done, on the magnitude of the various trades and employments, and on other circumstances of fact and of time—all of which must be carefully weighed" (42). Nevertheless there is stated here as a "general and perpetual law," "that Workmen's Associations must be so organized and governed as to furnish the best and most suitable means for attaining what is aimed at, that is to say, for helping each individual member to better his condition to the utmost, in body, mind and property" (42).

On balance, it seems apparent that this entire last portion of the encyclical also involves a preview of the kind of "workmen's association" far more in harmony with the Church's view of how these should eventually take shape, than with what was emerging in a society that was becoming increasingly secularistic and preoccupied with a struggle between the classes. This is apparent also from the appeal for "foundations of the organization being laid in Religion," and also from the subsequent remark that: "It is not rash to conjecture the future from the past," since, "the events of one century are wonderfully like those of another...." (43). This aspect of the social teachings, like the principle of subsidiarity, and the central role of social justice and social charity in the reordering of the society was to be further articulated and developed in the next social encyclical addressed to the economic order, *Quadragesimo Anno.*

Conclusion

While there is a dominant thrust toward justice in its various applications throughout *Rerum Novarum,* the ultimate appeal by Leo XIII, as by subsequent popes in their papal teachings, is to the specifically Christian contribution to resolving the social problems of the time: "Charity, the mistress and queen of virtues." That appeal provides, at one and the same time, the keynote for the entire body of social teachings addressed to the economic order, and also the most fitting possible conclusion to our discussion of this pioneer among the papal encyclicals which treat economics as if God matters.

> For the happy result we all long for must be chiefly brought about by the plenteous outpouring of Charity; of that true Christian Charity which is the fulfilling of the whole Gospel law, which is always ready to sacrifice itself for other's sake, and which is man's surest antidote against worldly pride and immoderate love of self: that Charity whose office is described and whose God-like features are drawn by the Apostle St. Paul in these words: 'Charity is patient, is kind,...seeketh not her own,...suffereth all things,...endureth all things.' (45)

Notes

1. The so-called "law of markets," proclaimed by the early French economist, Jean Baptiste Say (1767-1832), stated that supply generates its own demand. Facile reasoning led Say to believe that since the income from producing any supply was equal to the price of what was supplied, it would therefore eventually constitute an equivalent demand for it. This "law" remained the basis for much of classical and neo-classical economics until modern times, when John Maynard Keynes made it the focal point of his challenge to neo-classical economics during the Great Depression in the 1930s. Largely as a reaction to Keynesian economics, it has since been revived in recent times as the central dogma of what has come to be referred to as "supply side economics" which proposes that if you take care of the supplier (entrepreneur, investor, capitalist, businessman), demand would take care of itself. If this were so, the mega-billions spent on advertising would, of course, make little sense. The economic process starts with people's needs and wants expressed as effective demand, not with supply.

2. Adam Smith and the early classical economists did not hesitate to make "value judgments." Indeed, the *Wealth of Nations* was to a large extent a negative value judgment of the Mercantilist system. The British economist, Nassau Senior (1790-1864), began the tradition of treating economics as a purely deductive science. More recently, Max Weber (1864-1920) was an important influence in establishing economics, like the other social sciences, as a pure, positive science, regarding "value judgments" as legitimate, but not as "scientific."

3. The term, *capitalism*, was not used in *Rerum Novarum.* Indeed, the expression was not yet in vogue. Even Karl Marx had not used the word, "capitalism," only "capitalist," "capitalistic system," and "capitalistic production." Making "isms" out of ideological systems and systems of belief became common practice only later in the 20th century, when we began hearing of fascism, nazism, communism, and also capitalism.

4. Claudia Carlen IHM, ed., *The Papal Encyclicals, Vol I: 1740-1878,* (N.p.:

McGrath Publ. Co., 1981), 17.

5. For a definitive scholarly treatment of the Church's teachings on interest and usury, see B.W. Dempsey, S. J., *Interest and Usury* (Washington: American Council on Public Affairs, 1943).

6. Carlen, 214.

7. The process by which modern societies create most of their money supplies is described in most standard textbooks on money and banking. One of first scholars to describe the process in detail was Chester Arthur Phillips in his work, *Bank Credit* (New York: Macmillan, 1928). Perhaps the most distinguished critic of this system of money creation by the banking system was the noted American economist, Irving Fisher, in his book: *100% Money* (New York: Adelphi, 1935). Bernard W. Dempsey, in his work cited above, came to the conclusion that, "a Scholastic of the seventeenth century viewing the modern monetary problems would readily favor a 100% reserve plan...": Dempsey, 210. An analysis of how money came to its present state may be found in: Rupert J. Ederer, *The Evolution of Money* (Washington, DC: Public Affairs Press, 1964).

8. For an enlightened discussion of how Western attitudes in labor relations puzzle the Japanese, see Wm. G. Ouchi, *The M-Form Society* (Reading, PA: Addison-Wesley, 1984).

9. Cf. Aristotle, "Politics," *The Basic Works of Aristotle*, ed. Richard McKeon (New York: Random House, 1941), bk. II.

10. St. Thomas Aquinas, *Summa Theologica*, 2, 2ae Q. lxv. art. 2.

11. This theme is developed expertly by Nicolas Berdyaev in *The Origin of Russian Communism* (London: Geoffrey Bles, 1937).

12. Our society could still derive much benefit from a careful study of the long forgotten encyclical by Leo XIII *On Human Liberty* (*Libertas Praestantissumum*, 1888). It provides an antidote to the ritual incantations about liberty which is so misunderstood and therefore so much abused in our own time. See Carlen, pp. 169-181.

13. Claudia Carlen, IHM, ed., *The Papal Encyclicals, Vol. III: 1903-1939*, 547 (par. 51).

14. Aristotle, bk. 5, chaps. 1-11.

15. Cf. St. Thomas Aquinas, *Commentary on the Nichomachean Ethics,* trans. C. I. Litzinger (Chicago: Henry Regnery Co., 1964), 1: 381ff.

16. The Industrial Workers of the World represented a classic and rare example of a "revolutionary union," in the history of American organized labor. It began in 1905 and faded out soon after World War I. The I.W.W., as it came to be known, caused large waves for a time in certain sectors of the U. S., by its radical agenda and methods. However, the concept of unionism that it represented never caught hold among American workers who, in the main, preferred to improve their lot within the existing social system.

17. *Rerum Novarum,* par. 40.

18. This is especially prevalent, but not certainly not limited to the food industry, all of the way from the vast fields of so-called "agri-businesses" where children labor side-by-side with their migrant worker parents to harvest it, to the far-flung empire of "fast food chains" where youngsters prepare and serve it, usually after school hours.

19. It is a demographic fact of life that this requires the willingness to have more than two children. Two children would simply replace the mother and father; but that would not compensate, even in healthy societies where there is not widespread abortion and contraception of human life, for those who never marry, for those who are unable to have two, one, or any children, and for whatever natural unevenness there may be in the distribution of the two sexes, as well as for infant and child mortality.

20. Cf. Lenin, *On the Emancipation of Women* (Moscow: Progress Publishers, 1934). This 136-page book contains a series of essays gathered from various of Lenin's writings by his wife, N. Krupskaya. The actual expression, "emancipation of women," is found innumerable times throughout. That the concept, taken in the manner as it is usually understood in our time, is obviously not of Christian origin, is clear from a reading of papal encyclicals, especially since the time of Leo XIII.

21. Aside from the ideological factor, the tremendous toll of casualties during World War II in the Soviet Union also put pressure on an already inefficient economic system to put women into the work force in order to assure the kind of performance the economy was supposed to achieve.

22. The just wage doctrine was affirmed and developed further in *Quadragesimo Anno*. Pope John XXIII also made reference to it in *Mater et Magistra*; and in *Laborem Exercens*, Pope John Paul II actually made the just wage a central criterion for judging the effectiveness of a national economy.

23. Pius XI rejected this flawed theory explicitly in *Quadragesimo Anno* (par. 68). Karl Marx, the author of the so-called "labor theory of value," apparently found it difficult to avoid contradicting himself when dealing with the relationship of labor to value. On page 45 of the English translation of his major work, *Das Kapital*, he wrote: "The use-value, or useful article, therefore has value only because human labour in the abstract has been embodied or materialised in it." Three pages later (p. 48) we find: "Lastly, nothing can have value, without being an object of utility. If the thing is useless, so is the labour contained in it; the labour does not count as labour, and therefore creates no value." The first statement clearly suggests that labor causes value; but the next one makes labor useless unless there is utility. Obviously it is the utility of an object which confers value, not the labor expended on it, which could be "useless," as in the case of a boondoggle! Cf. Karl Marx, *Capital* (Chicago, Charles H. Kerr & Co.: 1918), vol. 1.

24. "Quantity and Cost Budgets for Two Income Levels," issued by The Heller Committee for Research in Social Economics, University of California, 1962, p. 5.

25. United States Department of Labor, Bureau of Labor Statistics, *Workers' Budgets in the United States: City Families and Single Persons, 1946 and 1947* (Washington: Government Printing Office, 1948), 3.

26. The CWF Budget, as the Labor Department's budget came to be known, called for a $6,304 income for city workers in the San Francisco Bay area for 1959. The Heller Committee Budget, designed for the San Francisco Bay area, called for $6,271. Both figures were for a family of four.

27. Unfortunately, during the Reagan administration, funding was no longer made available to the U. S. Labor Department for this venture, so that it appeared for the last time in 1983. The Heller budgets had been discontinued previously, perhaps because the results they sought to achieve were being accomplished by the Labor Department's City Worker's Family Budget.

28. In the encyclical *Quadragesimo Anno* by which Pius XI commemorated the 40th anniversary of *Rerum Novarum*, depending on the particular translator, these hoped-for successors of the medieval guilds were called "functional groups" or "vocational orders." In the original Latin they appeared as *ordines*.

29. The right of workers generally to organize was first stated explicitly and protected by the National Labor Relations Act of 1935 (known generally as the Wagner Act). The Railway Labor Act of 1926 had protected that right to organize, but only for railroad workers. (Later this law was made applicable also to airline employees.)

30. So-called "labor priests" who established "labor colleges" for workers and special institutes in certain dioceses, as well as at some Catholic universities, where they taught courses on the social encyclicals, were not uncommon during this time.

Chapter 2
Pius XI
Quadragesimo Anno

The second encyclical addressed to the economic order, or, in terms of our subtitle, treating economics as if God matters, was issued by Pius XI to commemorate the 40th anniversary of *Rerum Novarum.* According to the established practice of designating encyclicals by the first words of the original text, it is known as *Quadragesimo Anno* which translates as: "In the fortieth year." The vernacular titles generally try to capture the basic thrust of encyclicals, so that this one has the English title: *On Reconstructing the Social Order.* In addition, the words, "on reconstructing the social order" do actually occur in the formal opening statement of the encyclical's purpose.

It is interesting to note at the outset of this commentary a certain evolution even in the way papal encyclicals are addressed. For *Rerum Novarum,* Leo XIII still followed the traditional mode: "To Our Venerable Brethren, All Patriarchs, Primates, Archbishops and Bishops of the Catholic World." *Quadragesimo Anno* added to this standard form also: "...and to All Faithful of the Catholic World." It was left to John XXIII to expand the dimensions of that form, "To All Men of Good Will," in his encyclical, *Pacem in Terris.* One may interpret this change as reflecting either the increasing urgency of the problems dealt with in the social encyclicals, or the growing ecumenical endeavor of the Catholic Church as it moved toward the Second Vatican Council. Indeed, these two factors may well be related: as economic disorder became more widespread and critical, the need to come to grips with them became a matter of obvious, serious concern for all of mankind. In any case, all subsequent social encyclicals have included the expanded, more ecumenical format.

By 1931 the advanced nations of the world had, in fact, slipped into a worldwide economic depression. Moreover, the effect of the widespread economic collapse had its impact also on the remainder of the world—a world then still divided to large a extent into a few empire-building nations on the one hand, and their colonial possessions on the other. The latter had never actually derived significant benefit from the Industrial Revolution and from the wealth that began to flow from the mines, mills, and factories of the developed nations in the century following it. They had served merely as the suppliers of cheap raw materials for those mines, mills, and factories; and frequently they also served as reservoirs of cheap labor. Indeed, some economists saw the Great Depression as stemming, at least to some degree, from a severe imbalance between the pattern of distribution of the growing production made possible by the continuing advances in technology and industry, and the dire, unfulfilled needs of a vast portion of mankind. Others traced it to the severe economic and political dislocations caused by World War I. Once again, the two factors are not unrelated, since that War was calculated, at least in part, to protect the colonial interests of the victorious nations.

For the United States, which had not joined the ranks of the European empire-builders to any significant degree, the ensuing tide of events which upset its very economic foundations became cataclysmic to the extent that it is now referred to widely in capital letters as the "Great Depression." That distinguishes it from all subsequent, recurrent economic setbacks, which are referred to in more benign terms as "recessions."

The Great Depression was marked by widespread unemployment raging side-by-side with dire need, not only in the poorer countries, but also in the wealthy and highly developed ones. In the United States, it reached a level approaching one-fourth of the work force. Monetary systems collapsed disastrously with results ranging from runaway inflation in the vanquished powers, Germany, Austria, and Russia, to the loss of one-third of the commercial banks in the United States, along with the then uninsured savings of millions of depositors.[1] Other casualties of the collapse were the stock exchanges where vast fortunes were wiped out overnight, and also the hallowed gold standard, deemed by some to be indispensable for maintaining a proper monetary system. The economic turmoil was so severe that it inevitably led to disturbances also in the political *status quo*. By 1930, the previously existing order had already been upset by the Communist Revolution in Russia and by Mussolini's Fascist takeover in Italy. Similar collapse was threatening in Germany and elsewhere. All of this disorder in the world prompted Pius XI to issue a second social encyclical addressed to the economic problem, and he used the occasion of the fortieth anniversary of *Rerum Novarum* to do so.

The new encyclical reviewed much of what Leo XIII had presented in *Rerum Novarum*: All that was important in the Leo XIII encyclical, and which was still relevant to the fast-changing world in 1931, can be found again in *Quadragesimo Anno,* often in a more highly developed form. The approach in the encyclical, in fact, incites an interest in reviewing *Rerum Novarum,* which successors of Leo XIII, including Pius XI, have declared to be by no means outmoded. Indeed, the latter designated it as "the *Magna Charta* on which all Christian activities in social matters are ultimately based" (39). Meanwhile, he indicated that much of the world, even the Catholic segment, had not been able to absorb all of the counsel contained in that pioneer encyclical, or to accept it. "These men either slander a doctrine of which they are entirely ignorant, or if not unacquainted with this teaching, they betray their failure to understand it, or else if they understand it they lay themselves open to the charge of base injustice and ingratitude" (39). Such failure and, in some cases, recidivism, is precisely one important factor prompting popes time and again to issue anniversary encyclicals repeating the same basic themes, but adding updated applications. In any case, Pius XI felt called upon to do so because: "In the course of these years...doubts have arisen concerning the correct interpretation of certain passages of the Encyclical or their inferences, and these doubts have led to controversies even among Catholics, not always of a peaceful character" (40). Along with such remedial work, the Pontiff indicated that, "...the new needs of our age and the changed conditions of society have rendered necessary more precise application and amplification of Leo's doctrine" (40). Thus, we have first a cursory review of what was accomplished since and in the name of *Rerum Novarum.*

The Review

In his own landmark social encyclical, Pius XI always took great pains to accredit the pioneer builder, Leo XIII. Thus he started out by listing six Leonine encyclicals which preceded *Rerum Novarum,* and which set forth the principles for correcting the errors in society also in family life and in the political order.[2] There is also, according to some translations, the very significant first use of an important concept *solidarity* which was to become commonplace in subsequent social encyclicals. Thus, we find: "*Rerum Novarum,* however, stood out in this, that it laid down for all mankind unerring rules for the right solution of the difficult problem of human solidarity, called the social question, at the very time when such guidance was most opportune and necessary" (2). The concept, human solidarity (Latin: *humana consortio*), came to be used subsequently with increasing frequency by Pius XII, John XXIII, Paul VI, and Pope John Paul II, with the latter designating it as a "Christian virtue"[3] and making it a pivotal principle for sound social order.[4]

We shall have more to say about that principle later in our commentary on the various succeeding encyclicals where it occupies an important position. It is worth noting at this point how Pius XI was equating the "problem of human solidarity" with what was referred to widely by then and in the time of Leo XIII as "the social question." Briefly, that social question involved relations among the classes. It had to do with the encroaching class conflict, widely hailed and incited by the socialists, between the workers and their employers. It was a conflict which fed on the abuses by the "capitalist class," and which was conditioned by the parameters of a harsh, disordered system.

Pius XI again addressed the plight of society which Leo XIII had referred to, where one class "small in numbers enjoyed practically all of the comforts so plentifully supplied by modern invention," whereas the second class, "the immense multitude of workingmen, was made up of those who, oppressed by dire poverty, struggled in vain to escape from the straits which encompassed them" (3).

In developing this theme, Pius XI prophetically struck a note which should draw our attention to a problem confronting and troubling the Catholic Church in recent times. It is the cult of "liberation theology" which has misled well-intentioned persons, including priests and religious, especially in missionary lands where the extreme contrasts between rich and poor are most glaring.[5] How resonant this section of an encyclical, now more than eighty years old, sounds! Referring to the grave economic inequality between workers and "the wealthy" who were easily persuaded to regard the sad state of affairs as "the consequence of inevitable and natural economic laws," Pius XI wrote: "Others, whom a solid Christian training restrained from such misguided excesses, convinced themselves nevertheless that there was much in all this that needed a radical and speedy reform" (4). Referring to "many Catholics, priests and laymen who with admirable charity had long devoted themselves to relieving the undeserved misery of the laboring classes, and who could not persuade themselves that so radical and unjust a distinction in the distribution of temporal goods was quite in harmony with the designs of an all-wise Creator" (5), the Pope indicated that all of this nevertheless resulted in a "grave conflict of opinions...accompanied by discussions not always of a peaceful nature" (7). Thus, Leo XIII had felt the need to provide some authentic social teaching in conformity with Christian principles. Regrettably, the same "grave conflict of opinions" erupted again in our own time when so-called "liberation theology" led to discord even among parties who proposed to have the interests of the Church at heart. Even more regrettably, we were now dealing with people who, unlike their counterparts before 1891, were in possession of a significant body of their Church's authentic social teachings which were being declared either irrelevant or passé by some of the contenders.[6]

At this point, Pius XI again established his Church's social teaching on its course between opposing evils, indicating that Leo XIII had "sought help neither from Liberalism nor Socialism." This was because, "The former had already shown its utter impotence to find a right solution of the social question, while the latter would have exposed human society to still graver dangers by offering a remedy much more disastrous than the evil it was designed to cure" (10). Needless to say, that too was a prophetic statement, given the turn of events in the years which followed. Nor is it entirely a matter of history; because, even while systems based on socialism have collapsed, after having indeed "exposed human society to still graver dangers by offering a remedy much more disastrous than the evil it designed to cure," the liberal ideology, despite having proven its "impotence to find a right solution to the social question," has experienced a remarkable revival in our time.[7] That is true even among those who have been privy to the wisdom of Leo XIII over the past century, and who should be aware that he long ago, in Pius XI's words, "boldly attacked and overthrew the idols of Liberalism." (14). Regrettably, however, what Leo XIII taught "was so far and so unexpectedly in advance of its time, that the slow of heart ridiculed the study of the new social philosophy, and the timid feared to scale its lofty heights" (14).

Although Pius XI was to use the specific term "capitalist" and "capitalistic," later in his encyclical, during the portion in which he reviewed what Leo

XIII had contributed and what was accomplished subsequently, he adhered to the theme, "liberalism."[8] It is almost as if the Pontiff had anticipated the dogged persistence of this flawed cult, which would later survive even socialism and claim a victory over it.[9] When reviewing what had been done by civil authorities since *Rerum Novarum*, Pius XI again pointed out how

> Leo XIII boldly passed beyond the restrictions imposed by Liberalism, and fearlessly proclaimed the doctrine that the civil power is more than the mere guardian of law and order, and that it must strive with all zeal "to make sure that the laws and institutions, the general character and administration of the commonwealth, should be such as of themselves to realize public well-being and private prosperity" (25).

To be sure, the *laissez faire* cult was one of the "idols of Liberalism," which Leo XIII dared to overthrow. In the years that followed, civil authorities in various parts of the world slowly resumed playing an active role in the economic life of states.

Even in the United States, with its predominantly Protestant cultural background, social legislation began to emerge, first at the state level, and later at the federal. Under the aegis of the constitutional right to "regulate interstate commerce," we had began to regulate our railroads even before *Rerum Novarum*, in 1887 after a period of wild and destructive competition. Later, in the name of preserving competition—another of the "idols of Liberalism"—we launched a period of "trust-busting," by a series of laws designed to break up large industrial combinations which dominated certain markets by agreements on pricing and market areas, etc. The first such law—the Sherman Act—came coincidentally in the same year as *Rerum Novarum,* 1891, with the Clayton Act following several years later. States also had begun passing laws to improve the lot of workers and to insulate them from the ravages of "free competition." Following the lead of Massachusetts which passed a minimum wage law in 1912, eight states had such legislation by 1923. Michigan and Montana actually passed laws in 1919 requiring "equal pay for equal work" for women. Also, states began passing laws requiring workmen's compensation, starting with Maryland in 1903, followed by 10 other states by 1911 and by the federal government in 1916. Other laws set limits on the hours of work by women and exempted them from hazardous occupations, etc. Therefore, inasmuch as "the Encyclical *Rerum Novarum* completely overthrew those 'tottering tenets of Liberalism,'" which, according to Pius XI, "had long hampered effective interference by the government," (27) there came into being "a new branch of jurisprudence unknown to earlier times, whose aim is the energetic defense of those sacred rights of the workingman which proceed from his dignity as a man and as a Christian" (28).

Turning to Leo XIII's suggestions about what the workers and employers could do for themselves, Pius XI again indicted "Liberalism," because it had "deeply infected...rulers of not a few nations," who accordingly "regarded...unions of workingmen with disfavor, if not with open hostility" (30). Indeed, the more colloquial term, "labor unions," began appearing with increasing frequency in *Quadragesimo Anno,* whereas in *Rerum Novarum* the common reference had been to "associations."[10] There was also recognition of the situation in which workers in non-Catholic cultures found themselves, where they "seem to have no choice but to enroll themselves in neutral trade unions." It was left to the judgment of "the Bishops to permit Catholic workingmen to join these unions" (35). A leading U. S. churchman, Edward Cardinal Gibbons, had interceded with Leo XIII to lift Rome's ban on the American labor union known as the Knights of Labor. The organization had certain Masonic trappings, like passwords, secrets, and titles like that of its leader, "Grand Master." Subsequently it was up to bishops heading dioceses to complement or counteract whatever "non-neutral" influence labor unions might demonstrate. As indicated earlier, this was accomplished in some dioceses by the establishment of complementary bodies known variously as "labor schools, colleges, institutes."

Beyond labor unions, there was mention of other "excellent organizations," as those "amongst farmers and others of the humbler classes" (37). However, "associations of employers and captains of industry...did not meet with the same success" (38).

Before moving into an updating of the Leonine teachings on private property and the just wage, Pius XII set the record straight regarding the Church's competence to speak on what seemed to some critics to be purely mundane matters. Once again, it found itself criticized by both sides: on the one hand, for not acting, and on the other, for interfering. The socialists criticized religion generally for providing an "opiate for the masses," so that they did not feel the pain of social oppression and arise to better their condition. On the other side, one which included unfortunately members of the same Church for which Leo XIII and Pius XI spoke, objected that these social encyclicals involved non-doctrinal, secular matters about which the Church was not in a position to speak with authority. Therefore, such persons regarded themselves as exempted from taking its pronouncements seriously. In addition, the persistent, ever-present nationalistic element also entered in. For example, there was the dogged Americanist factor in the United States, according to which the matter was sometimes expressed in such blunt terms as, "What do those Italians buried away in the Vatican know about actual conditions in alien cultures and faraway places like the United States?"

Thus, Pius XI felt compelled to repeat what Leo XIII had already insisted on, apparently without complete success, that the Church is within its competence and authority in "all those (matters) that have a bearing on moral conduct" (41). This went along with its disclaimer with regard to "technical matters, for which she has neither the equipment nor the mission." There was also the acknowledgment that "economic science and moral discipline are guided each by its own principles in its own sphere" (42). However, sensible persons must also acknowledge that these "spheres" do overlap often; and where they do, each science must respect the competence of the other. Justice, for example, is a virtue, and it is a part of the object of the moral science of ethics. What is more, it is a part of the science of moral theology, as is its companion social virtue, charity. Therefore, the Church has something to say to the economist. One does not pursue economic well-being at the expense of justice. Whereas theft may make the thief prosper economically, he does so at another's expense, and with possible consequent damage to the overall welfare of society. Thus the laws of morality—the moral law, in other words—must be given the same emphasis as the laws of economics. It is interesting that the Pope here referred to these as, "The laws of economics, as they are called…." (42). Economists should not take offense at this reference. Instead, they would do well to examine the loose way in which the term "law" has been used in their science from its beginnings: e.g., the "iron law of wages," the various Malthusian population laws (or principles) and, for that matter, the "laws of supply and demand" which are tendencies far more than they are "laws" in the same ineluctable sense as the term applies in the natural sciences. In any case, the matters discussed in the social encyclicals involve the moral law which "reason clearly deduces from the nature of things," also with regard to "the end and object of the whole economic order assigned by God the Creator" (42).

The Right of Private Property

In his affirmation of what Leo XIII taught about the double character of private ownership—its individual and social aspects—Pius XI felt compelled to deal with certain challenges to that position. Again, they came from opposite sides: the one, here referred to as "Individualism," denying the social aspect, and the other—"Collectivism"—denying the private one. At this point, we find reference to something beyond what was contained in *Rerum Novarum*: a warning about rushing, "headlong into the quick-sands of social modernism with its moral, juridical and social order, which we condemned in the Encyclical Letter issued at the beginning of Our Pontificate." (46). The Pontiff was referring to his first encyclical, *Ubi Arcano*, issued in 1922 where the expression "social modernism" was first used. *Modernism* refers to the theological heresy which flared up in its full fury during the pontificate of St. Pius X who condemned it in his encyclical *Pascendi* (1907). Reduced to its simplest and most general terms, it is the fallacy that calls for religion and the Church to continuously update and adapt to a shifting cultural and moral climate. The concern of Pius XI at this point was the growing denial by various parties of one or the other aspect of the principle of property ownership: the private one or the social one. Thus what he was denouncing now in *Quadragesimo Anno* was precisely this flexible, constantly adaptive spirit as applied to teachings on the social order. It represented precisely the kind of performance he had targeted in *Ubi Arcano* (60) ten years previously: while protesting

> that they believe in and hold fast to Catholic doctrine on such questions as the right of owning private property, on the relations between capital and labor, on the rights of the laboring man…they speak, write, and, what is more, act as if it were not necessary any longer to follow, or that they did not remain still in full

> force, the teachings and solemn pronouncements which may be found in so many documents of the Holy See, and particularly in those written by Leo XIII, Pius X, and Benedict XV.[11]

Such persons were at large in 1931, as they still are today. Pius XI felt the need to refer specifically to left-leaning types who were accusing the Church of allowing a "pagan concept of ownership to creep into [its] teachings...and that another concept must be substituted which in their astounding ignorance they call 'Christian'" (45). The "pagan concept" that the critics were alluding to was the so-called absolute notion of private ownership associated with Roman law, which we referred to earlier.[12]

With that interpretation of private property rights inserted into the liberal capitalistic framework of society came the leading emphasis on commutative justice which, as the Pope indicated here, calls upon us to "faithfully respect the possessions of others, not encroaching on the rights of another and thus exceeding the rights of ownership" (47). However, as Leo XIII had already pointed out, there is also an application of the virtue of justice, which transcends commutative justice. While not yet designating this application in specific terms, Pius XI recalled simply that, "The putting of one's own possession to proper use, however, does not fall under this form of justice, but under certain other virtues, and therefore it is 'a duty not enforced by courts of justice.'" Although Leo XIII never used the specific term "social justice," he did outline its meaning and some of its applications. Now Pius XI was moving closer to the point in *Quadragesimo Anno* where he would name it and designate it, along with social charity, as "a true and effective guiding principle" for economic life (88).

Thus we have a reaffirmation of the double character—individual and social—of private property. The Church found itself wrestling perennially with the two opposing forms of rejection: the individualistic one which sought to absolutize the right of private ownership and to reduce all obligations to those required in commutative or strict justice, and the collectivistic one which proposed to do away with obvious and horrendous abuses of the right of private ownership, by abolishing the right itself. To introduce some moderation into the discussion, Pius XI alluded to the historic fact that "the right of ownership, like other elements in social life, is not absolutely rigid..." (49). Through the course of history different people in different cultures applied sometimes more, sometimes less social control over property rights. In some cultures there was more communal property than in others. The first Christians during Apostolic times provide an obvious example where *voluntarily*, "Those who believed shared all things in common..." (Acts 3:44). In early Germanic societies, woodlands, meadows, etc. were withheld from private ownership, for use in common, a practice that carried over into medieval society, and beyond. Even in the most individualistic of times, there have been public parks, libraries, and the like. Indeed, an aspect of social control over private ownership which is perhaps too seldom noted (even while it is sometimes flagrantly abused!) is the right of the state to levy taxes. By the power to tax, civil authorities are, in effect, telling citizens that a certain portion of what they own is to be removed from their own discretionary capacity to spend, with the state taking over that jurisdiction for the common good. However, Pius XI repeated the warning by Leo XIII, that it is "unlawful for the state to exhaust the means of individuals by crushing taxes and tributes" (49). This upholds the common-sense right to tax, at the same time as it indicates that the right must be exercised by public authorities in a fair, prudential manner. What remains in place, however, is the basic right to private ownership which nature, not the state, conferred on man, so that the state has no right to take it away.

Not at all in harmony with our contemporary "capitalistic" culture is the stern admonition with regard to "superfluous income." Contemporary man tends to bristle at the admonition that, "a man's superfluous income is not left entirely to his own discretion." At this point, the primeval urge asserts itself to say some equivalent of: "What's mine is mine to do with as I please," perhaps even with an appended, emphatic, "by God!" Not "by God," in any case! Christian teaching, as presented in this important paragraph of *Quadragesimo Anno,* clearly has a different view with regard to "that portion of his income which he does not need in order to live as becomes his station." We learn here that, "the grave obligations of charity, beneficence and liberality which rest upon the wealthy are constantly insisted upon in telling words by Holy Scripture and the Fathers of the Church" (50).

As if to reassure those living in a capitalistic society which has gone a long way toward being post-Christian, the succeeding paragraph indicates that the use of "superfluous income in searching favorable opportunities for employment" falls within the norms of liberality indicated above. Indeed, it is fair to say that the bulk of people's "superfluous income" in our times does not characteristically take the form of idle hoards which have a detrimental effect on the economy; nor is such income used, by and large, for profligate consumption spending. Instead, it typically takes the form of money capital, which, more or less aggressively, seeks investment outlets that, at least potentially, may provide employment for others. Thus, Pius XI stated appropriately that such investment is "an act of real liberality particularly appropriate to the needs of our time" (51).

At this point the Pontiff turned to the question of how ownership is acquired, and how capital and labor may both end up making unjust claims to their share of produced wealth. Original acquisition of property, we are told, comes by *occupation* and by *industry*. The former applies, of course, to things which are "unclaimed and which belong to nobody." Industry, as a claim to things, may take two forms: that which a person applies as "his own master, and by which some new form or new value is produced" (52). Most persons in modern industrial society are not involved in this latter mode of production. Therefore, they find themselves in the more typical situation of "the labor one man hires out to another and which is expended on the property of another" (53). At this point the contest begins: to determine who gets how much of the goods which are produced jointly by labor and capital, aided by the "wealth and resources of nature, its treasures and its power" (53). Represented here are what economics textbooks typically refer to as the three primary factors of production: land, labor and capital. And from this arises the third step in the economic process—income distribution—following the first two: production and exchange. In the context of modern individualistic social philosophy, it is this step primarily which gives rise to the bitter contest between labor and capital, in other words, the so-called "social question."

While repeating the Leo XIII dictum that "It is only by the labor of workingmen that states grow rich," Pius XI indicated that unjust claims to the results of what is inherently a joint productive effort can come from labor as well as from capital. However, those who owned and controlled capital enjoyed what is intrinsically a more powerful position for exercising their demands. "Capital...was long able to appropriate to itself excessive advantages; it claimed all the products and profits and left to the laborer the barest minimum necessary to repair his strength and to ensure the continuation of his class" (54). Here the Pontiff outlined what came to be referred to in economic literature as the "subsistence theory of wages." This, he pointed out, had come to be regarded by certain economists as "an inexorable economic law" which held that "all accumulation of riches must fall to the share of the wealthy, while the workingman must remain perpetually in indigence or reduced to the minimum needed for existence." The subsistence theory was proposed in Adam Smith's *Wealth of Nations,* in David Ricardo's economic theory, and in Malthus' works. It was the socialist, Ferdinand Lassalle, who christened it "the iron law of wages." Accordingly, Pius XI referred to it as one of "the Liberalistic tenets of the so-called Manchester School" (54), even while he indicated that things were "not always and everywhere" as "deplorable" as this theory or "law" proposed. Nevertheless, actual conditions for workers were deplorable enough to provoke certain "intellectuals" to spin off an equally false theory: that "all products and profits, excepting those required to repair and replace invested capital, belong by every right to the workingmen." In other words, we had the so-called "labor theory of value," discussed previously in our commentary on *Rerum Novarum.* Pius XI then turned to formulating his own principle of just distribution, and it centered predictably on the just wage principle.

It is in this portion of the encyclical (pars. 56ff.) that the specific expressions "social justice" and "capitalists" are used for the first time in the social teachings of the Church. Pius XI indicated here what just distribution implies: "Wealth...which is constantly being augmented by social and economic progress, must be so distributed amongst the various individuals and classes of society that the common good of all...be thereby promoted." He continued: "By these principles of social justice one class is forbidden to exclude the other from a share in the profits." In violation of them, we have "an irresponsible wealthy class who...deem it a just state of things that they should receive everything and the laborer nothing.... But they are also violated by a propertyless wage-earning class who demand for themselves all the fruits of production as being the work of their hands." Such vehement worker reaction, according to Pius XI, was due to "the violation of justice by capitalists."

What follows in *Quadragesimo Anno* is a continuing development of the important principle that the virtue of social justice is a critical element for restoring social order. Although Leo XIII never used the term itself, he had already stated what was its essence: the common good.[13] That was reaffirmed now by

Pius XI with explicit mention of *social justice.* Indeed, the unmistakable link between social justice and the common good is indicated by his statement that "the distribution of created goods must be brought into conformity with the demands of the common good and social justice" (58).

We have in *Quadragesimo Anno*, therefore, what amounts to a further development of the Church's traditional teaching on the virtue of justice; and moral theologians ought to take serious account of it in their treatment of this important cardinal virtue. *Social justice* was clearly implied by Leo XIII; and it was also implicit in the works of St. Thomas Aquinas and of Aristotle before him, even though none of those three used the same expression. The standard distinctions in the application of the virtue of justice have included commutative justice, distributive justice, and legal justice. *Commutative justice* has as its object the particular good of another individual, as in a routine exchange transaction, the repayment of a debt, the return of borrowed goods, and the like. *Distributive justice* involves persons who are in some position of authority over others, assigning to those persons what is their due. What is due involves both benefits and obligations or burdens, as in taxation. Now, persons in authority are entrusted with the overall good of whatever society they are at the head of, ranging from the relationship of the father to his family, to rulers and legislators at the various levels of government. Therefore, distributive justice already has as its object a certain common good, rather than the specific good of some individual person. *Legal justice,* finally, represents the reciprocal obligation of persons who are subject to authority, to the common good of whatever legitimate society they are members. Since, in current usage, the designation "legal" implies laws —in other words, positive legislation—legal justice has come to be understood more or less narrowly as the due observance of such laws and legislation.

A moment's reflection will make it clear that, since both distributive and legal justice have as their object the common good in one or another of its aspects, they represent two specific applications of the broader concept, social justice, which has as its object precisely the common good. However, as the virtue of social justice is used in the social encyclicals with reference to the just distribution of income, it becomes equally clear that something beyond the mere passage of laws and their observance are involved here. Nowhere is it proposed by popes in their social teachings that, for example, the civil authorities should determine income shares for the various parties in production. Indeed, that would represent a violation of another key social principle, the principle of subsidiarity. Yet the demands of social justice and of the common good represent a most urgent category of what is required for reconstructing the social order. Two things are possible now: extending the concept "legal" in legal justice to include also all more or less obvious requirements of the natural law; or else, we may come up with another expression to cover that ground without the handicap involved in the way the term, legal, is currently used. Pius XI used the term, social justice, to include the broader category of the common good which clearly exceeds what is required simply by "laws," in the narrower sense.

The Jesuit economist, Heinrich Pesch (1864-1926), who is responsible to a large degree for some of the pivotal concepts introduced in *Quadragesimo Anno*, added another expression to the standard ones. First, he correctly subsumed distributive and legal justice, as commonly interpreted, under the general category social justice, because both have the common good as their object. These he therefore juxtaposed to commutative justice which has the good of a particular individual as its object. Then he went a step further by proposing that we may distinguish between *contributive* and *distributive* social justice. *Contributive justice* covers demands of the common good on the part of all who are members of society at its various levels, and who derive benefits from membership in societies and from the respective common good which each involves.[14] Pesch also pointed out that while social justice was often simply equated with *social order,* this was already a metaphorical usage of the term. Unfortunately, it appears that now this metaphorical usage has come to predominate, so that social justice has become for many little more than a slogan. At best, there is a confusion of means with the end. Social order results from the widespread application of the virtue of justice in its various dimensions throughout society. This obfuscation is regrettable, since it will become clear as we progress in our commentary on *Quadragesimo Anno* that social justice is a critical operative principle in the papal program for reconstructing the social order.

Indeed, the term "social justice" appears again in the next paragraph in *Quadragesimo Anno* where its use appears synonymously with the "demands of the common good." It is installed at the very heart of the proposed principle of just distribution. That principle is formulated here in the words: "Each class, then, must receive its due share, and the distribution of created goods must be brought into conformity with the demands of the common good and social justice, for every sincere observer is conscious that the vast differences between the few who hold excessive wealth and the many who live in destitution constitute a grave evil in modern society" (58). Here the "demands of the common good and social justice are linked" in such a way as to make it clear that social justice has as its object "all that is necessary for the common good," as the virtue was subsequently defined in the Pius XI encyclical, *Divini Redemptoris*, in 1937 (51).[15]

Notwithstanding the babble of liberalistic economics which came to be enshrined as "classical economics," common sense would have indicated that since most people on God's earth are working people, most of them of modest means, no national economy could long prosper if that vast majority of mankind is not allowed a modest degree of prosperity. Unfortunately, the nonsense proposed by that school, sometimes referred to as the Manchester School, suggested otherwise in the name of liberty, in this case, economic liberty.[16] It not only triggered the rise of equally absurd socialist theories, but it also led to the eventual breakdown of social order.

Incidentally, it was in this section of *Quadragesimo Anno* that the terms "proletariat" and "proletarianism" were also used for the first time in papal social teachings. They stem from the Latin word, "*proles,*" meaning "offspring," and they were introduced into common parlance by socialist theorists referring to the condition where "Capital...left to the laborer the barest minimum necessary to repair his strength and to ensure the continuation of his class" (54). This implied furthermore that the workers were a "propertyless" class. Thus, the socialists were provided with a clear track for abolishing the right of private property because, as they perceived matters, the workers who made up the majority of mankind were already basically without property. Pius XI proposed instead: "Every effort...must be made that at least in the future a just share only of the fruits of production be permitted to accumulate in the hands of the wealthy, and that an ample sufficiency be supplied to the workingmen" (61). The "effort" to improve the plight of the proletariat then brought the Pope to new high ground in developing further the just wage principle first presented by Leo XIII in *Rerum Novarum.*

That modest property ownership was a part of such a program was indicated by the words: "...by thrift they may increase their possessions and by the prudent management of the same (they) may be enabled to bear the family burden with greater ease and security, being freed from the hand-to-mouth uncertainty which is the lot of the proletarian." Indeed, Pius XI was proposing that the workers would therefore "not only be in a position to support life's changing fortunes, but will also have the reassuring confidence that when their lives are ended, some little provision will remain for those whom they leave behind them" (61).

The Just Wage Doctrine

Pius XI placed the just wage doctrine at the heart of his program for just income distribution, which was, in turn, critical in his overall plan for "reconstructing the social order." He made this clear when he opened the discussion of the just wage with the words: "This program cannot, however, be realized unless the propertyless wage-earner be placed in such circumstances that by skill and thrift he can acquire a certain moderate ownership.... But how can he ever save money, except from his wages and by living sparingly, who has nothing but his labor by which to obtain food and the necessities of life" (63)?

When Leo XIII launched the just wage discussion in *Rerum Novarum*, he offered a rudimentary statement of the principle. Needless to say, his presentation evoked criticism on opposing sides! These sides included also those who approached the problem too simplistically without taking into account what the pioneer social teacher had said: "Before deciding whether wages are fair, many things have to be considered."[17] Pius XI was about to deal with some of these "many things," and he began by addressing again the issue of whether the mere fact of a "free" agreement between workers and their employers is sufficient to assure the just wage. Leo XIII had conceded that "as a rule, workman and employer should make free agreements, and in particular should freely agree as to wages."[18] However, he also indicated in the same statement that the just wage requirement was presupposed here because "there is a dictate of nature more imperious and more ancient than any bargain between man and man." The Pontiff went on to indicate that oftentimes "necessity or fear of a worse evil," in fact, made the agreement less than truly free from the standpoint of the worker. In other words, what is at issue here is that old "chestnut" of the liberalistic philosophy, *freedom*. It comes down to the question of how free is "free," and whether there is real freedom for the worker in the typically unequal bargaining position between him and his employer who owns the tools of production.

Pius XI affirmed again the essential validity of the wage contract between workers and employers. Indeed, he admonished those who were now proposing that what "must be introduced" in its place is a "contract of partnership" (64). Then comes a significant proposal, which nevertheless certainly does not have the same magisterial sanction as the obligation to pay the just wage. It amounts instead to prudential, benevolent, conditional advice:

> In the present state of human society, however, We deem it advisable that the wage contract should, when possible, be modified somewhat by a contract of partnership, as is already being tried in various ways to the no small gain both of the wage-earners and of the employers. In this way wage-earners are made sharers in some sort in the ownership, or the management, or the profits (65).

That this is conditional advice is clear from the expression, "In the present state of human society," and from the proviso, "when possible." That it is prudential is clear from the expression, "We deem it advisable." That it is an eminently wise and prophetic bit of advice has been made clear retrospectively by the fact that the three kinds of sharing mentioned here represent what are until now perhaps the most advanced, progressive kinds of labor-management initiatives already in operation. Indeed, they have become widespread enough that there are acronyms in vogue among those who are knowledgeable in the field of labor-management relations, to facilitate discussion about them. Employee ownership of stock, i.e., a form of sharing in ownership, is known widely as ESOP (Employee-Stock-Ownership-Plan). Management-sharing is also widely known in terms of one of its most common forms as LMC (Labor-Management-Committee). And profit-sharing, perhaps the oldest of the initiatives, is often referred to among those involved in it simply as PS.

However, when all is said and done, none of these approaches *must* be followed in order to assure payment of the just wage. Nor may they be employed as substitutes for the basic just wage or to dissuade workers from joining or forming a labor union, as was not infrequently the case. The obligation to pay a just wage, on the other hand is *not* a prudential matter. It is, as Pius XI indicated, required "according to strict justice" (69). He did, however, propose certain conditions which, if not fulfilled, would make it impossible to equitably appraise or properly recompense workers "according to strict justice" (69-75). They are conditions stemming from the fact that labor has both an individual and a social character. This means that: "human society forms a truly social and organic body"; that "labor be protected in the social and juridical order"; that, "the various forms of human endeavor, dependent upon one another, are united in mutual harmony and mutual support"; and finally that, "above all, brains, capital and labor combine together for common effort."

This was a large order; but the Pope made it clear that unless these conditions were fulfilled, "man's toil cannot produce due fruit" so it could "be neither equitably appraised nor properly recompensed according to strict justice" (69). The year was 1931, and it is no exaggeration at all to say that none of these conditions were then entirely fulfilled. Therefore if we accept the papal premise, it is small wonder that workers at the time were not being "equitably appraised, nor properly recompensed according to strict justice." In the United States, for example, workers and their employers were engaged in bitter struggles for union recognition. Even despite significant changes in the "juridical order" brought about by long overdue labor legislation to protect the rights of workers to organize, the rank-and-file American worker still lacked the kind of social respectability enjoyed by other occupational groups.[19] Hence, he did not yet enjoy the kind of protection in the social order which the Pope was talking about. Indeed, an unbiased appraisal of the situation nearly a century later indicates that organized labor even now has a poor public image, and that the worker, despite a significant degree of protection in the juridical order, still does not enjoy the kind of social acceptance which honest labor deserves and would get in a well-ordered society. Also, even though there have been scattered bold and encouraging initiatives to bridge the gap between workers, owners, and management, those operate along the outer fringes of the overall American labor relations scene.

Given the lack of workplace and occupational group solidarity, what the Pope said, in effect, was that worker productivity and efficiency would not reach the level which it could attain in a more harmonious atmosphere. Thus, the worker's potential worth to the employer, as well as to the national economy, is too often not realized, limiting also what even a well-intentioned employer can offer him in pay. Significant traces of class conflict engendered and exploited by the social critics of capitalistic society linger, even after socialism itself has proven its long-run non-viability in real life. Class conflict is implicit in the expression "adversarial relationship" which is all too often still upheld with pride in depicting American labor-management relations. In other words, even now more than a half century after Pius XI warned about its debilitating effects with regard to the payment of just wages, the *individual* character of labor is still too much emphasized in our society, as opposed to its *social* character which has been shamefully neglected.

Viewing the entire matter in proper perspective—in other words, considering both the individual and social character of labor—Pius XI began putting the ingredients of the just wage principle in place. His proposals came under three headings: one having to do with the support of the worker and his family; the second, taking into account the condition in which a business may find itself; the third, considering the requirements of the common good. It is important to note that these factors do not represent conditions determining whether the just wage *should* be paid. They are instead factors to be considered in determining the wage which justice requires *must* be paid.

The first plainly makes the just wage a *family* wage, i.e., one which will support not only the worker himself, but also his wife and children. Ruled out is "abuse [of] the tender years of children or the weakness of woman." What is more, "Mothers will above all devote their work to the home and the things connected with it; intolerable, and to be opposed with all Our strength, is the abuse whereby mothers of families, because of the insufficiency of the father's salary, are forced to engage in gainful occupations outside the domestic walls to the neglect of their own proper cares and duties, particularly the education of their children" (71).

Needless to say, this papal admonition will not play well in contemporary society where a misguided feminist ideology is rampant. The erroneous view is sad enough, taken by itself; but equally distressing are the unfortunate economic realities which all too often virtually force mothers to work outside the home, "because of the insufficiency of the father's salary." Thus any number of fine women, while not allowing themselves to be deluded by the radical feminists who want to "emancipate" womankind from home and children, nevertheless feel compelled out of economic necessity to leave their positions in the home as wives and mothers, in order to earn the second paycheck—if not the only one!

Pius XI presented *Quadragesimo Anno* during the Great Depression. What he had to say then is certainly no less valid now. However, he did not excuse non-payment of the just wage, even while acknowledging the practical impossibility of doing so which some employers undoubtedly faced. Indeed, it afforded him the opportunity to emphasize again the ineluctable demands of *social justice*. Referring to that wage which was sufficient to support not only the worker, but also the mother of his children and the children, he stated: "If in the present state of society this is not always feasible, social justice demands that reforms be introduced without delay which will guarantee every adult workingman just such a wage" (71). In other words, when economic conditions in society are such that it is difficult, if not impossible, for the employer to pay his workers a just wage, both are victims of an unjust social order. Then the common good requires that "reforms be introduced without delay which will guarantee every adult workingman just such a wage." There is no yielding on the just wage principle here, only a shifting of blame and of the obligation, from the area of commutative justice which is binding on the individual employer, to that of social justice which is binding on other persons in society who share in some way in either the problem or the solution, or both. The widespread inability and also unwillingness, in many cases, to pay the just wage to workers even in our time so many years after *Quadragesimo Anno* called for reforms "without delay," suggest that we are not dealing here with an obsolete, irrelevant document.

"The condition of any particular business and of its owner" (72) also becomes a factor to be considered in arriving at the just wage. Once again, the sorry condition in which a business may find itself is not an excuse for non-payment of the just wage. It may, however, result in a shifting of blame from the particular employer. Whether or not it does depends on whether the poor state of the business is due to "...bad management, want of enterprise or out-of-date methods," or if it is "overwhelmed with unjust burdens, or...is compelled to sell its products at an unjustly low price" (72). In the former case, guilt obviously remains with the employer, so that he ends up violating strict justice in failing to pay his employees the just wage. In the latter case, other elements are at fault: "...those who thus injure it are guilty of grievous wrong, for it is they who deprive the workingmen of the just wage and force them to accept lower terms." This could apply to other business competitors operating in the same market area or industry. It could also involve those who are entrusted with keeping the national economy in good repair, and who may have allowed general economic conditions to deteriorate to such an extent that a widespread inability to pay just wages occurs. Thus, once again, social justice (whatever the common good calls for) requires action on the part of all such persons to remedy the bad situation. Ultimately, if conditions persist, "counsel must be taken whether the business can continue, or whether some other provision should be made for the workers." In other words, the inability to pay the just wage for reasons stemming from outside the business itself does not justify continuance of a business, anymore than does internal bad management of the business. Since the just wage is required in commutative justice, we have a situation similar to one where a customer honestly cannot afford the price of the product. Assuming that the price is just in the first place, the merchant is not therefore required to sell him the product at a lower price. In the just wage situation, it is the worker who is the "merchant," and he should not be forced to accept what is less than the just "price" for his product: labor. Indeed, he should not even be placed in a position where he "volunteers" to accept less than the just wage, because, as indicated earlier, labor is both "individual," and "social." It is the means whereby workers generally earn their livelihood, and even if I personally do not happen to need the minimum required just wage, it is a legitimate assumption that most others do; and I may not violate the common good in which I am a participant and sharer by "spoiling" the labor market for them.

It is precisely that third factor—the common good—to which Pius XI turned with his statement that: "The exigencies of the common good finally must be regulated with a view to the economic welfare of the whole people." It appears that now the Pontiff was moving the just wage doctrine beyond the minimum just wage to which every adult, full-time workingman is entitled, no matter how modest his level of skill or experience. It is implicit in the very nature of the common good to not ever require or tolerate a wage below that minimum level. However, there are also just wages for older, more skilled, more experienced workers which allow wider levels of tolerance depending on the particular exigencies of the common good in different situations. It is these exigencies which the negotiating parties must keep in mind in various concrete applications of the doctrine.

First of all, demanding too high a level of wages can seriously restrict or even dry up "opportunities for work." There is an implicit admonition here for powerful labor unions which may permit themselves to be carried away by their own power in the bargaining process, so that they are led to exact wages which are too high for the common good of the firm, of the industry, and eventually of the economy overall. Indeed, the admonition also applies to those who are in a position to contract individually for exorbitant rates of pay. This includes executives, professional persons like physicians and lawyers, various kinds of brokers and agents who work for commissions and, especially in our disordered times, the whole wide world of entertainers in sports and in the various media, who earn incomes which are beyond the wildest dreams of what entertainers in past ages would have thought possible![20] Such distortions in the overall income distribution pattern do grave damage to the overall economic common good, since they leave that much less of the finite, available amount of national wealth for the rest of humanity. Therefore, large numbers of workers may simultaneously end up with "a scale of wages" which is "too low." The Great Depression provided a tragic example of where the scale of wages was, by and large, too low to allow economic recovery. Regrettably, the developing situation at present appears to be moving in the same direction so that, among other things, wives are often forced to seek work outside the home so as to generate enough income to operate the household.

There is bounteous economic wisdom in the brief statement: "All are aware that a scale of wages too low, no less than a scale excessively high, causes unemployment" (74). Unfortunately, it appears that all were *not* aware of that basic economic truth then or even now so many years later. If people are required to work for substandard wages, this means, by definition, that they cannot maintain an adequate standard of living. This means, in turn, that they cannot purchase the quantities of goods and services which need to be purchased in order to maintain something like a full level of employment throughout the economy. Thus, when working people who do, in fact, make up the majority of buyers in the national economy do not earn wages above the bare subsistence level, the economic mechanism will grind to a halt for lack of sufficient purchasing power in the hands of the majority of people in the economy. It was in this context that Pius XI mentioned social justice for the fourth time in this encyclical. Referring to the lowering or raising of wages unduly, "with no consideration for the common good," he indicated that this is "contrary to social justice which demands that by union of effort and good will such a scale of wages be set up, if possible, as to offer to the greatest number opportunities of employment and of securing for themselves suitable means of livelihood" (74).

Pius XI referred to unemployment, "particularly if widespread and of long duration," as "a dreadful scourge," which "causes misery and temptation to the laborer, ruins the prosperity of nations, and endangers public order, peace and tranquility the world over" (74). It was to alleviate and remove that "scourge" that he alluded to "a reasonable relationship between different wages," and as "intimately connected with this...a reasonable relationship between the prices obtained for the products of the various economic groups, agrarian, industrial, etc." While some schools of economics have tended to adopt too mechanistic a view of the interrelationships between wages and prices among themselves and with each other, it is an undeniable fact that these represent variables which do have important relationships to each other. Indeed, the next papal encyclical addressed to the economic order, *Mater et Magistra* by John XXIII, went further in developing this matter. It had as its main theme the matter of *balance,* or to use the term economists have preferred, *equilibrium.* In *Quadragesimo Anno* it was applied principally to the obvious relationships between various wages and prices within a given national economy, whereas the next generation of encyclicals took it beyond national borders and extended it to the worldwide economy.

In the final analysis, the entire just wage issue lies at the heart of the economic problem; in fact, of the whole economic system. It brings us to the "chicken or the egg" dilemma of economic life. Does supply generate its own demand, as an early exponent of so-called classical economics proposed when the modern economic science was first being formulated?[21] Rephrased in terms of the more contemporary Keynesian and post-Keynesian discussion: does investment or does consumption act as the principal engine for generating full employment or, more broadly, economic prosperity? It is obvious that all of these variables are essential components of the economic process; and when the economy is performing well they all operate in simultaneous harmony. However, when the process breaks down or fails to function as smoothly as it should, we look for the source of the problem. Then the motive force—what starts the process and keeps it running smoothly—becomes a critical consideration. Ultimately, people do not buy things simply because they are supplied. Instead, people supply things because they perceive that they are needed, i.e., that there is a *demand* for them. So the "chicken" here is demand, and the "egg" is supply. Or again, in more contemporary Keynesian terms: people do not consume because someone has invested; instead, sensible, perceptive entrepreneurs invest because they perceive that what they produce will be purchased by consumers who have wants along with the buying power and the will to satisfy those wants. Now since most people must depend on their wages or salaries to fulfill their demand or their consumption needs, it seems clear that what is critical for the smooth, continuous operation of the economic process is the widespread payment of adequate wages, i.e., wages which make it possible for "fathers of families (to) receive a wage sufficient to meet adequately ordinary domestic needs" and "by skill and thrift (to) acquire a certain moderate ownership...." In other words, we have now, more than a century after *Rerum Novarum,* and approaching a century after *Quadragesimo Anno*, reverted to a distortion of economic literacy which a brilliant economist sought to set right when the leading economies of the world collapsed in the Great Depression.[22] And if someone chooses, perhaps understandably, not to accept the word of an economist, such a person may wish to reflect on the wisdom of perhaps the greatest political genius the United States has ever produced:

> It is the eternal struggle between these two principles—right and wrong—throughout the world. They are the two principles that have stood face to face from the beginning of time; and will ever continue to struggle. The one is the common right of humanity, and the other the divine right of kings. It is the same principle in whatever shape it develops itself. It is the same spirit that says, "You work and toil and earn bread, and I'll eat it. (Abraham Lincoln in the seventh Lincoln-Douglas Debate, October 15, 1858).

Reconstructing the Social Order—The Triad of Principles

The balance of *Quadragesimo Anno* deals with the particular, cardinal principles which need to be operational for reconstructing the social order overall. Pius XI indicated that the "right distribution of property and a just scale of wages" was "concerned directly with the individual," and only "indirectly with the social order." However, he also pointed out that Leo XIII, in presenting those doctrines, had made "A happy beginning" toward "reconstructing the social order"—the theme for *Quadragesimo Anno* (77). And he proceeded to present three specific ingredient principles for that reconstruction: *the principle of subsidiarity*; the *principle of occupational organization*; and the installation of the twin social virtues: *social justice and social charity, as the regulating principles for economic conduct.* As we indicated previously, all of these had been suggested by Leo XIII, but not in the precise terms as Pius XI now did. Their explicit formulation and installation as principles for reconstructing the social order may, in fact, be regarded as summarizing what is distinctive and new about *Quadragesimo Anno.* These three principles may be viewed as constituting a triad—three elements which support each other reciprocally like the three legs of a tripod.

The first of these delineates what is to be the role of the government or, more broadly, of the state and other social bodies comprising society. It is now widely known as the *principle of subsidiarity*. Depending on the translation, the original Latin, "*servato hoc 'subsidiarii' officii principio*" is rendered either as, "this principle of subsidiarity is followed" or, "this principle of subsidiary function" (80).[23] Leo XIII already provided specific guidance regarding the role of the public authorities in the economic life of the nation. It was his significant contribution, disturbing to many at the time, to indicate that the state was not to be reduced to something like "night-watchman" status in economic affairs, so that it was to play not merely a negative role, but also a positive one. Nevertheless, he cautioned "that the State must not absorb the individual or the family" (28). Pius XI now offered a further indication as to why he and his Predecessor felt a need to restore to the state an active role in the social order.

> Not indeed that all salvation is to be hoped for from its intervention, but because on account of the evil of Individualism, as We called it, things have come to such a pass that the highly developed social life which once flourished in a variety of prosperous institutions organically linked with each other has been damaged and all but ruined, leaving thus virtually only individuals and the state (78).

Here the Pope was, in fact, establishing the historical context also for the second principle for social order. Proper limitation of the role of the state implied that other social organs, present in the earlier ages, should take over some of the regulative functions that would otherwise be attempted by the state. That such social organs, when restored, would take a different form than the guilds is apparent: "It is indeed true, as history clearly proves, that owing to the change in social conditions, much that was formerly done by small bodies can nowadays be accomplished only by large corporations" (79). The Pope was not talking about "corporations" as this is commonly understood in American society at present.[24] He was referring to the corporate bodies made up of all who worked in the same industry or occupation: the vocational groups which comprised a second part of the triad. These would be adapted to the needs and mentality of post-medieval, modern society. They would make it possible for the state and the public authorities to "mind their own business," so as to conform to the *principle of subsidiarity* which is then stated explicitly. "None the less, just as it is wrong to withdraw from the individual and commit to the community at large what private enterprise and industry can accomplish, so, too, it is an injustice, a grave evil and a disturbance of right order for a larger and higher organization to arrogate to itself functions which can be performed efficiently by smaller and lower bodies" (79).

The Pontiff referred to this quite solemnly as "a fundamental principle of social philosophy, unshaken and unchangeable." To be sure, it is a principle which did not originate with *Quadragesimo Anno*; it is, instead, a common sense, i.e., natural law, principle. We may cite once again, Abraham Lincoln, who in many respects embodied quintessential common sense. He said many years before, in 1854:

> The legitimate object of government is to do for a community of people whatever they need to have done but cannot do at all, or cannot so well do for themselves in their separate and individual capacities. In all that the people can individually do as well for themselves government ought not to interfere.[25]

Obviously, if individuals and smaller bodies in society take care of "business of minor importance," then the state will be better able to "carry out with greater freedom, power and success the tasks belonging to it, because it alone can effectively accomplish these, directing, watching, stimulating and restraining, as circumstances suggest or necessity demand" (80).

The destruction of the old guild system which played a major role in regulating economic life in medieval cities left a vacuum in the social order. Inevitably, the state, growing more and more absolute and claiming rule by "divine right," moved in to fill the vacuum. That oppressive condition led to the liberalistic flirtation with economic chaos that has been going on to a greater or lesser degree since the end of the 18th century. And this flirtation and resultant economic disorder, in turn, provided a rostrum for socialists and other proponents of state control of economic life, if not all of social life, to bring a restoration of state absolutism, now called totalitarianism. As if to substantiate the Hegelian dialectical theory,[26] the inefficiency and oppressiveness of the latter has again made liberalism seem plausible. Had the world paid more attention to what Pius XI was proposing in 1931, such see-sawing attempts to restore social order could perhaps have been averted. What exactly was he proposing?

It was time now for "the state" and "all good citizens...to abolish conflict between classes with divergent interests and thus foster and promote harmony between the various ranks of society" (81). In retrospect, we feel entitled to apply that to both the socialists who advocated class hatred and the eventual abolition of the "capitalist class," but also to those who have remained content with the *status quo*, while even extolling the so-called "adversary relationship" between workers and their employers.

Pius XI then took a bold step—one which for various reasons even some who helped to formulate it later regarded as stillborn![27] He called for the installation of the second of his triad of principles for reconstructing the social order. This involves intermediate bodies between the individual and the state, which were designed to lift much of the burden of economic regulation from the overburdened state. "It is necessary, then, that social policy be directed toward the establishment of functional groups" (82).

Once again, the weakness of translation makes itself felt in this very important matter. The Latin word used is "*ordines,*" literally, "orders." It has come to be translated variously as "vocational orders," "vocational groups," "functional groups," "corporate orders," etc. More important than the term used is the idea that is clearly regarded by Pius XI as critical for the reestablishment of order in economic life. The idea is easily ascertainable from the context. It is seen in the juxtaposition of this idea to the present condition where "the demand and supply of labor divides men on the labor market into two classes, as into two camps, and (where) the bargaining between these parties transforms this labor market into an arena where the two armies are engaged in combat." Thus, the Pope affirmed, "But there cannot be question of any perfect cure, except this opposition be done away with, and well ordered members of the social body come into being anew, vocational groups namely, binding men together not according to the position they occupy in the labor market, but according to the diverse functions which they exercise in society" (83). It is this organization according to specific economic *function* which led some commentators and translators to turn from calling them "vocational groups" to use of the term. "functional groups."[28] Clearly what Pius XI was calling for here was an organization of intermediate bodies in society organized according to what people do for a living or on the basis of their specific function in the economic life of the nation. Such bodies could accomplish a large part of the task of regulating the economic conduct of their participants, specifically, seeing to the quality of their products, their pricing and competitive practices, the rate of pay, the adjustment of disputes among workers and employers, establishing uniform rules about observing Sunday rest, etc.

If the term, "vocational groups," seems alien, perhaps even other-worldly, to persons in contemporary industrial society, it is nevertheless worth noting that the author of *Quadragesimo Anno* was bringing us face to face once again with the natural law, something much older than any social encyclical. He represented such bodies as analogous to the political ones which people form because they live in close geographical proximity. "For as nature induces those who dwell in close proximity to unite into municipalities, so those who practice the same trade or profession, economic or otherwise, combine into vocational groups" (83). Indeed, Pius XI stated that such groups, "in a true sense autonomous, are considered by man to be, if not essential to civil society, at least its natural and spontaneous development." While it is not absolutely "essential" for man to always do what is "natural," he does violence to his own fulfillment by ignoring natural laws. An ancient saying by the poet Horace indicates that one cannot indefinitely frustrate nature: "*Naturam expellas furca, tamen usque recurret* (You may expel nature with a pitchfork, but it will always return)."[29] Once again, there is no better evidence for all of this *naturalness* than the example of the new ventures in labor relations in the years following World War II in Japan. There, such "vocational orders" were put in place, and they were called "industry councils."[30] And they did indeed play an important role in regulating the economic affairs of respective industries in the successful reconstruction of that war-devastated national economy. Yet, it is unlikely that in non-Christian, Japanese society the inspiration came from *Quadragesimo Anno.* It is far more likely that it came from promptings from "nature"; and the reason that "nature" does not prompt Western, ostensibly Christian, nations may lie in their having become not only post-Christian, but also unnatural in their approach to social order. People do not always do what is natural; and what is natural is not always absolutely essential. Obviously, a one-legged man can walk with a crutch indefinitely; but he suffers a considerable handicap in what he can do in that unnatural state.

What may have been a fatal flaw in the way some nations sought to carry this proposal for organization according to occupations into effect soon after the encyclical appeared, was the way in which it was attempted in certain cases. Pius XI stated that just as in choosing the appropriate form of political government, "Here too men may choose whatever form they please, provided that both justice and the common good be taken into account" (86). Attempts were made to establish vocational orders in predominantly Catholic countries like Austria, Portugal, and Spain. Even prior to the appearance of *Quadragesimo Anno,* Fascist Italy had established a so-called corporate state, which in some ways reflected the idea of the vocational orders. All of these efforts failed eventually for various reasons. Some sought to impose the orders in a peremptory manner from above; elsewhere they were attempted in situations where the cultural soil or the political climate was yet not prepared for them. In Austria, for example, attempts by the government of Engelbert Dollfuss were cut short by his assassination and the Nazi *Anschluss* in 1938.

A predictable objection to the kind of self-regulation implied in this papal proposal is the threat which it poses for the "free competition" installed as the ultimate regulating principle for economic life by what the Pope referred to here as the "'Individualistic' school" (88). According to that principle, workers should be allowed to compete one against the other in dealing with their employers; and the latter should also be allowed full freedom in competing with each other for workers, in the pricing of their products, etc. This philosophy was first introduced into the infant science, economics, by the French Physiocrats who were products of the Enlightenment. It reflected their deistic naturalism which did not tolerate even the Creator of the universe to meddle with so-called "natural laws" which, according to that philosophy, he had originally set into operation to govern both the physical universe and the social order. *Laissez faire et laissez passer, le monde va de lui même.*[31]

There is much wisdom for economists in what Pius XI had to say at this point: "This school, ignorant or forgetful of the social and moral aspects of economic matters, teaches that the state should refrain in theory and practice from interfering therein, because these possess in free competition and open markets a principle of self-direction better able to control them than any created intellect" (88). With that, among other things the whole positivistic orientation of modern social sciences, disdainful of so-called "value judgments," is swept aside, and ethical implications are restored to their proper place in a science which involves human, and not merely mechanical, actions.

Now obviously, if entire industries or occupational groups are united for pursuing their own particular common good, this would limit "free competition." It could even introduce in its place a power struggle by one self-interested group against another, with possible serious consequences not only for the weaker contestants but for the overall common good. In other words, group power struggles would replace what the reign of free competition had already accomplished by the start of the 19th century—a power struggle among self-interested individuals, where the most powerful (or the most ruthless) survived. Thus, we would be encouraging precisely the kind of situation which the anti-trust laws in the United States, for example, sought to prevent.[32] Here, then, was the proper context for the Pope to introduce the third part of the triad of social principles for reconstructing the social order.

It is important to remember that Pius XI and his successors in the social teachings never condemned competition outright as a valid force in economic life. In fact, the author of *Quadragesimo Anno* made it clear that "Free competition...within certain limits" could be "just and productive of good results." But it "cannot be the ruling principle of the economic world." Therefore, "it is...very necessary that economic affairs be once more subjected to and governed by a true and effective guiding principle" (88). Acknowledging that the inevitable consequence of unrestrained competition had, in the meantime, already occurred, the Pope hastened to point out that "the economic supremacy which within recent times has taken the place of free competition" also could not serve in place of the "true and effective guiding principle" which he now proposed. He spoke of "More lofty and noble principles...social justice and social charity" (88).

The third part of the triad of social principles—the third leg of the triad, or tripod—is now in place. It becomes clear how the three reinforce each other reciprocally. If the state is to be relieved of a multitude of tasks that can be done as well or better by individuals or lower social bodies, such bodies, like the vocational orders, must be in operation. However, if these are not to become simply self-seeking agents in power struggles driven by a kind of group egotism, they and their individual members must be motivated not only by a concern for their own narrower common good, but by an ongoing, active concern for the broader common good, up to and including the common good of the entire national economy. Here is where the third element in the triad, the virtues of justice and charity as applied to the common good—in other words, social justice and social charity—must play their role. These virtues, acting as "more lofty and noble principles," can, first of all, relieve the state of much burden which it would otherwise have to assume if all of its members operated simply in their own selfish interests. Social justice and social charity would serve to prevent the intermediate bodies, if and when those became operational, from acting simply as selfish interest groups. At the same time, the state, being relieved of a multitude of tasks by the intermediate groups, could function more effectively in the surveillance of such groups, to prevent them from giving in to the temptation of acting contrary to the overall common good.

We have already dealt at some length with the virtue, social justice, indicating that it involves the specific application of justice to the common good, as distinct from the individual good which is the object of commutative justice. But here Pius XI offered us for the first time with an additional concept: *social charity.* As presented here, he obviously intended it to operate in tandem with social justice. Now charity, the theological virtue, has as its object God Himself. However, in its second dimension, requiring us to love our neighbor as ourselves, it too has various possible applications. It may be defined as love for, or active concern for, whoever or whatever the object of charity in its specific application may be. Thus, the virtue of social charity is an active, continuing concern for the common good of any and all societies of which we are members. What then is its role in the context of reconstructing the social order? Justice requires or demands. Charity motivates or prompts (cf. 2 Cor. 5:14). Accordingly, the encyclical provides us with a guideline at this point. We are told that justice "must build up a juridical and social order able to pervade all economic activity." At the same time: "Social charity should be, as it were, the soul of this order" (88). There was no further elaboration on the meaning and precise function of this virtue at this point. Many years later in *Sollicitudo Rei Socialis* (1987), Pope John Paul II would elaborate on the meaning and implications of what he termed the "Christian virtue" of solidarity (40); and in *Centesimus Annus* (10) he in fact identified the "principle of solidarity" with "social charity."

While social justice is mentioned specifically on several more occasions during the remaining portions of the Pius XI encyclical, social charity is mentioned alongside it just one more time, nevertheless in a most significant manner. When inviting Catholics who have deserted to socialism to return to the fold, Pius XI urged them to dedicate themselves to "unremittingly endeavor to reform society according to the mind of the Church on the firm basis of social justice and social charity" (126).

However, charity, as such, does come up for earnest discussion near the end of the document. There we find important clues as to what the Pontiff quite probably had in mind when he linked social charity with social justice. After an important, unequivocal statement that "Economic life must be inspired by Christian principles," we are warned, in words which are as relevant in our own times as in 1931, that

> Mere sordid selfishness, which is the disgrace and the great crime of the present age, will be opposed in very deed by the kindly and forcible law of Christian moderation, whereby man is commanded to seek first the Kingdom of God and His Justice, confiding in God's liberality and definite promise that temporal goods also, so far as he has need of them, will be added unto him (136).

Since charity is central to the Christian Gospel, it is appropriate that the Pope turned his attention to it in his summation of the encyclical. To bring about the desired reform, then, we are told that "charity 'which is the bond of perfection' must play a leading part" (137). Although justice cannot accomplish everything, we are nevertheless reminded that "charity cannot take the place of justice unfairly withheld." This is an obvious reference to the kinds of persons that we seem to have among us always who, while withholding what they owe in justice, then dispense it as charity, not always without the ostentatious display that is sometimes characteristic of philanthropy. Yet, even if justice is in place everywhere, the complexities of everyday life and the possible collisions of even equal rights, which may occur even in the best of societies, make it certain that "a wide field will nevertheless remain open for charity" (137). Charity will ease frictions and make it possible to avert unnecessary confrontations over what may appear to be conflicting rights. In other words, justice, by itself, can be quite harsh and cold. Charity enlivens even a just structure; and needless to say, it also promotes and makes easier the practice of the virtue of justice. The critical point is then made: "For justice alone, even though most faithfully observed, can remove indeed the cause of social strife, but can never bring about a union of hearts and minds." That appears to contain the core of what the relationship of the twin social virtues, justice and charity, is all about. Justice without charity is like a body with a head, but without a heart. And charity substituted for justice is the body with a heart but without its head on straight. The "union of hearts and minds... binding men together, is the main principle of stability in all institutions, no matter how perfect they may seem, which aim at establishing social peace and promoting mutual aid" (137).

At this point the Pope, true to his office as head of the largest and oldest Christian church, spoke in scriptural and theological terms. He reminded us that we are all "members of a single family and children of the same Heavenly Father," and that we are also "one body in Christ and everyone members one of another." Furthermore, we are to follow "in the footsteps of Him, Who, being in the form of God, chose to become a Carpenter among men, and to be known as the Son of a Carpenter." This is proposed as the ultimate message which Christians have to bear in mind in order "to unite all in harmonious striving for the common good..." The message has special urgency given that, "we are confronted with a world which in large measure has almost fallen back into paganism" (141).

At the conclusion of the encyclical, we have an indication of why a Church whose mission is primarily directed to men's eternal salvation would get so heavily involved in developing a body of teachings addressed to the social order, and specifically, to its economic aspect. It is a lesson which all missionaries, starting with the First, have appreciated: that one cannot hope to inspire authentic religious sentiments in people without showing active concern also for their most pressing temporal needs.

> For herself the Church of Christ, built upon the solid rock, has nothing to fear, for she knows that the Gates of Hell shall not prevail against her: and the experience of centuries has taught her that storms, even the most violent, pass, leaving her stronger and triumphantly victorious. But her maternal bosom cannot but be stirred at the thought of the countless ills which tempests of the world occasion to so many thousands; at the thought, above all, of the immense spiritual evils which ensue, entailing the eternal ruin of so many souls redeemed by the Blood of Christ. No stone, then must be left unturned to avert these grave misfortunes from human society (144-145).

Casualties and Survivors

Since *Quadragesimo Anno* appeared in 1931, some violent storms have indeed passed over the Church; and one appears to be in the process of passing, not without much uncertainty and unsettling conditions. Fascism and Nazism, both of which evoked special encyclicals by the same Pope who authored this one, have become history.[33] Fascism was already in place in the Pope's beloved Italy when *Quadragesimo Anno* made its appearance.[34] Hitler's National Socialist government was to come to power in Germany two years later, in 1933. Both of these terminated by the end of World War II.

Meanwhile, socialism had found itself a victim country in 1917 where its twisted theories could finally be put into operation.[35] That disastrous experiment has now also faded into history in the lands which used to be parts of the Soviet Union—coincidentally so, just a century after the Church's social teachings on economic order began! Thus, the portion of *Quadragesimo Anno* addressed specifically to socialism in its various aspects and transformations, being historically conditioned, are now less relevant than in the period between 1931 and 1991.[36]

Yet, succeeding popes have continued to develop further the body of social teachings addressed to the economic order begun by Leo XIII. That is because the basic problem—the so-called "social question"—has not yet been favorably resolved. Could that be because the "parent" of social disorder is still alive? Consider this important statement by Pius XI: "Let us bear in mind that the parent of this cultural Socialism was Liberalism, and that its offspring will be Bolshevism" (122). The Pope was referring to an insidious approach by certain socialists whose "main aim is the formation of minds and manners" (121). Actually, that was merely to provide a training ground for full-fledged socialism, what the Pontiff referred to here simply as "Bolshevism." But let us turn our attention finally to the "parent," Liberalism.

Amid the death struggle of socialism, the liberalist cult persists; indeed, it thrives and is being proposed for imitation by many as the victor in the ideological combat which has occupied the center stage of history through most of the past century. Therefore, the portion of the encyclical which employed for the first time in social encyclicals the terms, "capitalist economic regime" (103), and the "capitalistic economic order" (104), remains very important for dealing with and evaluating precisely the situation we now face.

Pius XI used those expressions while referring to the fact that Leo XIII was addressing "chiefly...that economic regime in which were provided by different people the capital and labor jointly needed for production" (100). And he indicated that his predecessor's "whole endeavor was to adjust this economic regime to the standards of true order" (101). Accepting as the definition of capitalism suggested here: the system where the capital and labor "jointly needed for production" are provided by different people, we need to pay close attention to the important follow-up statement that, since Leo XIII's "whole endeavor was to adjust this economic regime to the standards of true order, ...it follows that the system itself is not to be condemned." Since "it is not vicious of its very nature...it violates right order only whenever capital so employs the working or wage-earning classes as to divert business and economic activity entirely to its own arbitrary will and advantage without any regard to the human dignity of the workers, the social character of economic life, social justice and the common good" (101). In other words, we are not talking about an economic system which is intrinsically evil ("vicious of its very nature"), like the Communist system, but about one which may become perverted ("violates right order") when, as indicated, "capital so employs the working or wage-earning classes as to divert business and economic activity entirely to its own arbitrary will and advantage without any regard to the human dignity of the workers."

What follows clearly suggests that historically the "capitalist economic regime" has indeed allowed itself to become perverted. And that perversion stems from the inherently flawed liberalist ideology, which Leo XIII opposed from the outset, and which has taken possession of its soul. In referring to changes which have taken place in the capitalist regime since *Rerum Novarum,* Pius XI referred to the accumulation of wealth and also immense power and despotic economic domination "in the hands of a few," who "are frequently not the owners, but only the trustees and directors of invested funds, who administer them at their good pleasure" (105). We have here an allusion to the prevalent structure of modern corporations where the actual owners—the stockholders—become more and more passive rentiers who await generous dividends, while managers chosen by directors, who, in turn, elect the directors, are actually in charge of these large industrial and financial empires.[37] The Pope then alluded to what may be even a more sinister force at work behind the scenes, the modern banking system which arose in principle simultaneously with modern capitalism (106). He identified them as "...those who, because they hold and control money, are able also to govern credit and determine its allotment," and who, "for that reason supply, so to speak, the life-blood of the entire economic body...grasping, as it were, in their hands the very soul of the economy, so that no one dares to breathe against their will.[38]

This accumulation of power in the modern capitalistic economies has been, according to Pius XI, the "natural result of limitless free competition that permits the survival of those only who are the strongest, which often means those who fight most relentlessly, who pay least heed to the dictates of conscience" (107). In a word, at the root of the problem is not the structure of the capitalistic regime as such. Depending on the historical context, it is perhaps inevitable that one or the other group in society will achieve a certain dominance, as feudal lords did during the Middle Ages, and capitalists did in the following period. Neither feudal lords nor capitalists must, of their nature, be wicked and preside over an evil form of society. Unfortunately, the capitalistic order came to be perverted by its liberalistic philosophy—"this individualistic spirit in economic affairs" (109). It resulted in a kind of economic Darwinism, where it was not necessarily the "fittest" but the least scrupulous who survived. Thus, the forceful statement: "Free competition has committed suicide; economic dictatorship has replaced the free market" (109). What is more, "Unbridled ambition for domination has succeeded the desire for gain; the whole economic life has become hard, cruel and relentless in a ghastly measure" (109). That is a significant observation, and it is extremely relevant still to our own times. Financial manipulation has become a hallmark or contemporary business wheeling and dealing. Greed alone cannot explain it, because many of the persons—some of which are caught in their corrupt practices—have more wealth than they could possibly spend in many lifetimes. A new avarice takes the place of simple greed—avarice for power and control. In the process, the ordinary worker, who generally aspires to little more than reasonable security in a job which will enable him and his family to live in the kind of modest comfort which our highly productive modern technology places within the reach of all, frequently becomes a pawn on some corporate chessboard. There he is moved about, sacrificed, and discarded in the manipulation and control games played by so-called entrepreneurs who are less concerned with producing a worthwhile product than with financial power and control. Thus, time and again the worker is reduced to insecurity unknown to even the serfs of the feudal era. And he must struggle to survive at a level of pay which forces also the mother of his children to leave the home and enter the work force. There she too becomes a part of the system where "bodily labor, which was decreed by Providence for the good of man's body and soul even after original sin, has everywhere been changed into an instrument of strange perversion: for dead matter leaves the factory ennobled and transformed, where men are corrupted and degraded" (135).[39]

Even while the worst predictions of Leo XIII were being fulfilled when Pius XI wrote such words—and as they are being fulfilled yet in our time—history moved ineluctably on its course. The boundaries of opportunity expanded on an unprecedented scale with the accelerated march of technology. By the end of World War II, we had entered an era when nuclear power changed the face of the earth, and when men traveled to the moon and back. Problems which had been predominantly national in scope, became global. Yet, as Leo XIII had been prophetic in foreseeing the problems which loomed ever larger and which bedevil mankind still, Pius XI, while mainly preoccupied with economic disorder within national economies, also foresaw with uncanny sense and warned that those problems would spread beyond national borders. These prophetic words, then, provided the keynote for a generation of social encyclicals in the years ahead: "Further, it would be well if the various nations in common counsel and endeavor strove to promote a healthy economic cooperation by prudent pacts and institutions, since in economic matters they are largely dependent one upon the other, and need one another's help" (89).

Notes

1. The Great Depression is generally regarded as having begun with the stock market crash in autumn of 1929. Actually, it had already gained momentum by that time, and the crash was a reflection of what was happening in the vital sections of the economy. Yet, things became much worse after the stock market broke, since banks, among others, had invested heavily in the market. They did this both directly on their own accounts, and indirectly through extensive lending to their customers. Thus, the nation's money supply, which came largely from the banking system, began to diminish; and before the worst was over, it had declined, as had the number of banks, by roughly one-third. There is disagreement about when the Depression ended. Actually there were slight spasmodic improvements within the 1930s, but full recovery did not occur until wartime spending brought about what the more modest pump-priming activities by the federal government during the New Deal era did not ever accomplish. Excellent works on this disastrous period in U.S. economic life include John Kenneth Galbraith, *The Great Crash* (1955); David A. Shannon, ed., *The Great Depression* (1960); Lester B. Chandler, *America's Greatest Depression 1929-1941* (1970).

2. These may be termed *social* encyclicals, since they are addressed to various aspects of the social order, specifically to the family and the political order: *Arcanum* (*On Christian Marriage*, 1880); *Immortale Dei (On the Christian Constitution of States*, 1885); *Sapientiae Christianae* (*On Christian Citizenship,*1890); *Quod Apostolici Muneris* (*On Socialism*, 1878); *Libertas* (*On Human Liberty*). Not mentioned, but referred to by Pius XI as "others of the kind") include: *Inscrutabili* (*On the Evils Affecting Modern Society*, 1878), and *Diuturnum* (*On Civil Government,* 1881). Serious students of Catholic social teachings should familiarize themselves with all of these, which are in various ways still relevant for present-day society.

3. Cf. John Paul II, *Sollicitudo Rei Socialis* (*On Social Concern*, 1987), St. Paul Editions, par. 40.

4. Cf. Oswald von Nell-Breuning, *Reorganization of Social Economy,* English by Bernard W. Dempsey, S. J. (Milwaukee: Bruce Publ. Co., 1936), 5. (Certain translations do not use the expression, human solidarity, at this point). The author of that work, who died in 1991 at the age of 101, is reputed to have been predominant in helping Pius XI to draft the encyclical *Quadragesimo Anno*. As an understudy of his fellow Jesuit Heinrich Pesch, Nell-Breuning was beholden to him for the ideas that were central to the encyclical. Pesch (1864-1926) developed the *solidarist* economic system in his exhaustive five volume textbook, *Lehrbuch der Nationalökonomie*, published in several editions by Herder in Freiburg, Germany between 1905 and 1926. The solidaristic system, opposed to both individualistic capitalism and collectivistic socialism was based on the *principle of solidarity.* Briefly, this principle involved reciprocal, mutual cooperation at all levels

of society, from the family to the workshop and the occupational group, and from the national economy to the entire family of nations worldwide, based on the *de facto* interdependence of all parties involved at all levels of economic life.

5. The liberation theology notion rests on the supposition that church teaching must provide the basis for "liberating" the millions throughout the world, especially in developing nations, from the dire poverty to which they have been reduced by manifold social injustice. In their impatience to accomplish this praiseworthy goal, some of the exponents have gone so far as to support Marxian tactics and even its philosophy, including class conflict which is diametrically opposed to Christianity.

6. The Catholic Church has seen fit to issue two documents related specifically to this "liberation theology" movement. The first (1984) was *An Instruction On Certain Aspects of the "Theology of Liberation"* by Joseph Cardinal Ratzinger, then Prefect of the Sacred Congregation for the Doctrine of the Faith. The second (1986) by the same author speaking as head of the same Congregation was entitled: *An Instruction on Christian Freedom and Liberation.* Both affirm the need to reform the social order and bring true liberation of mankind by applying the social teachings of the Church.

7. Paul VI, *Octogesimo Adveniens* (St. Paul Editions, 1971), par. 35.

8. For American readers especially, it is important to recall that the terms "liberal" and "liberalism" used in papal encyclicals reflects the original sense, as it is still used widely in European circles. It refers to the idea of economic liberty extolled in classical economics and dating back to the Physiocratic-Enlightenment *laissez faire* concept. In other words, these terms in contemporary American usage represent an almost diametrically opposite meaning.

9. In *Centesimus Annus* (42), Pope John Paul II cautioned against declaring the defeat of socialism in our time as a victory for capitalism. Much depends on how one chooses to define capitalism, and that Pope clearly preferred a different term, in own his words, "*business economy, market economy,* or simply *free economy.*"

10. In *Rerum Novarum* the Latin term, *sodalitia artificum,* appears suggesting worker associations. In *Quadragesimo Anno* the word *syndicatus,* was used, and also the more generic term, *consociationes*..

11. Cf. Pius XI, *Ubi Arcano Dei Consilio,* in *The Papal Encyclicals, Vol. 2, 1903-1939,* ed. Claudia Carlen, IHM (N.p.: McGrath Publ. Co. 1981), 236-7.

12. Nicolas Berdyaev, *The Origins of Russian Communism* (London: Geoffrey Bles, 1948), 30, 126.

13. Cf. *Rerum Novarum* , pars. 26, 27.

14. Heinrich Pesch S.J., *Lehrbuch der Nationalökonomie* (4th & 5th ed.; Freiburg: Herder, 1925), 2, 272-6. English Edition: *Lehrbuch der Nationalökonomie/Teaching Guide to Economics*, trans. Rupert J. Ederer), (Lewiston, NY: Edwin Mellen Press, 2002-2003), vol. II, bk. 1, 272–300.

15. *The Papal Encyclicals* 1903-1939, 547.

16. The terms "Manchester School" and "Manchester liberalism" derive their origin from the Manchester Chamber of Commerce in England which was especially active after 1819 when Parliament passed measures retaining tariffs between England and Ireland. It was made up of prominent merchants and manufacturers who, following Adam Smith's work, vigorously advocated *laissez faire* in domestic economic affairs and free trade internationally.

17. *Rerum Novarum*, par.17.

18. *Ibid.*, par. 24.

19. The most important general legislation protecting the right of workers generally to organize included the Federal Anti-Injunction Act of 1932 (Norris-LaGuardia Act),

and the National Labor Relations Act of 1935 (Wagner Act).

20. For example, it has become commonplace in our time for young men, directly out of college, to be offered multi-million dollar annual salaries for playing in professional sports.

21. The so-called "law of markets" (first formulated by J. B. Say) referred to earlier proposed that supply would generate its own demand in the long run.

22. Whatever one may think of John Maynard Keynes, no one can simply disregard his challenge to the old classical and neo-classical economic thinking, which led to a rephrasing of all of economic analysis following the publication of his book *The General Theory of Employment, Interest and Money* in 1935.

23. An early Paulist translation used the first; and a later one translated this as the "principle of subsidiarity." In the original Latin we find "*'subsidarii' officii principio,"* in other words, "by this principle of subsidiary function."

24. The business corporation is a form of business enterprise created by law with a legal personality of its own. Its liability is therefore limited to what the corporation itself owns; it has a life span separate from that of the owners—the stockholders.

25. *Fragments on Government,* 1854. This may be found in *Abraham Lincoln: Speeches and Writings,* ed. Don E. Fehrenbacher (New York: The Library of America, 1989), 301.

26. According to Hegel, history moves on its course by an ongoing clash between successive emerging opposing situations, which he termed *theses* and *antitheses*, resulting in a *synthesis* which, in turn, becomes the new *thesis*, and so on *ad infinitum.*

27. Nell-Breuning, who late in his long lifetime stated openly that he "wrote" *Quadragesimo Anno* for Pius XI, also allegedly told some who were close to him that the vocational order idea was moribund.

28. Heinrich Pesch, who originated the idea of such organization according to functions performed in the economy, based it on the application of the principle of solidarity among those who work at the same occupation. He used the German terms, "*berufsständische Organisation"* (Pesch, *Lehrbuch* IV, 265; Pesch/Ederer IV, bk.1, 290), and *"berufliche Korporation"* (ibid. II, 220; Pesch/Ederer II, bk.1, 242ff.). Literally, these translate as "vocational," or "occupational organization," and "vocational" or "occupational corporation." Since the words "vocation" and "vocational" have developed a more restrictive meaning in contemporary English usage, I prefer to translate Pesch's idea as "occupational organization."

29. From Horace, "You may drive nature out with a pitchfork, yet it will always return." (Epistles, I, x. 24).

30. William Ouchi, *The M-Form Society* (cited in the previous chapter). In an Appendix (pp. 231ff.) this work lists 38 advisory councils which operate in some key industries including electronics machinery, aircraft machinery, textiles, mining, electric utility, etc. Some are called *industry councils.* In their composition and function they resemble remarkably what Pius XI was proposing here in *Quadragesimo Anno*.

31. The expression is generally attributed to the French Physiocrat writer Jacques Claude Marie Vincent de Gournay (1712-1759).

32. The anti-trust laws were originally designed to prevent competing firms from entering into agreements on prices, output, etc. The purpose to was maintain "free competition." However, in 1911 a United State Supreme Court ruling toned down the enforcement of these laws by establishing what was called the "rule of reason." In essence, the Court declared that only "unreasonable" restraint of trade was subject to anti-trust prosecution. This reflected a gradual realization that exaggerated competition would in certain situations not be in the long-run best interests of either businesses or their customers.

33. The encyclical *Noi Abbiamo Bisogno* (1931) addressed the difficulties which Italian Fascism caused for the Church in Italy. *Mit Brennender Sorge* (1937) dealt with

the threat of Nazism for the faithful in Germany.

34. The section from pars. 98-103 in *Quadragesimo Anno* relates to Mussolini's attempts to install a so-called "corporate state" which some claimed as being in harmony with the vocational orders proposed in this encyclical. These paragraphs make it clear that the Fascist corporate state was not what Pius XI had in mind.

35. *Divini Redemptoris* (1937) was the definitive encyclical on atheistic communism in the Soviet Union. Thus, we have the spectacle of an aging Pius XI facing down three dictators, two of them among the most vicious in history.

36. The paragraphs, 119-140, deal with real or imagined transformations in socialism, e.g., "Christian socialism."

37. Cf. Robert J. Larner, *Management Control and the Large Corporation* (New York: Dunellen, 1970). This scholarly work demonstrates the extent to which, and the devices by which, management gets to control large corporations. The author concluded that of the 500 large non-financial corporations studied, 377 are management controlled by use of the proxy form. By use of this device, stockholders routinely authorize incumbent management to vote for directors. The directors, in turn, select or reinstate the incumbent managers.

38. Modern banking has been perhaps one of the most persistent and important hallmarks of the capitalistic system. It is generally regarded as having come into existence in its present form, i.e., where the commercial banking system is responsible for creating the bulk of the money supply in modern nations, during the 17th century. This corresponds roughly to the increasing predominance of capitalism especially in Holland (the Bank of Amsterdam) and in Great Britain (the Bank of England). Thus, bankers have ever since been in a dominant position not only because of the power to lend or to withhold money capital needed by businesses, but even more so because of the central position which they occupy as the nation's chief money creators. Their record in providing the important lifeblood for national economies has not been reassuring, as is indicated by their pivotal role in the Great Crash in 1929 along with the consequent Great Depression, and most recently in the economic collapse of 2008.

39. Pius XII favored and sometimes quoted that statement. This eminent pontiff never wrote a social encyclical in the generally accepted sense of the word. Yet he dealt incisively with problems affecting the social order at all levels: the family, the economy, and the political order. His thinking on such matters was keynoted by his first encyclical, *Summi Pontificatus* (1939); and it was updated annually in his 19 brilliant *Christmas Messages*. No study of Catholic social teachings is complete without a careful reading of these.

Chapter 3
John XXIII
Mater et Magistra

During his brief pontificate (1958-1963) Blessed John XXIII issued two major social encyclicals: *Mater et Magistra* in 1961, and *Pacem in Terris* in 1963. The first was addressed to the economic order in the tradition of *Rerum Novarum* and *Quadragesimo Anno*, and it bore the English title *Christianity and Social Progress*. The second was, like early Leo XIII encyclicals, focused largely on the political order, and its usual English title is simply a translation of the Latin: *Peace on Earth.*[1] We shall confine our commentary, therefore, to *Mater et Magistra* which commemorated the 70th anniversary of *Rerum Novarum*; and its subtitle provided an indication of its main thrust: *On Recent Developments of the Social Question in the Light of Christian Teaching.* It is clearly an updated application of basic principles established and developed by the two previous social encyclicals on the lingering "social question" in the economic order. And it begins and ends affirming the Catholic Church's role as the "Mother and Teacher of nations" (1, 262).

Blessed John XXIII opened his encyclical by defusing once and for all the standard Marxian complaint that religion is an opiate which lulls people to sleep with regard to their temporal welfare. He did so by his statement that, "...although Holy Church has the special task of sanctifying souls and of making them sharers of heavenly blessings, she is also solicitous for the requirements of men in their daily lives, not merely those relating to food and sustenance, but also to their comfort and advancement in various kinds of goods and in varying circumstances of time" (3). That is a clear and definitive defense, if any is needed, of social encyclicals being addressed to the economic order. It also affirms man's right to a standard of living which in modern times extends well beyond a primitive level of subsistence, as could perhaps be justified in circumstances where there was or is no access to what modern technology makes possible. The Pope also reaffirmed that the "solidly grounded principles, the norms of action, and the paternal admonitions found in the masterly Letter of our predecessor, even today retain their original worth" (9).

Part I

The main body of *Mater et Magistra* began with a clear rejection of the Enlightenment philosophy of the French Physiocrats who established the first principles of the then infant science of economics giving it its naturalistic bias by proposing that, "in economic matters, everything was to be attributed to inescapable, natural forces." That, the Pope indicated, led to the lingering positivistic orientation of economics according to which, "no connection existed between economic and moral laws." If that seems like a lesson in the history of a bygone era, people of our own time might well reflect on his description of the consequent naive faith that, "mutual relations between economic agents could be left to the play of free and unregulated competition." Then he related naive articles of faith by those theological deists like: "Consequently mutual relations between economic agents could be left to the play of free and unregulated competition" and "Interest on capital, prices of goods and services, profits and wages, were to be determined purely mechanically by the laws of the marketplace" (11). All of these foreshadow the words of Paul VI ten years later that "we are witnessing a renewal of the liberal ideology."[2]

Likewise, there is nowhere in papal teachings a more succinct statement of the "social question" than in the paragraphs which tell us about "the proud rule of the stronger regarded as legitimate, so far as economic affairs were concerned"; that "while a few accumulated excessive riches, large masses of workingmen daily labored in very acute need"; and that "wages were insufficient for the necessities of life, and sometimes were at starvation level" (12, 13). We also find in this first part of *Mater et Magistra* a restatement that the social teachings starting with *Rerum Novarum* are based "on the requirements of human nature itself and conforming to the precepts of the Gospel and reason" (15). In other words, we are dealing throughout in these social encyclicals with the natural law which of necessity conforms with the Gospel because both of these, as well as human reason, come from the same Source.

Finally, there was in this recapitulation of *Rerum Novarum* the admonition that, "Workers and employers should regulate their mutual relations in a spirit of human solidarity and in accordance with the bond of Christian brotherhood." *Human solidarity* is the operative term which will be used with increasing frequency in papal social teachings from this time on especially by Paul VI, and until its culmination in *Sollicitudo Rei Socialis,* where John Paul II designates it as a "Christian virtue."[3] Here John XXIII also reaffirmed the Church's position that both: "the unregulated competition which so-called *liberals* espouse, or the class struggle in the Marxist sense, are utterly opposed to Christian teaching and also to the very nature of man" (23).

In turning to what Pius XI accomplished in *Quadragesimo Anno*, the first of several encyclicals commemorating *Rerum Novarum*, Blessed John XXIII provided a succinct summary of its salient points. This involved an interesting change of terminology with regard to the occupational organization (vocational orders, functional groups) proposed by Pius XI to replace the condition where "the demand and supply of labor divides men on the labor market into two classes, as into two camps," and where the bargaining between them resembles, "two armies...engaged in combat."[4] The context in which *social justice* was mentioned for the first of several times in *Mater et Magistra* is significant. John XXIII astutely picked up the reference that Pius XI had made to the mutual dependence of nations on one another, in an encyclical devoted predominantly to economic reconstruction of domestic economies within particular nations.[5] Consequently, the application of the principles of justice and charity to relations among nations was to become a dominant theme in subsequent encyclicals, as keynoted by John XXIII in portions of *Mater et Magistra.*

Dutifully, John XXIII did not fail to mention also Pius XII who, although he wrote no social encyclicals as such, did deliver many important statements on social issues. Mentioned specifically was an important radio address to the whole world on Pentecost, June 1, 1941 marking the 50th anniversary of *Rerum Novarum.* It too declared the pioneer encyclical to be of "permanent value" and of "rich and abiding usefulness" (42).

Then, before launching into his own specific contribution to the body of Catholic social teachings, John XXIII explained why he felt that yet another social encyclical was called for. He referred to the almost literally earth-shaking events in the world emerging from World War II. Mentioned are the dramatic changes in science, technology, and economics: the discovery and application of atomic energy; the "almost limitless possibilities opened up by chemistry in synthetic products; the growth of automation in the sectors of industry and services; the modernization of agriculture; the nearly complete conquest, especially through radio and television, of the distances separating peoples; the greatly increased speed of all manner of transportation; the initial conquests of outer space" (47). The shrinkage of time for communication and transportation, along with the threat posed by the use of nuclear force in warfare, had together renewed the face of the earth in a very threatening sense. At the same time changes in the techniques for providing for people's needs and wants also put an age of plenty, speaking relatively, within the reach of all of mankind—now made more keenly aware of what was available to it, by the transportation and communications revolution which was, perhaps ironically, a good effect coming out of World War II. Thus, imbalances within and among nations became more obvious and glaring, to some extent, because the means for resolving them were, now more than ever, placed within reach by the tremendous economic progress during the postwar era. Add to that the dissolution of the old colonial empires in Africa and Asia following the war period, and there was at large an urgent quest for the kind of economic development which could no longer be confined to a handful of affluent nations living along both sides of the north Atlantic. The gap between the northern and the southern hemispheres became glaringly apparent; and there was talk of a "third world," which wanted a share in the earth's bounty. The matter could be resolved peacefully; or else, there could be devastating results! Popes of the Catholic Church, starting with John XXIII in 1961, now began dealing systematically with this matter of unconscionable economic imbalance among nations, as Leo XIII had begun addressing the problem of economic imbalance *within* nations in 1891. And they all did so now by applying the same principles of justice and charity, specifically in their application to the common good, to the "social question" in both its domestic and now ominous worldwide dimensions.

Part II

This second part of *Mater et Magistra* explains and develops further in the context of changing society the basic doctrines first presented in *Rerum Novarum.* There is renewed emphasis, therefore, in an updated social context on the role of public authorities and the *subsidiarity* principle, on harmonious labor relations and the just wage, and on a balanced approach to the ownership of private property.

Lest anyone had gotten wrong impressions from the radical overtones in that encyclical, John XXIII affirmed clearly that "in economic affairs first place is to be given to the private initiative of individual men who, either working by themselves, or with others in one fashion or another, pursue their common interest" (51). That, lest some might be tempted to overemphasize social intervention, while losing sight of the role of the individual in working out his economic welfare. However, so that the individualism which was still a major force in the world of the 1960s should again lose sight of the common good present in all societies, including the political ones, which men choose to form for themselves, "it is necessary that public authorities take active interest, the better to increase output of goods and to further social progress for the benefit of all citizens" (52). Maintaining a balance between the individual, his interests and his pursuit of them, and the like interests of other individuals, but also the interests common to all, i.e., the common good, has been one of the principal balancing acts confronting mankind throughout its history.

The principle of subsidiarity is then repeated verbatim as stated in *Quadragesimo Anno.* That not only upholds a certain primacy of individual initiative; but it is used here also to substantiate Pope John's approval of "intervention of public authorities that encourages, stimulates, regulates, supplements and complements" (53). It should be noted that he was not proposing the kind of "night-watchman" state which Manchester liberalism upheld. Beyond the state's restrictive, negative role, John XXIII added the very positive ones of encouraging, stimulating, regulating and complementing private initiative. In fact, the Pope proceeded from this point to make statements about the role of "public authorities," which raised hackles in certain circles. He asserted that "recent developments of science and technology provide additional reasons why, to a greater extent than heretofore, it is within the power of public authorities to reduce imbalances, whether these be between various sectors of economic life, or between different regions of the same nation, or even between different peoples of the world as a whole" (54). Indeed, that statement outlines what is the substance of the remainder of this encyclical: imbalance, both within a nation's sectors and regions, and among the nations of the world. While warning that such developments should not only not infringe on the legitimate "freedom of

ments should not only not infringe on the legitimate "freedom of private citizens, but also increase it" (55), the Pope stated "that there cannot be a prosperous and well-ordered society unless both private citizens and public authorities work together in economic affairs" (56).

At this point the plain-spoken Pontiff sparked some controversy, largely because of the always thorny translation process. He wrote that "One of the principal characteristics or our time is the multiplication of social relationships, that is, a daily more complex interdependence of citizens, introducing into their lives and activities many and varied forms of association" (59). Some translations, including an early American version of the encyclical, used the word "socialization" for this "multiplication of social relationships."[6] The Latin expression in the original was "*socialium rationum incrementa,*" and it should present no difficulty. Also, the words which follow explain clearly enough what the Pope had in mind here. However, there was a growing hypersensitivity among those who were hoping for a comeback for the "liberal ideology" which did indeed reassert itself in the years ahead, specifically, in places like the United States and England. Actually the term "socialization" itself is legitimate not only for the kind of nationalization which occurs on a total scale in the Communist states, but also for the innocent and normal process of "socializing," when good fellows get together, so to speak. Children "socialize"; adults "socialize." Anyone who is not misanthropic "socializes." To avoid such difficulty, subsequent English translations expressed what the Pope was describing as a "multiplication of social relationships." He went on to explain that the tendency he was referring to applies to all manner of "organizations and institutes on both national and international levels," and that they involve "economic and social goals, as well as cultural and recreational activities," and also "athletics," "various professions," as well as "political affairs" (60). One has only to consider the vast number of professional associations which hold annual meetings in host cities to discuss advances in medicine, economics, and other academic fields. In athletics, there are the non-governmental associations which make rules for the sports, enact penalties for violations, conduct player drafts, and so forth. The quadrennial Olympic games are the result of a vast, voluntary, cooperative international effort. Health care in the United States has long been provided to a considerable extent through non-governmental group insurance programs devised according to various patterns.

Pope John was not advocating something here, as much as he was acknowledging a force at work in modern society perhaps more than in the past, again, because of vastly improved transportation and communication made possible by modern scientific breakthroughs. Indeed, he perceived the threat of mass organization, as Pius XII had before him.[7] In fact, he raised the question, "Will men perhaps then become automatons, and cease to be personally responsible, as these social relationships multiply more and more?" (62). The reply was: "It is a question which must be answered negatively" (62). This could be interpreted as an expression of hope by a pope who was reputedly a congenital optimist. Or it could be an imperative affirmation that this must not be so. The Latin appears to support the latter interpretation.[8] Also, Pope John went on to support the latter interpretation.[8] Also, Pope John went on to point out that the "increased complexity of social life...is the creation of free men who are so disposed to act by nature as to be responsible for what they do" (63). Either interpretation will not disturb the tone of the encyclical to this point. Indeed this discussion leads up to an important matter: an explicit definition of what is meant by the common good.

Indicating the course by which all of the desirable objectives of the "advances in social organization" (64)—in other words, of the "multiplication of social relationships"—could be achieved, the Pope observed that "public authorities must have "a correct understanding of the common good." *"This embraces the sum total of those conditions of social living, whereby men are enabled more fully and more readily to achieve their own perfection"* (65). The italics are added here to emphasize the importance of this contribution. The notion of "common good" has long been used in discussions, where it ranges from a platitudinous concept, to one that is subjected to ridicule by cynics. It is used also to simply designate the sum total of the good of all individuals—an interpretation which corresponds to the individualistic view of society: in other words, where the whole is seen as simply equal to the sum of its parts. Good mathematics, but poor social theory! In social life—the whole is decidedly greater than the sum of its parts. Otherwise self-interested individuals would have little cause or inclination to offer up a little of themselves or of their own immediate personal interests in order to promote some common good, or indeed, to multiply "social relationships." A symphony orchestra with its conductor, its score, and its many various musicians offers an appropriate example of a common good which could not be arrived at if each individual involved would not surrender a part of his or her own artistic inclination to the conductor's interpretation of the score in front of him. Without such surrender, there could be 100 simultaneous, expert, solo performances resulting in intolerable dissonance, but never in a beautiful symphony. And pertinent to our discussion here, every step of the economic process involves some yielding in order to gain far more than is given up, whether we are talking about our highly integrated, cooperative production process, the exchange process, or the income distribution process which, while thorny and complex, nevertheless reflects the results of successful efforts in the other two. In economic life, who could survive, living like Robinson Crusoe, at anything but the most abysmal primitive level of subsistence, if at all?

The definition provided here by Pope John XXIII therefore gives us an indication of the vast importance of the common good, which is often overlooked simply because it is so ubiquitous and taken for granted. It takes its place alongside the statement of the subsidiarity principle in *Quadragesimo Anno,* and the definition of social justice in *Divini Redemptoris,* as one of the critical, basic tools for understanding Catholic social teachings. Little perspective is required to realize the meaning and impact of this concept for those ultimate regulating principles of the social order—*social justice* and *social charity*—which have as their object the common good rather than the particular good of some individual. Since it is by definition a good that we all share in, it is immediately clear that it is also one to which we all have an obligation to contribute. The definition is repeated verbatim in subsequent social encyclicals—an indication of its definitive nature and importance.

Since Pius XI had made such a point of linking the need for the ability to pay the just wage as an urgent requirement of social justice, and therefore of the common good, it is appropriate that John XXIII moved on next to his own affirmation of the just wage doctrine. Now, seventy years after *Rerum Novarum* and thirty years after *Quadragesimo Anno,* he felt the need to state: "Our heart is filled with profound sadness when we observe, as it were, with our own eyes a wretched spectacle indeed—great masses of workers who, in not a few nations, and even in whole continents, receive too small a return from their labor" (68). In other words, what Pius XI had said in 1931 should be accomplished "without delay" (*Quadragesimo Anno*, par. 71) was still widely unfulfilled in 1961. What is more, John XXIII saw this problem not only in regions where "modern industrial techniques either have only recently been introduced or have made less than satisfactory progress" (68), but also in "economically developed countries" (70).

We have here a stern indictment of the chronic condition in, for example, many Latin American countries, where "as compared with the extreme need of the majority, the wealth and conspicuous consumption of a few stand out, and are in open and bold contrast with the lot of the needy" (69). The Pope took the opportunity to air a pet peeve: that often "a disproportionate share of the revenue goes toward the building up of national prestige, and that large sums of money are devoted to armaments." How often we see on televised news pitched battles fought in poverty-stricken countries where it is obvious that people do not have enough to eat and to wear, but where warring factions try to destroy each other with costly, sophisticated modern weaponry! It is an all too common situation which cries to Heaven.

More relevant to our own condition, however, the Pope indicted another widespread abuse; and it is one which has, if anything, become more flagrant since the encyclical appeared. Speaking of "economically developed countries," he said, "it frequently happens that great, or sometimes very great, remuneration is had for the performance of some task of lesser importance or doubtful utility" (70). We need not even speak of the obvious cases of criminal activities like drug-dealing, which enriches people also in poverty-stricken locales beyond the wildest imagination. We need only point out the outrageously high salaries paid to entertainers, including those in professional sports and in the various media—the rock stars, the screen idols, and much of the entertainment industry in general.[9] Then, although they perform services which are of higher level of productive importance, there are the exorbitant salaries which some business executives routinely pay themselves, the often inordinately high incomes in the medical and legal professions, the ridiculously high pay for "top fashion models." At the same time, policemen, teachers, health-care workers, all providing services that are critically important for society, along with farmers, the migrant workers who harvest our food, those who mine coal, produce steel, automobiles, and provide the services without which modern life is inconceivable, in the Pope's words, "are begrudged a decent income" and receive "too low a payment and one insufficient for the necessities of life, or else, one that does not correspond to the contribution made to the community, or to the revenues of the undertakings in which they are engaged, or to the national income" (70). Once again, we have here clear papal rejection of the absolute reign of so-called free market principles, in the words: "...remuneration for work cannot be left entirely to unregulated competition, any more than it can be decided arbitrarily at the will of the more powerful" (71). Actually, the so-called forces of the free market boil down in many instances to simply imposition of the arbitrary will of the more powerful. That conflicts directly with what could be termed democracy in the economic realm.

What follows is a restatement of the just wage principle as established in *Rerum Novarum* and developed further in *Quadragesimo Anno.* Added is the stipulation that the principle itself is "binding always and everywhere," even though the way it is applied must be adjusted "in concrete cases" with reference to "resources at hand" which do in fact "vary in quantity and quality among different peoples," and which "may even change within the same country with the passing of time" (72). In other words, it is clear that the just wage in 2005 in Uganda will not be equal to the just wage in the United States in that same year; nor would the just wage in the United States in 2005 be the same as it was in 1951. It must increase as national product and wealth increase. John XXIII stated specifically that social justice requires "a corresponding social development," which means that "all classes of citizens will benefit equitably from an increase in national wealth." And from this arises the important mandate that the "differences arising from disparity of wealth not be increased, but lessened so far as possible" (73). The qualification, "so far as possible," makes it clear that this is not a call for an egalitarian, "classless" society. It merely calls for a reduction of the glaring inequalities based, once again, on the arbitrary will of the more powerful, which goes hand-in-glove with unregulated competition.

At this point the Pope turned to differences in the size and structure of modern enterprises and to the implication of these differences for the payment of wages and the treatment of workers, generally. Once again we find the counsel that in large- and medium-size productive enterprises in particular, the workers should be granted "some share in the enterprise, especially where they are paid no more than the minimum wage" (75). While the specific approach to accomplishing this "sharing" is left open, what is not left open is "an innate need of human nature requiring that men engaged in production activity have an opportunity to assume responsibility and to perfect themselves by their efforts" (82). The Pope was prepared to call an economic order "unjust" if this innate need of human nature was thwarted so that "the human dignity of workers is compromised, or their sense of responsibility is weakened, or their freedom of action is removed, even though it produces a vast amount of goods whose distribution conforms to the norms of justice and equity" (83). Here is significant new ground, boldly taken, in the important area of labor-management relations. So long as the "[I]nnate need of human nature" among workers is ignored, even if the just wage is paid, the social order is declared "unjust"!

That we are dealing here with a "need of human nature" that is indeed "innate" can be substantiated by the fact that, in places like Sweden, and Japan, astute initiatives have been taken in this direction of worker-participation in management. It is not likely that the people involved were influenced by what is written in papal encyclicals, any more than it is likely that the more progressive persons shaping labor-management relations in the United States, who have been adopting such structures, were devotees of those teachings.[10] Here we have a Roman Catholic pope supporting such overtures even while stating that it is not "possible in economic affairs to determine in one formula all the measures...conformable to the dignity of man, or...more suitable in developing in him a sense of responsibility" (84). Nevertheless he upheld what Pius XI had to say about management-, profit-, and ownership-sharing, and what Pius XII recommended so that workers in "small and medium-sized holdings in agriculture, in the arts and crafts, in commerce and industry" might share in the "service and benefits of large-scale enterprises" (84).[11] What Pius XII proposed was that workers in such "small and medium-sized" operations should "join together in mutual-aid societies," in other words, into producer cooperatives.

John XXIII picked up that theme with reference to "artisan and farm enterprises" in urging that, where the common good and the state of technology make it possible, "family type" operations should be "safeguarded and fostered, as should...cooperatives that aim to complement and perfect such enterprises" (85). Over the years there have been enthusiasts of a somewhat romantic persuasion who saw in the cooperative form of enterprise the means for resolving the "social question." More mature consideration and actual experience have indicated that while there is a definite place for producer cooperatives (as well as consumer cooperatives), these are not a panacea to be applied in all times, places, and circumstances. That is why John XXIII, a champion of family- and small-scale operations, qualified his advocacy with the proviso: "conformably to requirements of the common good and the state of technology." He added also: "in order that they may survive and flourish," such enterprises "should be continuously adapted—both in their productive structure and in their operating methods—to new conditions of the times" (87). This was not always observed in all cooperative endeavors.

Turning to "medium-size and large enterprises," Blessed John XXIII reaffirmed the "justifiable desire of employees to be partners in enterprises with which they are associated and wherein they work" (91). Pius XII, after supporting "mutual aid societies" in "small and medium sized" operations, had added that in "larger enterprises...work agreements should in some way be modified by partnership arrangements."[12] John XXIII qualified that by stating: "We do not think it possible, however, to decide with certain and explicit norms the manner and degree of such partnership, since this must be determined according to the state of the individual productive enterprises" (91). There is an area left here for prudential judgment. However, the actual fact of introducing some form of worker participation—a degree of partnership—was apparently not left open to dispute.

What we have here appears to be important matter, actually new high ground in papal social teachings—proposed first by Pius XI in *Quadragesimo Anno,* affirmed and developed by Pius XII in certain addresses, and incorporated into this document on *Christianity and Social Progress*. What it amounts to, when all is said and done, is an extension to the principles of democracy from political life, into economic life and, specifically, into the work place where most people spend most of their waking hours during their adult years. Is it less important to have a say in one's everyday life as an economic producer, than to be able to vote for a political candidate once a year in November, or perhaps every four years? That proposition must be considered especially in the light of a papal statement that we are talking about "an innate need of human nature." And it must be considered in the light of the John XXIII statement: "But it is of the utmost importance that productive enterprises assume the character of a true human fellowship whose spirit suffuses the dealings, activities, and standing of all its members" (91).[13] It amounts to a proposal that those who work in the same industry or occupation must be relieved of that cold, impersonal situation where "those who work daily...are to be considered merely as servants, whose sole function is to execute orders silently, and [who] are not allowed to interject their desires and interests, but must conduct themselves as idle standbys when it comes to assignment and direction of their tasks" (92). That is an incisive indictment of a condition which became all too common in labor-management relations, especially in the giant corporate enterprises characteristic of the modern era. It is nevertheless not a proposal for "mob rule" in enterprise, nor for the abdication of the legitimate role of managers. Thus, we find: "Beyond doubt, an enterprise truly in accord with human dignity should safeguard the necessary and efficient unity of administration" (92).

There is also a hopeful suggestion that, aside from the "innate need of human nature," historical developments also point toward a "greater amount of responsibility desired today by workers in productive enterprises." John XXIII was referring to the "greater abilities and professional qualifications" demanded of more and more workers because of the changes which modern technology and science have brought into productive systems. Thus, there is less need for the untrained, unschooled mass-production workers than there was a generation ago. The more sophisticated the work force, the more it will call for a less disinterested, more active, role in its daily working life.

Finally, the Pope referred to labor unions, now widely protected by positive legislation. He cited apparent progress in this area inasmuch as these "no longer recruit workers for purposes of strife, but rather for pursuing a common aim...achieved especially by collective bargaining" (97).[14]

The Pontiff also appealed for workers to be given the opportunity to make their voices heard beyond the workplace in matters that are "helpful to the overall economic and social situation in each country" (98). He cited the obvious fact that those responsible for "safeguarding the rights, needs, and aspirations of workers" have as much right as "managers or agents of management" to be represented before public authorities and institutions "established either nationally or among a number of countries" so as to "function in various sectors of economic life" (99). The section closes with praise for the International Labor Organization, an example of how workers through their organizations have a role in matters related to "the over-all economic and social situation" in a body "which, for many years, has done effective and valuable work in adapting the economic and social order everywhere to the norms of justice and humanity" (103).

In upholding the traditional defense of private property, John XXIII directed attention to certain more recent developments. First, since the actual ownership of large corporations has been more and more separated from the managerial role, the need to exercise some control over the managers and directors with a view to the common good has become a relevant issue. The same applies also in cases where capital investment decisions are made for public enterprises.[15]

At the level of the employees, there has also been a change in the direction of their future security being provided for by "insurance programs and various systems of social security" (105). Thus, there appears to be less urgency to own property as a basis for that "future security." The Pope mentioned, along with this and to some extent because of it, that more premium is placed on the possession of skill and the income derived from it than from the private ownership of capital or other property. "This trend," said John XXIII, "indicates an advance in civilization" (108). That conforms with the traditional position in Catholic social teachings that human work is the most important source of economic wealth and prosperity, whereas all other factors of production, including capital, are simply instrumental causes.

Nevertheless, the right to and the advisability of owning private property, including the productive kind, is "permanently valid" (109). That is so because private ownership which "continually draws its force and vigor from the fruitfulness of labor…is an effective aid in safeguarding the dignity of the human person and the free exercise of responsibility in all fields of endeavor." Also, "it strengthens the stability and tranquility of family life, thus contributing to the peace and prosperity of the commonwealth" (112).

All of that reaffirmation of the traditional defense of private ownership as presented by his predecessors did not "preclude ownership of goods pertaining to production of wealth by State and public agencies, especially 'if these carry with them power too great to be left in private hands, without injury to the community at large'" (116).[16] And since there was apparent a tendency to more of such public ownership, the principle of subsidiarity was presented once again at this point as a limiting factor in such activity by the state. In addition, all of the traditional precautions by previous pontiffs about "social responsibility" in the exercise of the private property right are presented once again. These include even a quotation of St. Gregory the Great: "He who has a talent, let him take care that he hides it not; he who has abundance, let him arouse himself to mercy and generosity; he who has skill in managing affairs, let him make special effort to share the use and utility thereof with his neighbor" (119).

Part III

Here begins the distinctively "John XXIII portion" of this encyclical. In its most general terms, it addresses certain problems of imbalance within national economies and among the various national economies throughout the world. If one were to single out a *leitmotif* for *Mater et Magistra,* a good case could be made for this concern about various imbalances in the economic life of nations. The Blessed Pope opened with the statement that the norms of justice and charity must be applied also among "various types of economic activity and differently endowed regions within a country, and in the overall human community" (122). These indicate the three areas of concern with which this third, distinctive part of the encyclical deals.

For the first time we have a pope in a major social encyclical addressing the problems faced by agriculture in our time, whether in the poorer countries, or in affluent developed countries like the United States. Perhaps this was to be expected from a pontiff who came from the small, economically hard-pressed, rural village of Sotto il Monte, near Bergamo, in northern Italy. Acknowledging that the percentage, though not the total numbers of people remaining in agriculture has decreased almost universally, and that this is to some extent an inevitable by-product of "the very evolution of economic affairs," John XXIII also indicated with regret a not so inevitable element in this abandonment of the farms. It is the ubiquitous "itch" for the big city lights, broader horizons or, in the Pope's words, "a more comfortable life," "the quest for novelty," "quickly acquired goods and fortunes." However, there is an even more somber aspect: "rural dwellers leave the fields because nearly everywhere they see their affairs in a state of depression, both as regards labor productivity and the level of living of farm populations." The low labor productivity factor may be said to apply in lesser developed countries, or even in sectors within the same country, where such factors as poor transportation facilities, access to markets, and the absence of modern technological advances handicap productivity. Meanwhile in more developed countries it is actually high productivity which has often, ironically, become perhaps the worst enemy, so that *relative* overproduction causes the "state of depression."

After indicating his awareness of all of the relevant urgent problems, the Pope offered "some norms of permanent validity" indicating, however, that these "must be adapted as various circumstances of time and place permit, or suggest, or absolutely require" (126). They involved action by "everyone, and especially public authorities" to provide the "principal services needed by all, including: highway construction; transport services; market facilities; pure drinking water; housing; medical services; elementary, trade and professional schools; things requisite for religion and for recreation; finally, furnishings and equipment needed in the modern farm home" (127).

In broader terms, the Blessed John XXIII called for an appropriate economic policy to be determined by public authorities in matters including: "taxes and duties, credit, insurance, prices, the fostering of requisite skills, and finally, improved equipment for rural enterprises" (131). Specifically, he called for taxation "according to ability to pay" as "fundamental to a just and equitable system" (132).[17] Also mentioned is the need for special banks to "provide capital to farmers at reasonable rates of interest because of a twofold problem facing them: "...those with money to invest are more inclined to invest it in enterprises other than in the rural economy"; and farmers, on the other hand, cannot pay the higher rates of interest which this operation of the market mechanism therefore brings about. Finally, the Pope stated that, "it does not seem to be fully in accord with the norms of social justice and equity to provide farmers with insurance or social security benefits that are inferior to those of other classes of citizens." (135)

Certainly a bone of contention for so-called free marketeers is the call for "price protection" for farm products because they have "special characteristics." While farmers are urged to do whatever they can to help themselves in this matter, "public authorities cannot stand entirely aloof from the stabilization procedure" (137). At this point, John XXIII quoted Pius XI in his call for a "reasonable relationship between the prices obtained for the products of the various economic groups: agrarian, industrial, and so forth" (139).[18]

There is also a provident call for appropriate industries in rural areas which preserve, process and transport farm products. Such enterprises make it possible for farmers, some of whose work is seasonal in nature, along with their families, to "supplement their incomes, and that within the milieu wherein they live and work" (141).

After a call for preservation of the family-type farm, the Pope went on to urge farm workers themselves to play a leading role in improving their situation. He accomplished this in the context of praise for the work of the farmer, the great demands which modern farming makes for ever more knowledge in '"the mechanical arts, chemistry, and biology," so as to bolster the self-esteem of the people who feed their fellow human beings by their work which is often hard and economically uncertain. A major kind of self-help should stem from a "sense of solidarity," which would, among other things, prompt farmers to organize themselves in various ways. There is good bit of earthy wisdom by John XXIII here because, in his words, "today it is unquestionably true that the solitary voice speaks, as they say, to the winds" (146).

In addition to the sectoral imbalance between, for example, agricultural and other parts of the national economy, there are often also regional disparities. For example, in the United States until after World War II, the South, as compared with the North, was regarded as "the nation's leading economic problem." Ironically, the portion of the country which, prior to World War II, could be referred to with pride as its industrial heartland, is now designated widely as the "rust belt." In the Pope's own Italy, the regions south of Naples have persistently lagged behind in economic development and prosperity. Many countries have similar imbalances. To remedy the matter, there is an unabashed appeal in the name of "justice and equity" demanding "that the government make efforts either to remove or to minimize imbalances of this sort" (150). However, there is a precautionary reference again to the principle of subsidiarity. All remedial action should take into account the people involved so that they "feel themselves to be the ones chiefly responsible for their own progress" (151); and private enterprise should also be favored "to allow private citizens themselves to accomplish as much as is feasible" (152).

Where imbalances between land and population are involved, resolution of the difficulties begins to extend beyond national boundaries. However, there is often some serious maldistribution within the same country where, for example, vast landholdings may exist side-by-side with large land-poor populations reduced to being exploited, poverty-stricken tenant farmers. That is obviously an imbalance which cries out for prompt solutions. It is the kind of situation which gave plausibility to Marxian "liberation theology" in some nations, among those who were perhaps not sufficiently grounded in their own papal social teachings. If the greedy who had far more land than they could possible make use of could not act according to good Christian norms of social responsibility in the area of private property rights, it would seem that the same public authorities who are entitled to redistribute excess income by the normal taxation process are within their rights to redistribute such excessive landholdings.

In his third appeal to "solidarity," in this case, of the whole human race, Pope John XXIII now called for "a freer movement of goods, of capital, and of men" to lessen imbalances between nations (155). This implies less trade restrictions, but certainly not an endorsement of absolute free trade; and it also calls for the movement of capital across national boundaries; and finally, perhaps as a last resort because of the personally disruptive implications for human beings involved, it makes a case for the immigration and emigration of people. And such migration of peoples across national borders provided access to the pressing problem of imbalance among nations at different stages of economic development.

Pope John XXIII opened this section with the very significant statement: "Perhaps the most pressing question of our day concerns the relationship between economically advanced commonwealths and those that are in the process of development" (157). Indeed, this new aspect of "the social question" was to be the theme of two subsequent social encyclicals: *Populorum Progressio* by Paul VI in 1967; and *Sollicitudo Rei Socialis* by Pope John Paul II in 1987. It is also the theme which brought about the designation "third world." A "third" implied, of course, a first and a second even though these terms were used less frequently, probably because they referred to ideological opponents both of which would have been adamant about being classed as "second." In any case, one of these other "two worlds" was represented by the affluent nations in the so-called "free world," and the other was made up of the command economies under Communist rule.

Since modern technology and economic progress puts elimination of that problem of economic imbalance between developed and developing nations within the realm of what is clearly possible, the glaring contrast between dire poverty in the less economically advanced countries and the relative affluence in those which first enjoyed the fruits of the Industrial Revolution is no longer morally acceptable. What is more, it is no longer economically tolerable, since, as the Pope said, "countries each day seem to become more dependent on each other" (157). As severe maldistribution of income within a national economy can stifle its continued domestic prosperity, so now grave disparities in income worldwide can cause economic breakdown internationally. The affluent, technically advanced nations of the world have much that they could produce and sell in countries which still have many needs. Yet, the latter must develop to the point where they can produce and sell the things which their own economic resources and cultures would enable them to provide. That is the basic theme of this portion of *Mater et Magistra,* as well as of the subsequent teachings by Paul VI and Pope John Paul II.

Pope John XXIII therefore called for the two kinds of foreign aid that have come to represented by standard terms in discussing such assistance among nations. First, there is the emergency foreign aid, the first aid, so to speak, which handles the worst immediate situations: starvation and deprivation caused by natural disasters, wars, internal upheaval and the like. Few would quarrel with that; the people of the United States have little to be ashamed of in this regard. Few nations throughout history have been so willing to help even fallen enemies soon after they have engaged in armed conflict with them. And few have been more prompt in rushing food, medical supplies, and other forms of humanitarian aid to even the most distant parts of the world after natural disasters.

If there is some criticism of that kind of immediate assistance with food and other necessities, it stems from the argument that it does not help people to help themselves, and it perhaps even deters them from learning to do so. That implies the second kind of "foreign aid": helping people to help themselves. From this dichotomy was derived the now standard expression: "If you give a man a fish, you feed him for a day; if you teach him how to fish, you feed him for always." The Pope covered all of the bases. After praising "emergency assistance," he stated: "However, the underlying causes of poverty and hunger will not be removed in a number of countries by these means alone" (163). Then he proceeded to put the Church on record as defending foreign aid by the richer to the poorer nations. He proposed that this should involve "exploring all available avenues...to instruct citizens fully in necessary skills and in carrying out their responsibilities"; and also "to enable them to acquire the capital wherewith to promote economic growth" (163). What is more, this was not to be merely a government effort but, "we look to private enterprises and societies to exert daily more generous efforts on behalf of such countries, transmitting to them requisite productive skills" (165).

As happened to Leo XIII and his defense of the workers and their labor unions, the man who somehow came to be known spontaneously as "good Pope John" also suffered some vituperation at the hands of those who were often not yet fully reconciled even with what was called for in *Rerum Novarum,* and who now also considered foreign aid a waste.[19] Often even some Catholics joined the chorus of dissent by using the facile escape that what he said about such matters are matters of prudential judgment, and not strictly speaking moral pronouncements. Careful reflection on such teachings as developing from earlier teachings by Leo XIII and Pius XI suggests that they involve doctrinal activity by the Church's Magisterium on a serious moral matter. It appears to this commentator that what we have here is the application of the virtues of social justice and social charity to the broader area of international economic life in the changing context of the shrinking post-World War II world.

The need to help what used to be called "undeveloped nations," later "underdeveloped nations," and finally more euphemistically, "developing nations," comes along with a warning to avoid past errors. This applies to the countries themselves who have a grave responsibility to do all in their own power to lift themselves up, and to see that they do not repeat the mistakes made in other countries with regard to the equitable distribution of income, to avoiding imbalances among the various economic sectors, and to showing proper regard also for social advances beyond what are merely economic considerations. It also applies to the countries offering assistance: that they have respect for the individual characteristics of the various recipient nations and their varying cultures. What is more, foreign aid is not to be given for the donor nation's own political advantage, what the Pope here referred to as "but another form of colonialism" (172). We need not spell out how much foreign aid in the post-World War II era came with significant ideological strings attached. There were often at least implicit conditions that the recipient nations should adopt the donor nations' "capitalistic" system, or socialistic system, respectively, or their "democratic" form of government; and it is noteworthy that both ideological contenders promoted their own particular form of "democracy." Undoubtedly, this kind of conduct also helped to prompt the Pope's warning that economic assistance should not be offered as though it were the ultimate consideration, disregarding any higher values of which, incidentally, the people in developing nations are often keenly aware. This leads into a discussion of a most sensitive issue about which John XXIII offered some definitive teaching by the "Mother and Teacher of nations."

Much foreign aid in the period following *Mater et Magistra*, especially where certain western nations were involved, including the United States, came packaged with "family planning" propaganda and devices. Underlying was the implicit notion that foreign economic assistance will simply be a wasted effort if "you people don't do something to curb your inordinate birth rates." Now there is nothing wrong with family planning, *per se*. The question is: according to whose cultural values is such "planning" to take place, those of perhaps some post-Christian benefactor nation, or of the recipient nation whose culture on this particular matter has perhaps not yet been degraded to the same extent?

Pope John XXIII began the discussion by presenting the legitimate question raised widely in the period following World War II when population was growing more rapidly than before, especially among the developing nations: "how economic organization and the means of subsistence can be balanced with population increase, whether in the world as a whole or within the needy nations" (185). He then presented a statement of the problem, which was, demographically speaking, far more dispassionate and scientific than the tone of an ongoing, unprecedented torrent of alarmist propaganda about the "population bomb" and its imminent "explosion." Speaking of the "less developed nations," the Pope stated that, "because recent advances in public health and in medicine are there widely diffused, the citizens have a longer life expectancy consequent to lowered rates of infant mortality." And since "the birth rate, where it has traditionally been high, tends to remain at such levels, at least for the immediate future...the birth rate in a given year exceeds the death rate." These represent the cold, statistical, demographic facts explaining population growth in recent times. One is led to believe that birth rates are rising. They are not, as the "statistical records" to which the Pope referred here make clear. Thus, at its worst the present growth in population is a temporary one until death rates adjust again to the lengthened life expectancies, as they must inevitably after a period of time unless one believes that life expectancy will go on increasing indefinitely.

The question now shifts to whether the world, by and large sparsely populated and economically underdeveloped, has the capacity to provide for such a temporarily rising level of world population. No one who has looked recently at a population density map or at figures indicating population per square kilometer can be unaware of the imbalances which Pope John referred to previously, when he stated: "Some nations experience a shortage of citizens, but have rich land resources; others have many citizens but an insufficiency of agricultural land" (153). At this point in the encyclical (188) he affirmed modestly: "Now to tell the truth, the interrelationship on a global scale between the number of births and available resources are such that we can infer grave difficulties in this matter do not arise at present, nor will in the immediate future." It is a fact that, by and large, the most densely populated countries are also among the world's most wealthy and prosperous. This lends credence to the thesis that the pressure of population growth and of large populations relative to land area may indeed act as a motivating force to get people to become more diligent and ingenious in dealing with the problem—therefore, becoming economically more productive.[20] By comparison, some of the very poorest countries in the world rank low on the population density scale.[21] Therefore, the data itself shows no direct correlation between the level of national wealth and population density, since both poor and rich nations rank among both the densely populated and the sparsely populated ones.

Other factors must be found to explain the poverty of certain nations, besides population density; and these are often close at hand. Sometimes there is in place atrocious political corruption, or an ill-fated attempt to establish a flawed socialistic order; or else there is something approaching internecine warfare among contending parties. At other times, we find people attempting to feed growing populations with virtually the same stone-age agricultural technology in use during past millennia. That all suggests where the proper solutions lie.

Blessed Pope John XXIII proposed here that "God in His goodness and wisdom has, on the one hand, provided nature with almost inexhaustible productive capacity; and, on the other hand, He has endowed man with such ingenuity that, by using suitable means, he can apply nature's resources to the needs and requirements of existence." Also, "man should, by use of his skills and science of every kind, acquire an intimate knowledge of the forces of nature and control them ever more extensively." Besides, "the advances hitherto made in science and technology give almost limitless promise for the future in this matter." Thus, there is no need to resort to "a course of action…contrary to the moral law laid down by God" where the "procreative function is also violated" (189).

The encyclical *Humanae Vitae* issued by Pope Paul VI seven years later created a storm of controversy and dissent, even *de facto* schism in the Catholic Church, which has not yet subsided. It is often referred to simply as "the encyclical against birth control." Actually the kind of birth control (the use of contraceptives) implied here was already specifically rejected in the Pius XI encyclical, *Casti Connubii*, in 1930. And now in *Mater et Magistra* we have another presentation of that same doctrine in the context of the post-World War II over-population hysteria, although it comes couched in the kind of positive terms which some regard as characteristic of John XXIII.

First, we find: "Indeed, in a matter of this kind, first place must be accorded everything that pertains to the dignity of man as such, or to the life of individual men, than which nothing can be more precious" (192). Then comes the critical statement:

> In this connection we strongly affirm that human life is transmitted and propagated through the instrumentality of the family which rests on marriage, one and indissoluble, and, so far as Christians are concerned, elevated to the dignity of a sacrament. Because the life of man is passed on to other men deliberately and knowingly, it therefore follows that this should be done in accord with the most sacred, permanent, inviolate prescriptions of God. Everyone without exception is bound to recognize and observe these laws. Wherefore, in this matter, no one is permitted to use methods and procedures which may indeed be permissible to check the life of plants and animals" (193).

Theologians may wish to discuss whether this adds up to a solemn declaration of a moral doctrine. Another translation rendered the Latin "*Hac de re graviter pronuntiamus,*" as: "We must solemnly proclaim that..."[22] It would be another matter to question, in view of the deteriorating condition of marriage, family life and sexual conduct generally, along with the now apparent, frightening and even fatal consequences, the prophetic quality of the paragraph following that one: "Those who depart from this plan of God not only offend His divine majesty and dishonor themselves and the human race, but they also weaken the inner fiber of the commonwealth" (194).

Blessed John XXIII, like Paul VI after him, often expressed great discouragement with what the former referred to here as "two conflicting trends: on the one hand, the scarcity of goods is vaguely described as such that the life of men reportedly is in danger of perishing from misery and hunger; on the other hand, the recent discoveries of science, technical advances, and economic production are transformed into means whereby the human race is led toward ruin and a horrible death" (198). Reference is to the trillions spent worldwide since World War II on sophisticated weaponry to police and to proselytize the world in accordance with rival ideological positions. This has now resulted in the bankruptcy and near bankruptcy of the two leading contenders respectively, at the same time that it has greatly drained resources which could have been devoted far more wisely and productively to help bring the poor nations up to the economic level of the richer ones. However, we will have more to say about that in discussing the encyclical Paul VI devoted exclusively to this matter.

Pope John XXXII concluded this portion of *Mater et Magistra* by affirming the complementarity of interests—"whether in the fields of science and technology, or of economic and social affairs, or of public administration, or of cultural advancement"—which, "because they may exceed the capacities of individual States, very often affect a number of nations and at times all the nations of the earth" (201). Nor does this increasingly interdependent condition among nations exempt even the wealthier countries which, "though advanced in culture and civilization, in number and industry of citizens, in wealth, in geographical extent, are not able by themselves to resolve satisfactorily their basic problems." Since man is a social animal, he cannot solve his various problems, including the important economic one, in isolation from society. That clear expression of the principle of solidarity applies also to entire nations. "Hence, dire necessity warns commonwealths to cooperate among themselves and provide mutual assistance" (202).

What follows prepares the way toward the final part of the encyclical which returns, as is typical in social encyclicals, to the spiritual and theological dimensions involved in the solution of these various aspects of "the social question." The Pope referred to the general sense of frustration at large based on the deterioration of life in "the city of man." He indicated that this is not "because peoples lack scientific, technical, or economic means, but because they distrust one another," and in fact, they "stand in fear of one another" (203). It is a distrust and a fear based on the "differing philosophies of life." Thus, the *justice* and *demands of justice* to which all appeal take on different meanings and become mere "verbalizations" and therefore even the basis for "serious contentions" (206).

The remedy, easy in concept, difficult in practice, is that "the laws of truth and justice must first be acknowledged and preserved on all sides" (207), which brings us back to religion and God, because apart from Him "the guiding principles of morality and virtue...necessarily collapse" (208). This portion of *Mater et Magistra* ends on the hopeful note that "terrified men" having been betrayed by the limitless horizons promised by science may again "rightly conclude that things pertaining to the spirit and to moral life are to be preferred to all else, so that progress in science and technology does not result in destruction of the human race..." (210). At the same time there is a suggestion that people in the affluent societies are becoming "less and less satisfied with external goods." And all of these currents appear "to give some promise that not only individuals, but even peoples may come to an understanding for extensive and extremely useful collaboration" (211).

Part IV

This final part of *Mater et Magistra* affirms the role of religion and of God in the restoration of social order and economic balance within and among nations. Its author recalled the profound Augustinian lament: "Thou hast made us for Thyself, O Lord, and our hearts are restless until they rest in Thee." There is prophetic thunder in the statements by Blessed John XXIII in the final part of his encyclical: "Separated from God man becomes monstrous to himself and others" (215); and "no folly seems more characteristic of our time than the desire to establish a firm and meaningful temporal order, but without God, its necessary foundation." We find there also: "many systems of thought have been developed and committed to writing: some of these have been dissipated as mist by the sun; others remain basically unchanged today; still others now elicit less and less response from men" (213).

In two highly significant and important statements, John XXIII provided an important reminder also for those in his own Church who seem to regard its social message as somehow less cogent and doctrinal than its other teachings. "What the Catholic Church teaches and declares regarding the social life and relationships of men is beyond question for all time valid" (218). Also: "Above all, we affirm that the social teaching proclaimed by the Catholic Church cannot be separated from her traditional teaching regarding man's life" (222). Accordingly, he expressed his "earnest wish that more and more attention be given to this branch of learning…in Catholic schools on all levels, and especially in seminaries..." (223).

There was also wise counsel that the Church's social teaching, with "truth as its guide, justice as its end, and love as its driving force," is not only to be studied and explained, but also applied" (226). And there is the significant practical suggestion that such doctrines are to be put into effect in three stages: "first the actual situation is examined; then, the situation is evaluated carefully in relation to these teachings; then only is it decided what can and should be done in order that the traditional norms may be adapted to circumstances of time and place" (236). This program is summed up by the "three words: *observe, judge, act.*" In the process of cooperating with those "who do not share their view of life," Catholics are cautioned to "take special care to be consistent and not compromise in matters wherein the integrity of religion or morals would suffer harm" (239). That is significant counsel coming from John XXIII, especially in view of his own ecumenical inclinations as manifested, for example, by the Second Vatican Council which he convoked.

The Pope concluded on some somber notes that he nevertheless followed with his own expressions of hope for the future. First, we find repeated the trenchant statement by Pius XI: "And so, bodily labor, which was decreed by divine providence for the good of man's body and soul even after original sin, has too often been changed into an instrument of perversion: for dead matter leaves the factory ennobled and transformed whereas men are there corrupted and degraded."[23] Then there is the lament by Venerable Pius XII who, after noting "that our age is distinguished from others precisely by the fact that science and technology have made incalculable progress" (243), called it a "monstrous masterpiece" of this age "to have transformed man, as it were, into a giant as regards the order of nature, yet in the order of the supernatural and the eternal, to have changed him into a pygmy."[24]

Yet, even in a world rent by discord and living under the shadow of possible nuclear annihilation, John XXIII did not allow himself to become a "prophet of doom." He ended this encyclical with the conditional promise that: "If each one of you does his best courageously, it will necessarily help in no small measure to establish the kingdom of Christ on earth" (261). This was coupled with his "desire that, in a properly organized order of social affairs, all nations will at last enjoy prosperity, and happiness, and peace" (263).

Such sentiments are appropriate for the pope who entertained visions of a "new Pentecost" as mentioned frequently by his successors. At the close of the first session of the Second Vatican Council in 1962, John XXIII expressed his feeling that, "doubtless will dawn that new Pentecost which is the object of our yearning—a Pentecost that will increase the Church's wealth of spiritual strength and extend her maternal influence and saving power to every sphere of human endeavor."[25]

Notes

1. There are indeed some references to economic problems in *Pacem in Terris* as these relate to the maintenance of peace and justice among people and nations. In the main that encyclical provides a statement of basic human rights and directions governing the relationship of people to public authorities, and among nations for maintaining peace.

2. Paul VI, Apostolic Letter, *Octogesima Adveniens* (1971), par. 35.

3. John Paul II, *Sollicitudo Rei Socialis* (1987), par 40.

4. Pius XI, *Quadragesimo Anno* (1931), par. 83.

5. Ibid., 95.

6. The America Press edition of *Mater et Magistra* used the word "socialization" here. Its editors stated that they revised the English version released by the Vatican Press Office. Perhaps, in hindsight, they regretted their revision.

7. In his Christmas Message of 1952, Pius XII spoke of the "demon of organization" which "invades and tyrannizes man's spirit." Cf. Vincent A. Yzermans, ed., *Major Addresses of Pope Pius XII* (St. Paul: North Central Publ. Co., 1961), 2:163.

8. The original Latin reads: "*Est tale quid praecise negandum.*"

9. A report some time ago listed 22 major league baseball players who earned more than $4 million dollars a year. The highest was paid $7 million. These men "work" for slightly more than a half year, including their spring training in delightful climates. Such remuneration is explained and justified in terms of "demand and supply," and the "free market." The situation in other major league sports, and for other types of entertainment is, of course, similar.

10. Several colleagues and associates known to me personally during my years spent teaching labor relations come to mind. None of them were Roman Catholics; but their eminent good common sense led them to support and promote various kinds of initiatives which brought about a more active participation by workers in their daily working lives.

11. John XXIII quoted this verbatim from a radio broadcast by Pius XII on September 1, 1944.

12. Quoted by John XXXIII from an Allocution by Pius XII on October 8, 1956.

13. In Germany there has been in effect since the Adenauer-Erhard years a law passed in 1950 known as the *Mitbestimmungsrecht*. It requires that worker representatives participate in decision-making processes up to the top level for all firms beyond a certain size. Germany—thanks to its strong Catholic Center tradition—had been the seedbed for much of what later appeared in papal social teachings. The persons involved range from Bishop Wilhelm von Ketteler of Mainz, Karl Vogelsang, Johann v. Görres, and Franz Hitze, to the more recent figures including the three Jesuits, Heinrich Pesch, S. J., Oswald von Nell-Breuning, Gustav Gundlach, and also the Austrian priest, Johannes Messner. The Anglo-American cultural milieu, on the other hand, still appears to be more conditioned by the British classical and neo-classical tradition in economics, including Manchester liberalism.

14. Successful collective bargaining by unions with management is, of course, already a kind of management-sharing at a very significant level, i.e., a co-determinination of wages, hours and other working conditions.

15. Recently there have been initiatives, even proposals for legislation, on the part of stockholders who wish to regain some control over the salaries paid to executive officers of the corporations of which they, the stockholders, are the legal owners. Salaries are approved by directors who are themselves chosen by the top management people who cast decisive votes which the vast majority of stockholders entrust to them routinely by their proxy statements. The pressure for a say in this matter comes from highly publicized instances of the extremely high salaries paid to top executives even while their corporations post miserable earnings records and even losses.

16. This was a direct quotation from *Quadragesimo Anno* (par. 125).

17. This principle for taxation, once quite widely accepted, has been challenged more of late since the revival of the "liberal ideology." Given the high budgets which have become characteristic in contemporary society, the ability-to-pay principle implies the use of progressive tax rates, meaning rates which rise as the base, usually income, rises. To apply the same rate to all would involve inordinate burden for people with less ability to pay, i.e., those with lower incomes. Also, progressive rates have been used increasingly to bring about a certain redistribution of income when other socio-political measures are lacking to prevent gross maldistribution from occurring in the first place—a tacit acknowledgement that the income distribution mechanism is not functioning as it should!

18. One is entitled to ask the pertinent question here: Why are people willing to pay $100 and more for a ticket to a football game on a cold day—a game which, incidentally, they could often watch on television—at the same time that they protest vigorously any increase in the price of essential food grown and harvested by people who are, as a rule, grossly underpaid for their efforts? Where is the balance? It would appear to be a legitimate use of the tax mechanism to rectify the imbalance; i.e., people who can afford such luxuries could afford to pay taxes which would, for example, help to support farm prices.

19. The well-known magazine of conservative opinion, *National Review*, whose editor was nominally a Catholic, protested this entire encyclical editorially in the memorable words: "*Mater si; Magistra, no!*" And the publication made abundantly clear its own opinion by referring to the encyclical as a "venture in trivialities."

20. Examples are England, the Netherlands, Belgium, Japan, Germany, and Taiwan which rank among the most prosperous and, at the same time, the most densely populated nations on earth at this time. The thesis that population growth motivates economic growth has been supported by economists far apart in time and approach like the noted British economist Colin Clark, and the German Jesuit economist Heinrich Pesch. Cf.

Colin Clark, *Population Growth and Land Use* (New York: St. Martin's Press, 1968), 272-273. Cf. also Heinrich Pesch, *Lehrbuch der Nationalökonomie/Teaching Guide to Economics*, trans. Rupert J. Ederer (Lewiston: Edwin Mellen Press, 2002), vol. II, bk. two 77ff.

21. For example, the United States and Canada, as well as Australia, are sparsely populated countries, which nevertheless rank among the wealthy, developed nations. On the other hand, countries in the South American continent, by and large, as well as many stereotypically poor nations in Africa are also sparsely populated.

The reader should note that in this population discussion, the relevant information—population per square mile or kilometer—is often overlooked in favor of total population figures. The latter are more eye-catching and tend to weight the argument in favor of the alarmism about overpopulation, but they are less pertinent for analyzing the problem. There are also tendentious metaphors like "the spaceship earth." On earth, people are born and they die. In spaceships, at least as we have been able to envision them until now, adding more people would be like having a second and then a third person enter a telephone booth (a common appurtenance of the pre-cell phone era). The vast areas of the earth have little in common with either phone booths or spaceships, real or fancied.

22. This is the translation used in the 1958-1981 volume of Sister Claudia Carlen's fine five volume work: *The Papal Encyclicals,* 80. The *America Press* translation is similar: "On this point We solemnly proclaim that…."

23. Pius XI, *Quadragesimo Anno*, par. 135.

24. Pius XII, *Christmas Message of 1953* in Yzermans, 2, 177-178.

25. Cf. Staff of *The Pope Speaks Magazine*, *The Encyclicals and Other Messages of John XXIII* (Washington: TPS Press, 1964), 444-445.

Chapter 4
Paul VI
Populorum Progressio

Mater et Magistra was still addressed to a wide range of problems in the social order, where the application of the virtues of justice and charity are relevant and therefore a proper matter for popes to discuss in social encyclicals. While John XXIII did indeed launch into the area of imbalance between rich nations and poor nations, he also dealt with matters that Leo XIII first made the business of the modern Church, especially justice in the relations between employers and workers; and he ventured for the first time into the problems of agriculture in modern industrial society. *Populorum Progressio* (*On the Development of Peoples*) which appeared in 1967, on the other hand, may be designated as a single-purpose social encyclical. It picked up on the theme which previous pontiffs had suggested in one way or another, but which first took on the dimensions of a premier issue in the period following World War II. One may add parenthetically, that its author, Pope Paul VI, was the first modern pope to travel extensively outside the gates of Vatican City, thereby reflecting the name of the missionary apostle whose name he chose for himself as pope. He anticipated by his several travels abroad the peripatetic style of Pope John Paul II.

Perhaps no social encyclical was so much a Cassandra-cry as *Populorum Progressio*. That may possibly reflect a certain pathos in the character of Paul VI, as much as the special urgency which he sensed about the problem that he addressed. Indeed, this sense of urgency emerged no less than seven times during the course of the encyclical. In the opening paragraph we find: "...solidarity in action at this turning point in human history is a matter of urgency" (1). Next, the concerned Pontiff wrote: "The question is urgent, for on it depends the future of the civilization of the world" (44). Then he appealed to persons wielding political power: "Would that those in authority listened to Our words before it is too late" (53). Later we read: "But let everyone be convinced of this: the very life of poor nations, civil peace in developing countries, and world peace itself are at stake" (55). And there is a fateful diagnosis: "The world is sick" (66). Once again, we find: "...at stake are the peace of the world and the future of civilization" (80). Finally, the encyclical ended as it began on the note which best characterizes the entire appeal: "Yes, We ask all of you, to heed Our cry of anguish, in the name of the Lord" (87). *Populorum Progressio* was, to be sure, a "cry of anguish."

The encyclical is divided into 4 parts: a brief introduction; Part I calling "For Man's Complete Development"; Part II which is an appeal for "The Development of the Human Race in the Spirit of Solidarity"; and a short conclusion entitled: "A Final Appeal." Following the tradition begun by John XXIII in *Pacem in Terris,* it is addressed also "To all men of good will." Being the first social encyclical after the Second Vatican Council, it appears to reflect an awareness that since the grave problems facing us are now truly worldwide, their solution also calls for what may be termed an ecumenical approach.

The five introductory paragraphs simply state the central problem that Paul VI intended to address: "the development of those peoples who are striving to escape from hunger, misery, endemic diseases and ignorance" (1). The theme provided him with the occasion to establish "solidarity in action" as the critical element in resolving the problem. He began in this encyclical the practice of using almost reflexively the expression, "solidarity," in his writings and discourses, and we shall have more to say about that later.

After the customary deferential reference to the "great encyclicals" of his predecessor, Paul VI stated what may be termed the specific theme of this encyclical: "Today...the social question has become world-wide." Thus, it is necessary now "'to encourage social justice among nations, to offer to less developed nations the means whereby they can further their own progress'" (5).[1]

Part I: For Man's Complete Development

This part opens with what today anyone but a die-hard colonialist would admit is an accurate portrayal of the aftermath of colonialism. First, it scarcely stretches the truth to state that "colonizing powers have often furthered their own interests, power or glory, and that their departure has sometimes left a precarious economy, bound up for instance with the production one kind of crop." Nor should even the most rabid anti-colonialist deny that nevertheless the "qualities and achievement of colonizers who brought their science and technical knowledge...left beneficial results of their presence in so many underprivileged regions. In other words they left behind "structures" which "diminished ignorance and sickness, brought the benefits of communications and improved living conditions" (7).

All in all, however, the residuals of past colonial episodes leave a "situation...manifestly inadequate for facing the hard reality of modern economics." Thus, "rich peoples enjoy rapid growth whereas the poor develop slowly." Furthermore, the "imbalance is on the increase where some produce a surplus of foodstuffs, others cruelly lack them and see their exports made uncertain" (8). Add to that the fact that "social conflicts have taken on world dimensions" (9), and that "the temptation becomes stronger to risk being swept away towards types of messianism which give promises but create illusions," (11) and we have the basis for the Pope's fears for the future. One can only imagine the disillusionment among peoples in developing nations who have permitted themselves to be seduced by the Marxian siren-song, as they witnessed the decline of the vast empires built on that philosophy! And this brings up the question of proper solutions. It is that question which a prescient pontiff already addressed in *Populorum Progressio,* and which would appear to be all the more urgent at present. Although one temptation has been made less alluring by the course of recent events, other "types of messianism which give promises but create illusions" may still be lurking about.

Enter the Mother and Teacher of nations. At this point, Paul VI introduced the Church and the role which she has and can play in helping to resolve the staggering problem. First there are the undeniable, but often underappreciated efforts of its missionaries throughout the world and down through the ages.[2] They "have built not only churches, but also hostels and hospitals, schools and universities." And they have taught "the local populations the means of deriving the best advantages from their natural resources." The Pope took the step, unusual in encyclicals, of mentioning a specific person—Charles de Foucauld—who "edited an invaluable dictionary of the Touareg language" (12). One thinks of Damien the Leper and of our great contemporary missionary, Mother Teresa; but we may tend to lose sight of the many thousands of missionaries who labor and have labored in relative obscurity, sacrificing much, sometimes even paying the ultimate price. Along with the Gospel, they invariably bring modern medical care and some of the technical advantages their home countries have achieved.

Nevertheless, "local and individual undertakings are no longer enough." What is called for now is "concerted action based on a clear vision of all economic social, cultural, and spiritual aspects." And while the predominant mission of the Church is not politics, but its spiritual mission, it cannot sit by idly when she sees the "noblest aspirations of men…not satisfied." What she offers toward a resolution of the shortfall is "a global vision of man and of the human race" (13). That vision involves also the "integral" view of man which suggests: "Development cannot be limited to mere economic growth" (14).

What follows is a first tentative explanation of that solidarity which Pope John Paul II installed as a pivotal principle in *Sollicitudo Rei Socialis*, the encyclical which marked the 20th anniversary of *Populorum Progressio.* Paul VI described an important aspect of solidarity in this way: "We have inherited from past generations, and we have benefited from the work of our contemporaries: for this reason we have obligations towards all, and we cannot refuse to interest ourselves in those who will come after us to enlarge the human family." That "reality of human solidarity, which is a benefit for us, also imposes a duty" (17). Thus, we progress from the reality of human solidarity to the obligations to contribute to the common good which we all derive from it; hence, we are face to face again with the ultimate ordering principles proposed to us by Pius XI in *Quadragesimo Anno*: social justice and social charity.

After making a case for the minimum material welfare to which all people and nations are entitled, there is the attendant warning: "Individuals, families and nations can be overcome by avarice, be they poor or rich, and all can fall victim to a stifling materialism" (18). That is followed by the Pope's defense of "a new humanism," and a very significant statement involving an ascending scale of the conditions which such humanism implies. It begins with the "less human conditions," where people lack the minimum material necessities, while others are rendered morally deficient because they are "mutilated by selfishness." And it ends on the highest level where "faith, a gift of God [is] accepted by the good will of man, and unity in charity of Christ, Who calls us all to share as sons in the life of the living God, the Father of all men." In between are such conditions as "victory over social scourges, the growth of knowledge, and the acquisition of culture, cooperation for the common good, the will and desire for peace" (21). All in all, this paragraph adds up to an impressive manifesto of a true "new humanism."

The program for action which follows that manifesto involves the traditional Christian (and Aristotelian) view of private property. Supported by scriptural and patristic quotations, Paul VI restates that simply with the words: "...private property does not constitute for anyone an absolute and unconditional right" (23). Then there is the stern counsel of St. Ambrose: "'You are not making a gift of your possessions to the poor person. You are handing over to him what is his. For what has been given in common for the use of all, you have arrogated to yourself. The world is given to all, and not only to the rich.'" (*De Nabuthe,* c. 12, n. 53)

That statement stops just short of Proudhon's stern judgment that "property is theft"; and those who have never grasped the truly radical nature of Catholic social teachings were scandalized by such "hard sayings." Moreover, their chagrin was, no doubt, intensified when Paul VI continued with this counsel: "If certain landed estates impeded the general prosperity because they are extensive, unused or poorly used, or because they bring hardship to peoples or are detrimental to the interests of the country, the common good sometimes demands their expropriation" (24).

As if the justification of "expropriation" under certain blatantly unjust conditions were not enough, the Paul VI went on to stress the too easily fudged over distinction between the genuine blessings of the explosion in technological advances usually referred to as the Industrial Revolution, and the liberal economic philosophy which fastened itself to that Revolution at its outset. He referred to that philosophy as "unchecked liberalism"; and he pointed out that it "considers profit as the key motive for economic progress, competition as the supreme law of economics, and private ownership of the means of production as an absolute right that has no limits and carries no corresponding social obligation" (26). It is to be noted that the Pope used the present tense in this important statement; in other words, he was not intending to describe something that ended in the 19th century. Indeed, he denounced this state of affairs emphatically with the words: "One cannot condemn such abuses too strongly by solemnly recalling once again that the economy is at the service of man" (26).

A far more subtle, if not delicate, statement follows that directly: "But if it is true that a type of capitalism has been the source of excessive suffering, injustices and fratricidal conflicts whose effects still persist, it would also be wrong to attribute to industrialization itself evils that belong to the woeful system which accompanied it" (26). First of all, there is the conditional, "if," and then there is the word, "type," modifying capitalism. This appears to leave the door open to another "type" of capitalism which might cleanse, or have cleansed itself, of the philosophy of economic liberalism. That philosophy involves an exaggerated notion of an absolute right of private ownership, a justification of the quest for unlimited profits as the highest goal of private enterprise and of economic life generally, and the naive Darwinian notion that unlimited, free competition will lead to "the survival of the fittest" producers and merchants, so that these forces together would automatically result in the highest conceivable common good for all. Needless to say, all of such lack of restriction implies that the state or public authorities are to remain on the sidelines as merely the "night-watchmen" of society.

Such radical stuff was denounced editorially by the *Wall Street Journal* as "warmed over Marxism."[3] The same kinds of tempers which had barely cooled down from the discomfort caused by Leo XIII in *Rerum Novarum* were again inflamed, and the Mother and Teacher of nations has once again been summoned before the high priests and the Pontius Pilates of our time. The accusers were typically the ones who never could or never wanted to segregate the blessings of industrial society which came with increasing intensity during the 18th century and afterwards, from the wretched Physiocratic, Enlightenment naturalistic philosophy that was unhappily instilled in our culture at roughly the same time in history. Indeed, they are also not willing to acknowledge that capitalism in any meaningful sense of the word itself preceded this historical confluence by as many as two centuries, as we indicated earlier. Thus we find the common, convenient error of attributing the blessings of industrial progress to liberal capitalism, the "type of capitalism" which Paul VI spoke about as "the source of excessive suffering, injustices and fratricidal conflicts whose effects still persist." The Pope himself had no such problems. He clearly emphasized the differences in "the introduction of industry" which is "a necessity for economic growth and human progress" (25), and "unchecked liberalism," and "a type of capitalism" (26). And he proceeded from that to anticipate remarkably what Pope John Paul II would dedicate his first social encyclical to: the theology of human work (27). At the same time, the next paragraph reviewed what John XXIII had said about making "the enterprise a community of persons in the dealings, activities and standing of all its members." In this way, the continuing linkage between the social teachings that went before, and those that followed, was once again affirmed.

The paragraphs following that contain a papal statement suggesting what must also certainly have upset people with conservative political leanings. While pointing out that a revolutionary uprising typically "produces new injustices, throws more elements out of balance and brings on new disasters," there is the qualifying clause, "save where there is manifest, long-standing tyranny which would do great damage to fundamental personal rights and dangerous harm to the common good of the country" (31). One must suppose that this counsel parallels the "just war doctrine" but with equally, severely circumscribed conditions. Nevertheless, such social teaching could motivate the types of persons who were carried away by so-called "liberation theology," assuming they were at all familiar with it.

While implicitly including "individual initiative," the favorite solution of those who attacked this encyclical as well as its follow-up encyclical, *Sollicitudo Rei Socialis,* Pope Paul nevertheless stated that it and "the mere free play of competition could never assure successful development" (33). That he included it is clear from the next statement contained in the same paragraph: "Hence programmes are necessary in order 'to encourage, stimulate, coordinate, supplement and integrate' the activity of individuals and of intermediary bodies."[4] What is more we have here the resurfacing of the "intermediary bodies" first explicitly presented in the Church's social teachings by Pius XI and reaffirmed by his successors, Pius XII, and John XXIII. However, they are no longer referred to in what may be for the contemporary world the somewhat arcane terminology of *Quadragesimo Anno,* i.e., "functional groups" (*Quadragesimo Anno*, par. 82) and "vocational groups" (*Quadragesimo Anno*, par. 86). Henceforth they are cited simply as "intermediate" or "intermediary bodies." But they are intended specifically to "avoid the danger of complete collectivization or of arbitrary planning, which, by denying liberty, would prevent the exercise of the fundamental rights of the human person." (33). Thus, we again have the Church, in its social teachings trying to steer a course between "Tomorrow's technocracy [which] can beget evils no less redoubtable than those due to the liberalism of yesterday" (34). There could be no stronger reaffirmation of the individual human being and his personal initiative than this: "And man is only truly man in as far as, master of his own acts and judge of their worth, he is author of his own advancement, in keeping with the nature which was given him by his Creator and whose possibilities and exigencies he himself freely assumes" (34).

It is worth noting that what followed at this point in the encyclical was suggested by the same pope who one year later issued the controverted encyclical, *Humanae Vitae*. Acknowledging that "frequently an accelerated demographic increase adds its own difficulties to the problems of development: the size of the population increases more rapidly than available resources," Paul VI indicated his awareness that "the temptation is great to check the demographic increases by means of radical measures." It is possible to see how a careless reading of what followed could have helped lead to the kinds of measures and attitudes which caused a virtual schism in the Church. First, the Pope stated: "It is certain that public authorities can intervene, *within the limit of their competence*, by favoring the availability of *appropriate* information and by adopting *suitable* measures *provided that these be in conformity with the moral law* and that they respect the rightful freedom of married couples" (37). The italics are added to indicate what many developed a tendency to overlook in hastening to address the "difficulties" actually or supposedly stemming from "demographic increase." Paul VI nevertheless affirmed the "rightful freedom of married couples," which governments would be tempted to run roughshod over. The extreme case would be Communist China where parents are told how many children they may have, where "assembly-line" abortions occur to rectify "mistakes," and where there are severe penalties for disobeying the established norms. But elsewhere in the world there are also various kinds of pressures, some more subtle than others, infringing on "the rightful freedom of married couples."

The admonition that "it is for the parents to decide, with full knowledge of the matter, on the number of their children, taking into account their responsibilities towards God, themselves, the children they have already brought into the world and the community to which they belong," also led many into believing that the Church had finally changed its longstanding opposition to contraceptive birth control. The temptation was not removed by the sentence which followed: "In all this they must follow the demands of their own conscience *enlightened by God's law authentically interpreted,* and sustained by confidence in Him" (37). Once again, the italics are added to indicate what many often conveniently overlooked or interpreted so as to become inconsequential, in upholding the sovereignty of the individual conscience. In any case, *Humanae Vitae* rectified whatever misunderstanding—or more to the point—what misinterpretation there was of this paragraph in *Populorum Progressio.* Furthermore, ironically it was in the wealthy nations which were already well along on the road to demographic decline, where the most opposition arose to the Church's teaching. There, it was fondly hoped, that the Church would now at last sanction an all-too-common reprobate lifestyle.

It is difficult to determine whether the "professional organizations" mentioned at this point in the encyclical are co-extensive with the "intermediary bodies" mentioned above. There is no question that the latter category includes the former. Here they are cited as subsidiary to the family; and their suggested objective is "to promote the interests of their members," and that their task is "educative." That they are not coextensive with labor unions seems clear from the subsequent statement that "a pluralism of professional organizations and trade unions is admissible" (39).

This portion of the encyclical ends with the Pope's warning lest the temptation to materialism would vitiate the legitimate quest for economic development. There is explicit counsel here for "[L]ess well-off peoples" to the effect that they "can never be sufficiently on their guard against this temptation which comes to them from wealthy nations" (41). But, by the same token, there is an implicit admonition for those "wealthy nations," which by their success in arriving at "a highly technical and culturally developed civilization...provide the model for a way of acting that is principally aimed at the conquest of material prosperity." While rampant "consumerism" was not yet so far advanced, especially in the European nations still struggling to dig out from under of the rubble of World War II, its advanced indicators were already in evidence by 1967. It was the Church's ardent wish, expressed here by Paul VI, that this virus would not now also afflict the "developing nations." Help, yes; but not at the expense of "true human values" in the latter.

The Pope concluded with a warning that "What must be aimed at is complete humanism," not one that is "closed in on itself, and not open to the values of the spirit and to God Who is their source..." (42). Thus, lest anyone suspect that Paul VI was himself becoming entrapped by the prevailing secularism humanism, there is this splendid concluding statement:[5]

> "An isolated humanism is an inhuman humanism." There is no true humanism but that which is open to the Absolute and is conscious of a vocation which gives human life its true meaning. Far from being the ultimate measure of all things, man can only realize himself by reaching beyond himself. As Pascal has said so well: 'Man infinitely surpasses man' (42).

Part II
The Development of the Human Race in the Spirit of Solidarity

This heading comes from the opening paragraph of the second part of *Populorum Progressio.* As indicated earlier, solidarity became a favorite theme of its author—one which has been adopted with equal persistence by his successor, Pope John Paul II. Having stated the problem in the first part of the encyclical, Paul VI was now ready to propose the solution: achieving "a true communion among all nations" (43). He indicated that doing so is a duty "especially of better-off nations," and that it stems from "a brotherhood that is at once human and supernatural" (44). The three elements involved in accomplishing the task are listed as:

> the duty of human solidarity—the aid that the rich nations must give to developing countries; the duty of social justice—the rectification of inequitable trade relations between powerful nations and weak nations; the duty of charity extended now on a global scale—the effort to bring about a world that is more human towards all men, where all will be able to give and receive without one group making progress at the expense of the other (44).

Combined here are the three salient principles of social order: solidarity, social justice, and universal charity, whether applied at the internal, domestic level, or at the international, worldwide one.

Specific remedies involve: supporting out of one's "own pocket works and undertakings organized in favor of the most destitute"; being prepared "to pay higher taxes so that the public authorities can intensify their efforts in favor of development," and readiness "to pay a higher price for imported goods so that the producer may be more justly rewarded." Enthusiastic supporters of the "free market" should note that in Catholic social teaching the lowest possible price is not always necessarily the best price or the highest good to which an economy can aspire. Ultimately, the just wage for work is a far more predominant consideration; and payment of such a wage sometimes calls for a higher price than a producer might otherwise be in a position to charge for his product. Thus, as in this case, the well-to-do buyers in developed nations may be expected to pay a higher price than they have perhaps become accustomed to paying for the products of developing nations.

Beyond those considerations, there is even a challenge to the occasional intrepid soul, "to leave his country, if necessary and if he is young, in order to assist in this development of the young nations" (47). In other words then, the papal program covers private initiative as well as action by public authorities. Clearly, the problem is viewed as extending far beyond what private initiative could accomplish, because the Pope pointed out that "the same duty of solidarity that rests on individuals exists also for nations" (48). Lest there be any doubt about the specificity of that mandate, "We must repeat once more that the superfluous wealth of rich countries should be placed at the service of poor nations" (49). And lest there be any doubt that it is a *common good* which is being discussed here, we are told: "Besides, the rich will be the first to benefit as a result" (49).

In economic terms, this means that unless the poor nations are drawn into the worldwide marketplace and enabled to become a functioning part of it, the wealthy nations will soon experience a surfeit of their goods so that their economies will stifle and go into decline. That is true quite simply because the goods of this world and the economic process are not intended for the benefit of a privileged few, but for all people. Now that simple economic truth is being applied in the enlarged context of worldwide solidarity in a second generation of Catholic social teachings. We are talking about social justice and social charity with their object, the common good, on a global scale.

In view of the magnitude and urgency of the problem, Paul VI called for "concerted planning." This has aroused the anxiety of those who still place their faith in economic liberalism; in other words, in the haphazard actions of self-interested individuals and the magical forces of the free market. In retrospect, there has been a "see, we told you so" reaction when some foreign aid initiative went awry sometimes because of the inefficiency or even corruption of the officials who were entrusted with administering the programs at either end. We are dealing with the same mentality which, a century after *Rerum Novarum,* still regarded with suspicion and hostility workers exercising their natural right to unionize, because *some* union officials *sometimes* became corrupt. So, what befell Leo XIII also happened to Paul VI. For his efforts, he brought vituperation on his head.[6]

The Pope's emphasis on international collaboration to deal with this worldwide economic imbalance is based on certain valid considerations. Such cooperation would, he felt, put the efforts beyond suspicion of "political pressures and economic suzerainty aimed at maintaining or acquiring complete dominance" (52). In other words, we are dealing with the "neocolonialism" to which John XXIII already alluded in *Mater et Magistra* (171-172). Additionally, expenditures "prompted by motives of national or personal ostentation" would be minimized, specifically: "every exhausting armaments race," which in his words, "becomes an intolerable scandal" in view of the widespread, desperate destitution in many developing nations. With regard to military expenditures, Pope Paul had previously, in Bombay, India, "called for the establishment of a great 'World Fund' to be made up of a part of the money spent on arms, to relieve the most destitute of this world" (51). Here he called also for "rates of interest and time for repayment of the loan" to be arranged so as not to overwhelm recipient nations. On the other hand, "guarantees could be given to those who provide the capital that it will be put to use according to an agreed plan, with a reasonable measure of efficiency..." (54). Indeed, since this "common task will not succeed without concerted, constant, and courageous efforts" (55), it involves also "the men and women who must be helped, who must be persuaded to work for their own betterment and endeavor to acquire gradually the means to that end." In other words, since the entire program is not designed to encourage "parasites or the indolent" (54), the recipient peoples are themselves expected to be heavily engaged in the development process.

Assistance from the rich to the poor nations also involves another consideration: fairness in trade relations. Pope Paul indicated that that former would be "illusory" if the latter are not adjusted in keeping with the requirements of social justice. Pointing out that since the underdeveloped countries must until now rely mainly on their export of raw materials, whereas the industrialized nations export mostly manufactured goods, the former remain at a considerable disadvantage. That is so because the prices of their raw materials "are subject to wide and sudden fluctuations," whereas those of industrial products are "progressively increasing" (57). Thus, the "poor nations remain ever poor while the rich ones become still richer." Here, Paul VI put his finger on one considerable factor which some critics of the papal plea for help by the rich nations to the poor ones lose sight of. Then he moved into the highly controversial territory of free trade versus protectionism, that "old chestnut" in economic theory that persists and polarizes, and which is even now again an important issue.

The Pope drew an intriguing parallel between the free-market, free-contract ideology as it is applied in this area and also in the just wage discussion initiated by Leo XIII. Invariably, the same ideology and its supporters come to the fore here as then, more than a century earlier! Doggedly, however, the teaching Church holds to its position that "the rule of free trade, taken by itself, is no longer able to govern international relations." That represents major heresy, given the terms of the present-day revival of "the liberal ideology."[7] Paul VI was well aware that, "it is the fundamental principle of liberalism, as a rule for commercial exchange, which is questioned here" (58). As in the just wage issue, "Its advantages are certainly evident when the parties involved are not affected by any excessive inequalities of economic power." However, "when economic conditions differ too widely from country to country: prices which are 'freely' set in the market can produce unfair results." The use of quotation marks is the paramount indication of what the Pope was talking about. Indeed, he explicitly applied the "teaching of Leo XIII in *Rerum Novarum*" here as "always valid," meaning that "if the positions of the contracting parties are too unequal, the consent of the parties does not suffice to guarantee the justice of their contract, and the rule of free agreement remains subservient to the demands of the natural law" (59). That is a powerful tonic against the ancient Manchester liberalism, which its surviving ideologues could not stomach! To make matters worse, the Pope went on to state that "an economy of exchange can no longer be based solely on the law of free competition, a law which in its turn too often creates an economic dictatorship" (59). The regulating principle for economic life established by Pius XI is reaffirmed here: "Freedom of trade is fair only if it is subject to the demands of social justice" (59).

We are talking here about that principle which John XXIII and Paul VI began applying to the worldwide economy, whereas Leo XIII and Pius XI were still concerned predominantly with the internal disorder which was then devastating national economies. What is more, Pope Paul now took the occasion to remind the "developed nations" that they themselves have adjusted the old free trade theories "to re-establish within their own economies a balance, which competition, if left to itself, tends to compromise" (60). He referred to price supports for farm products, "at the price of sacrifices imposed on economically more favored sectors"—an appropriate parallel. And there are also the obvious concessions among nations in the process of establishing common market arrangements. These generally adopt common tariffs toward "outside" nations, while moving toward free trade among member nations. The conclusion: "In this area one cannot employ two systems of weights and measures." Therefore what "holds for a national economy or among developed countries is valid also in commercial relations between rich nations and poor nations." The standard Catholic social teachings approach to competition follows: "Without abolishing the competitive market, it should be kept within the limits which make it just and moral, and therefore human" (61).

From those economic considerations, the tone of the encyclical changes in the direction of other types of threats to "universal solidarity:" nationalism and racism. "Nationalism isolates people from their true good," and it can be an unfortunate handicap especially "where the weakness of national economies demands rather the pooling of efforts, of knowledge and of funds" (62). Racism is also divisive; and it takes various forms, sometimes hiding "beneath the rivalries of clans and political parties." Then there is the persistent, nagging tension which it has created "between the colonists and the indigenous population" (63).

It is perhaps not saying too much if we suggest that racism, by and large, originated in the first encounters between colonizers and the "backwards" aspects of the cultures they experienced among those whom they subjugated and colonized. There was the all too predominant tendency to associate such retarded elements in the native cultures with some inherent racial characteristics, which has caused the persistent irrational feeling of racial superiority and all of its subsequent, attendant problems. Inevitably, given the presence of such attitudes, there was less than adequate motivation to try to bring the native peoples up to economic equality with their "superiors." The temptation then is to use the "inferiors" as mere means for the enrichment of their overlords. The trenchant observation of Abraham Lincoln about the unfortunate yet perennial principle in human affairs comes to mind: "You work and toil and earn bread, and I'll eat it."

Pope Paul turned next to the need to apply universal charity to the problem at hand. More than "the unproductive monopolization of resources by a small number of men," he perceived the root of the problem in "the lack of brotherhood among individuals and peoples" (66). Turning from the large picture, he addressed the "duty springing from human solidarity and Christian charity," to welcome people from other countries whether they are young students or emigrant workers. The presence of foreign students from developing nations has become a widespread phenomenon in the post-World War II era. Emigrant workers are characteristic of certain European countries, where they form large population pools in some large cities. While the money they earn and send home, or return home with, after some years of service improves their economic lot, the conditions of their life abroad often ranges from the sadness of homesickness to a truly pathetic condition. A great opportunity for the practice of charity is thus presented to the host nations; and, needless to say, some of them and some of their people perform more admirably than others.

Another set of admonitions is reserved for the reverse flow of people from the developed to the underdeveloped nations. The Pope was referring specifically to "industrialists, merchants, leaders or representatives of larger enterprises," as well as to the "experts…sent in larger and larger numbers on development missions." This included a warning taken from the Vatican II document *Gaudium et Spes,* that "they ought not to conduct themselves in a lordly fashion, but as helpers and co-workers" (71).

Conclusion

The final part of *Populorum Progressio* sums up the case its author tried to make throughout, with the words: "Development is the new name for peace." There is also the significant statement: "Peace cannot be limited to a mere absence of war, the result of an ever precarious balance of forces" (76). Instead, we are reminded of the ancient scriptural wisdom that peace is the work of justice: "No, peace is something that is built up day after day, in the pursuit of an order intended by God, which implies a more perfect form of justice among men" (76).

Laying to rest criticisms about the papal program leading to "handouts" which would tend to enervate the ambition of the people in the poor nations to work at developing their own economies, we find: "The peoples themselves have the prime responsibility to work for their own development." That is always a given in all of the Church's social teachings whether applied to domestic or international economic considerations. Personal responsibility and initiative are kept in the foreground of the discussion. However, the proposal of help from outside is all too often used as a pretext by critics who, impregnated by the old liberal philosophy, would prefer to shrug off any responsibility to share their wealth in goods and know-how with people who, by various flukes of history, are left in less fortunate circumstances. And it should come as no shock to Christians that they have an ongoing responsibility to help their fellow man, individually and collectively, because nothing is accomplished, as Paul VI said, "in isolation." We are required to shake off the torpor induced by the primitive economic philosophy of the 18th century before we can begin to appreciate the commonality of the *common* good and what it is all about, and the obligations which everyone has to it.

As popes in their social teachings typically return to pastoral theological terms in the final portions of their encyclicals, Paul VI also recalled the fact that it is actually the doctrine of the Mystical Body of Christ, which underlies the "universal solidarity of mankind" (79).

The "Final Appeal" at the conclusion of *Populorum Progressio* calls first on Catholics ("all our sons"), segregating "the laymen [who] should take up as their own proper task the renewal of the temporal order," from "the Hierarchy" which "is to teach and to interpret authentically the norms of morality to be followed in this matter." There is special counsel for laymen, that they are "to take the initiative freely and to infuse a Christian spirit into the mentality, customs, laws, and structures of the community in which they live." And they are to do so, "without waiting passively for orders and directives" (81). Pope Paul also appealed to "all Christians," then to "all men of good will who believe that the way to peace lies in the area of development," with specific mention of "delegates to international organizations, government officials, gentlemen of the press, educators" (82-84). And there is the dramatic closing appeal: "Yes, We ask you, all of you to heed our cry of anguish, in the name of the Lord" (87).

That the "cry of anguish" was not heard and responded to in an adequate manner is clear from a review of the world situation as reported to us daily by our media. In any case, the two immediate successors of Pope Paul VI saw fit to draw attention to it pointing out its continuing urgent relevance. Pope John Paul II used the occasion of the 20th anniversary of *Populorum Progressio* to commemorate it with the second of the trilogy of his own social encyclicals, *Sollicitudo Rei Socialis* in 1987. More recently Pope Benedict XVI cited its great importance in his social encyclical *Caritas in Veritate* issued in 2009 in response to an economic crisis which reminded the older generation of the major upheaval which Pius XI addressed in 1931. Its entire first chapter—*The Message of Populorum Progressio*—extolled the importance of Pope Paul's social teaching, which the German pope cited and reaffirmed frequently in his own social encyclical. We will examine that after turning our attention first to what the Polish Pope wrote in his three brilliant encyclicals addressed to the continuing "social question" within and beyond national economies.

Notes

1. Pope Paul VI was quoting his own *Motu Proprio* establishing the Pontifical Justice and Peace Commission.

2. For example, objections were raised against the recent beatification of the Franciscan missionary to the Indian population in Mexico and California, Junipero Serra. This appears to be in keeping with of a trend at present to decry what missionaries (and also explorers like Columbus) allegedly did to denigrate or obliterate the culture of the "native peoples," and to foist on them European "values," presumably including Christian ones. In the process, some very negative aspects of those primitive native cultures are sometimes overlooked in dwelling on whatever positive aspects there may have been. For example, there is an excellent account by a distinguished contemporary historian, of the large-scale, ritual human sacrifices performed by the Aztecs in Mexico. Cf. Warren Carroll, *Our Lady of Guadalupe and the Conquest of Darkness* (Front Royal, VA : Christendom Publications, 1983). Carroll estimates that there were at least 50,000 such human sacrifices each year on altars set up atop the giant stone pyramids, which are now tourist attractions.

3. Cf. the leading editorial in the *Wall Street Journal,* "A Blessing for Secular Error," March 30, 1967, 14.

4. Paul VI was quoting from *Mater et Magistra.*

5. Paul VI relied heavily on certain French scholars for his social thinking. On this matter of humanism, the encyclical had footnote references to Jacques Maritain (*L'humanisme intégral,* 1936), and Henri de Lubac, S.J. (*Le drame de l'humanisme athée,* 1945).

6. Cf. for example a book which echoes the kind of criticism contained in the aforementioned *Wall Street Journal* editorial: George Weigel and Robert Royal, eds., *A Century of Catholic Social Thought* (Washington: Ethics and Public Policy Center, 1991),115-130.

7. Cited by Paul VI in his Apostolic Letter, *Octogesima Adveniens* (par. 35).

Chapter 5
John Paul II
Laborem Exercens

This encyclical, with the English title *On Human Work*, was born amid frightful circumstances. It was originally scheduled for release on May 15, 1981, the 90th anniversary of *Rerum Novarum.* On May 13, in St. Peter's Square, however, Pope John Paul II was shot, almost fatally, in an assassination attempt. After a recovery which some considered miraculous, the Pope issued the encyclical belatedly on the Feast of the Triumph of the Cross on September 14 of the same year.

We have indicated that Paul VI was an enthusiastic admirer of thinkers, several of which are mentioned in footnotes to *Populorum Progressio.* It appears that Pope John Paul II too had a scholar on whom he relied for many of his views on economic matters, even though, for what are certainly his own good reasons, he never revealed the identity of the person publicly. However, anyone familiar with the remarkable work of the German Jesuit economist, Heinrich Pesch (1864-1926), will recognize the concordance between his work and the trilogy of social encyclicals by John Paul II which began with *Laborem Exercens.*[1]

Pesch's influence in encyclicals addressed to the economic order began with *Quadragesimo Anno*, into which it was infused by two of his Jesuit confreres who served as principal advisors to Pius XI in drafting that encyclical. They were Oswald von Nell-Breuning (d. 1991) and Gustav Gundlach (d. 1963), both proponents of Pesch's solidarist economics. Indeed, the man entrusted by Pius XI with overseeing that project was then the Superior General of the Jesuits, Wlodimir Ledochowski, who assigned the task of formulating *Quadragesimo Anno* to the two German Jesuits. Thus, the process has come full circle, and the first Polish pope in the history of the Church has now established human work as the main force in economic life, with solidarity as the dominant dynamic principle.

As indicated previously, the principle of subsidiarity, social justice and social charity as ultimate regulating principles, and the organization of people according to their vocations and occupations in the economic process are all found in Pesch's massive, five volume *Lehrbuch der Nationalökonomie.* Ultimately, however, human work was placed at the center of the system which he devised and called the *social system of human work.*[2] And so, 90 years after the papal social teaching addressed to the economic order was begun with an encyclical *On the Condition of Labor*, these teachings came full circle with an encyclical *On Human Work.* And the statement in the introductory paragraph, that "work bears a particular mark of man and of humanity, the mark of a person operating within a community of persons," expresses precisely, if not in so many words, Pesch's theme that man is destined by his Creator to be lord over the world of nature by his work performed in the context of society.[3]

The main body of *Laborem Exercens* is divided into five parts: an Introduction; Work and Man; Conflict Between Labor and Capital in the Present Phase of History; Rights of Workers; Elements for a Spirituality of Work.

I. Introduction

Pope John Paul II established his theme as: "*human work* and, even more...*man* in the vast context of the reality of work" (2). He felt that another encyclical was needed on the matter because: "fresh *questions* and *problems* are always arising," and "there are always fresh hopes, but also fresh fears and threats, connected with this basic dimension of human existence." Therefore, "the Church considers it her task always to call attention to the dignity and rights of those who work" and, "to condemn situations in which that dignity and those rights are violated..." (3).

After a summary recapitulation of the flow of social teachings since 1891, in which he indicated the shift from the "'labor question' within individual nations" to *the 'world' question,*" John Paul II moved on to his own theme "that human work is *a key,* probably *the essential key,* to the whole social question" (10). He turned to what he calls "the gradual solution" of that persistent social question, by developing what some have called his "theology of human work."

II. Work and Man

Theology examines God, His nature and His works in the light of Divine Revelation. And so Pope John Paul II began his "theology of human work" with *"the very first pages of the book of Genesis"* as the basis for the Church's "conviction that work is a fundamental dimension of human existence on earth" (12). By the mandate of the Creator to "fill the earth and subdue it" (Gen. 1:28), man, created as "male and female," begins the role shared with the Creator to carry on the process of creation. Implicit here is a corrective for those excesses stemming from the present-day preoccupation with safeguarding our natural environment, which would reduce man to a kind of passive steward of the natural order. Man is designated by his Creator to be, as Pesch often expressed it, the "lord of the world," and not to be ruled by the inanimate and animate resources of nature.

Nevertheless, as is stated at various times in the Church's social teachings, this implies a responsible exercise of that dominion which takes into account also the future needs of mankind.

The Pope proceeded to make a significant distinction between what he called "work in the objective sense," and "work in the subjective sense." Treated in ascending order, he dealt first with the "objective sense," meaning all of what is accomplished by man's labor: ranging from the primitive stage where animals are domesticated and natural resources are extracted from the land and the seas, to the stage of industrialization where increasingly sophisticated machinery is brought into use, and finally to the most recent "electronics and microprocessor technology" that are referred to as "post-industrial changes." Lest we are bedazzled by all of the objective outcome of human work, John Paul II inserted the reminder that "even in the age of ever more mechanized 'work,' *the proper subject of work continues to be man"* (18). And that is the theme of the next important paragraph of *Laborem Exercens.*

Work in the subjective sense means precisely that work is, in the final analysis, by and for man. It is man who subdues the earth according to God's mandate, and it is man for whom all of the subduing takes place. We are not here to serve nature or to preserve it in its primordial condition, but to hunt, fish, extract, and to change the forms of resources by our industry, so as to make it useful for man's purposes. Only man can act "in a planned and rational way." And only he is "capable of deciding about himself, and with a tendency to self-realization," so that, "*As a person, man is therefore the subject of work"* (23). We are told that "This truth...constitutes the fundamental and perennial heart of Christian teaching on human work." And the Christian teaching is contrasted with certain ideas in the ancient world, for example, where people were categorized into two segments: "free men" and "slaves." To the latter, as inferior beings, were left all the work involving the "exercise of physical strength, the work of muscles and hands." Needless to say, "Christianity brought about a fundamental change of ideas in his field..." After all, its Founder "devoted most of the years of His life on earth to manual work at the carpenter's bench." This "most eloquent 'Gospel of work'" demonstrated once and for all that it "is not primarily the kind of work being done, but the fact that the one who is doing it is a person," in other words, the "subjective dimension" rather the "objective one," which is the source of the "dignity of work."

All of that Christian theology of work does not imply a false egalitarianism in the world of work. Work in the objective sense may still be "rated and qualified," but the *primary basis of the value of work is man himself,* who is its subject. Accordingly, work is "for man" and not man "for work." Thus, "in the final analysis it is always man who is the purpose of work, whatever work it is that is done by man—even if the common scale of values rates it as the merest 'service,' as the most monotonous, even the most alienating work" (27).

This "Gospel of work" has significant implications for the just wage doctrine presented first by Leo XIII, and updated in this encyclical and in previous ones, as we shall see presently. The reason eventually why there was and continues to be a "social question" is the total objectivization of human work, where people lost sight of its "subjective" side. The Pope indicated that the especially relevant period in history, prescinding from the pre-Christian era where slavery was accepted as natural by even the most brilliant philosophers relying solely on their natural reason, is the "industrial age" and "especially the "first half of the nineteenth century" (29). Unfortunately that also happens to be the age when the science of economics in its modern form began. With this came "the various trends of *materialistic and economistic* thought, which the Christian truth about work had to oppose."[4] Respectively, those trends of thought see economic life and, indeed, life overall exclusively in terms of material bounty and profitability. Thus human work too became simply "merchandise," which is bought and sold on the market. That view was, in the Pope's words, an "error of early capitalism" which paralleled "various forms of collectivism." Socialism, by its very philosophy, whereby everything was reduced to material, could not rise above regarding also the work of human beings as mere material—a fact which its sad history amply demonstrates, despite reverential paeans about the working class by its theorists. While John Paul II gave to capitalism a certain benefit of the doubt here by referring to "early capitalism," he nevertheless warned that we have here an error which "can be repeated wherever man is in a way treated on the same level as the whole complex of material means of production, as an instrument." Thus, even if we defer to the present non-socialistic societies by calling them "market economies," they are subject to the same pitfalls of "materialism" and especially "economism." What is critical is whether man is treated "in accordance with the true dignity of his work," in other words—as "subject and maker," and therefore as the "very purpose of the whole process of production." This "analysis of human work in the light of the words concerning man's 'dominion' over the earth," according to the Pontiff, lies "at the very heart of the ethical and social question."

He turned then to a theme which has come to be associated with his pontificate by virtue of his support of the Solidarity Movement in his own native Poland during the critical years, when the valiant Polish workers initiated the process of gradually weaning Eastern Europe away from the Soviet Union.[5] The word, solidarity, is used nine times in this eighth paragraph of *Laborem Exercens.* Even though the Pope was, at this point, speaking of "solidarity" as a generic element which may be brought to bear generally in economic life and also specifically to the efforts of workers to unite, who can doubt, especially in hindsight, but that there was also at least oblique reference to *Solidarność*?

Its application here is undoubtedly to the worldwide reaction by workers "*against the degradation of man as the subject of work,* and against the unheard-of accompanying exploitation in the field of wages, working conditions" (33). Included is a timely reminder that in Revelation denying the worker of his just wage was pronounced to be an injustice "that cried to heaven for vengeance." (Deut. 24:15; James 5:4). Such denial became a commonplace state of affairs because it

> was favored by the liberal sociopolitical system, which, in accordance with its "economistic" premises, strengthened and safeguarded economic initiative by

> the possessors of capital alone, but did not pay sufficient attention to the rights of the workers, on the grounds that human work is solely an instrument of production, and that capital is the basis, efficient factor and purpose of production.

Although the Pope did not use the term "capitalism" at this precise point, his term, "liberal sociopolitical system," is significant. In any meaningful sense of the word, capitalism is the system where ownership and control of the material factor of production, capital, conferred a dominance on those who owned and controlled it, which extended beyond industry and the economy to the entire sociopolitical system. Thus, John Paul II was identifying capitalism with far greater precision and relevance than is accomplished even in many economic textbooks. He also made it clear that the workers are its prime victims because of the "economistic" (meaning, the primacy of profit) premises from which capitalism proceeds.[6]

Gradually, "worker solidarity" did bring about "profound changes," some more promising than others. The Pope referred to these as "various forms of neo-capitalism or collectivism," and also to "new systems," where workers "can often share in running businesses and in controlling their productivity" and where they also "exercise influence over conditions of work and pay, and also over social legislation." What follows makes it clear that there is enough blame to go around, notwithstanding the changes that have occurred. Nor does blame rest exclusively on systems inspired by "collectivism." There are "other forms of injustice, much more extensive than those which in the last century stimulated unity between workers for particular solidarity in the working world." That applies to developed as well as underdeveloped countries. For example, there is reference to an "unemployment of intellectuals" in what has become a most painful phenomenon also in the United States. We do, in fact, have what the Pope called a "working 'intelligentsia,'" brought about by "ever wider access to education and an ever increasing number of people with degrees or diplomas...accompanied by a drop in demand for their labor." The Pope referred to that development as, "in effect 'proletarianization.'" Such results occur when an educational system—and these seem of their nature somehow to be ponderous and slow to adapt—is out of touch with "the types of employment or service required by the true needs of society, or when there is less demand for work which requires education, at least professional education, than for manual labor, or when it is less well paid."

At this point the term "social justice" is found for the first time in *Laborem Exercens*. Pointing to a "continued study of the subject of work and of the subject's living conditions," John Paul II called for "*new movements of solidarity of* the workers and *with* the worker....in order to achieve social justice in the various parts of the world." No one is exempted here, not the rich, nor the poor; not the then-collectivist East, or the neo-capitalist West! Conditions mentioned here clearly apply around the world. As the Pope indicated, "the 'poor' appear under various forms; they appear in various places and at various times." Specifically, they often appear "as a *result of the violation of the dignity of human work*: either because the opportunities for human work are limited as a result of the scourge of unemployment, or because a low value is put on work and the rights that flow from it, especially the right to a just wage" (37). The stage is set for an updating and reaffirmation of the just wage doctrine, but that will be the subject of the next part of this encyclical. First there is more "theology of work."

It appears that Pope John Paul II, a one-time youthful worker in the stone quarries of Poland, took pains in this encyclical to exonerate work from the status of being a curse. Exegetes have perhaps dwelt excessively on the stern judgment by the Creator after the Fall: "In the sweat of your face you shall eat bread" (Gen. 3:19). The Pontiff stressed here that "God's fundamental and original intention with regard to man...was not withdrawn or cancelled out even when man, having broken the original covenant with God," heard those awful words. His plan for us, "being created in His image and after His likeness," was to "subdue the earth." It was in this way that we are to carry on as persons made in the image of the Creator. After the Fall, processes like human work and childbirth were to be less pleasant. Nevertheless, work was ordained from the beginning, whether or not man conducted himself as he should have.

John Paul II then demonstrated that he knew something about the world of toil—about the "thorns and thistles"—by listing many kinds of hard labor. But he did not exclude even here the work of "scientists," of "those who bear the burden of grave responsibility for decisions that will have a vast impact on society," and also of "doctors and nurses, who spend days and nights at their patients' bedsides." Finally, and significantly, since the modern world tends to denigrate their kind of toil at present, the Pope mentioned "women who, sometimes without proper recognition on the part of society and even of their own families, bear the daily burden of responsibility for their homes and the upbringing of their children" (39). There is an implicit reminder here that the Church has, since the start of its modern social teachings, called for a social order where mothers of families are able to stay at home to spend full time at their unique, important responsibility.

This discussion culminates in the exoneration of work from being simply a kind of punitive tedium, to its being "a good thing for man—a good thing for his humanity—because through work man not only transforms nature, adapting it to his own needs, but he also achieves fulfillment as a human being and indeed, in a sense, becomes 'more a human being'" (41). Yet, the Pope, painfully aware of another way in which work can be degraded, did not fail to mention that in our time it has been used on a massive scale precisely as punishment "with the system of forced labor in concentration camps." But that was not its original purpose, nor is it its central purpose even after the Fall.

Indeed, work is destined not only for the personal fulfillment of the human being, but it also "constitutes a foundation for the formation of family life, which is a natural right and something that man is called to" (42). In addition, the "family is simultaneously *a community made possible by work* and the first *school of work,* within the home for every person"—an intriguing enlargement of the Church's social teachings on the link between labor and family life.

Finally, the significant role of work extends beyond the person's own fulfillment and its importance for family life to "the *great society* to which man belongs on the basis of particular cultural and historical links" (44). We are now talking about the "membership of a nation" within which man "intends his work also to increase the common good developed together with his compatriots..." This is, among other things, a fine illustration of the *common good* as defined first by John XXIII in *Mater et Magistra.* But John Paul II also extended the importance of work and the resultant common good beyond national boundaries, as John XXIII began doing in that encyclical, "to add to the heritage of the whole human family, of all the people living in the world" (44).

The section ends therefore with a final admonition: that we not allow ourselves to be carried away by the *objective* dimension of human work—"an immense development of technological means...in recent centuries"—so as to allow ourselves to lose sight of its all-important *subjective* dimension as indicated in that final paragraph.

III. Conflict Between Labor and Capital in the Present Phase of History

Prefatory to detailing the rights of workers now outlined and supported, as the Pope indicated, by both national legislatures and on the international level by, for example, the International Labor Organization, he turned first to a matter relating to "this latest period," first addressed in *Rerum Novarum.* The reason is that this period with its specific problem is, in the opinion of John Paul II, "by no means yet over" (48). Indeed, the widespread unwillingness among so-called conservative circles to even now accept labor organization as a basic right of workers, substantiates his view, as does the volume of criticism which greeted this encyclical.

The specific problem of the age then, is the "great *conflict...between 'capital' and 'labor.'*" What is meant by these two categories is "the small but highly influential group of entrepreneurs, owners or holders of the means of production, and the broader multitude of people who lacked these means and who shared in the process of production solely by their labor." A not surprising result, given the inherent nature of capitalism and of market economies, was the fact that "the entrepreneurs...following the principle of maximum profit, tried to establish the lowest possible wages for the work done by the employees." According to the principles of economic liberalism, this should have led to the maximum attainable good of all concerned. Historically, it did not! Indeed, the period brought with it also "other elements of exploitation, connected with the lack of safety at work and of safeguards regarding the health and living conditions of the workers and their families." Hence the protracted period of conflict.

The Pope referred to this as "the *ideological conflict* between liberalism, understood as the ideology of capitalism, and Marxism, understood as the ideology of scientific socialism and communism." He then presented a brief analysis of the Marxian position and its eventual goal, stating that, even though it is an "extremely important field of issues," he would not "go into the details," since the theses are already widely known "both from the vast literature...and by experience." Instead, he returned to "the fundamental issue of human work...the main subject of the considerations in this document" as relevant to the topic of this section of the encyclical. Not at all pleasing to some conservative observers was the Pope's forthright statement of what is simply an ontological fact: *"the principle of the priority of labor over capital"* (52). That is so because "labor is always a primary *efficient cause,* while capital, the whole collection of means of production, remains a mere *instrument* or instrumental cause." Some have wrongly interpreted this as making the ordinary worker somehow superior to those who are in charge of production—the managers. The juxtaposition is rather between those who work for a living, which includes the managers, and the material instruments of production, which will do nothing unless workers first produce them and then activate and maintain them. Production calls for a hierarchy of producers: some manage and direct; others carry out their instructions and directions. Democracy in the workplace does not abolish authority any more than it does so in political governance. However, capital is, in any valid economic sense, a produced, material means of production; and its owners are entitled to a fair return for providing it to the productive process, as are the owners of land and natural resources. However, the material capital itself is obviously in no way superior to the workers; and, even if less obviously, neither are the human beings who own and control it.

A development which brings the priority of human work to the fore is the way managers, themselves working human persons, have come to predominate in the corporate world. Thus, the actual owners of capital have more and more been relegated to the status of passive rentiers who await quarterly dividend payments for providing capital to the corporate enterprises. Even in small corporations, the characteristic of management on the part of the typical owner-manager—in other words, his work at directing the enterprise—tends to loom larger than his ownership. Various experts have written significant works on this emergent aspect of corporate life in modern society.[7] Nevertheless, the juxtaposition of "capital vs. labor" still persists in popular perceptions about capitalism.

It appears that we now have a papal effort to clarify matters by making the distinction between the materials put in the hands of workers (including managers), and the people, at all levels, who make the economy work. John Paul II designated as capital, "not only the natural resources placed at man's disposal but also the whole collection of means by which man appropriates natural resources and transforms them in accordance with his needs (and thus in a sense humanizes them)" (55). The emphasis is on the fact that "*these means are the result of the historical heritage of human labor.*" And that is reemphasized, using italics liberally, with the words: "Thus *everything that is at the service of work,* everything that in the present state of technology constitutes its ever more highly perfected 'instrument,' *is the result of work.*" The objective of the Pope here, clearly, was to place human work at the center of the economic system and, more broadly to "emphasize and give prominence to the primacy of man in the production process, *the primacy of man over things.*" Even a more specific scientific use of the term, *capital,* would help in the process, since, as he states: "Everything contained in the concept of capital in the strict sense is only a collection of things." He concluded with the statement: "Man, as the subject of work, and independently of the work that he does—man alone is a person" (57).

Next, the Pope returned to the concepts mentioned early in the encyclical, which marked the beginning of the industrial age: "materialistic and economistic thought." Here the two terms used in combination are clarified. According to John Paul II the basic social question stemming from when "labor was separated from capital and set in opposition to it" began when, "the principle of the primacy of person over things...*was broken up in human thought...*" (60). And that resulted from the two errors: *"the error of economism"* and *"the error of materialism."* He indicated that the former sprung from the latter, "in that economism directly or indirectly includes a conviction of the primacy and superiority of the material, and directly or indirectly places the spiritual and the personal (i.e., man's activity, moral values and such matters) in a position of subordination to material reality." Economism, he defined, as the error of "considering human labor solely according to its economic purpose."

An important distinction was made here between *"theoretical materialism,"* and *"practical materialism"* which is "a materialism judged capable of satisfying man's needs, not so much on the grounds of premises derived from materialist theory, as on the grounds of a certain hierarchy of goods based on the greater immediate attractiveness of what is material." The distinction is especially relevant now since the "empire" that was based on "theoretical materialism" has collapsed, even while practical materialism (consumerism, included) and economism persist. As if gifted with prophetic foresight about what was to come less than 10 years later, John Paul II stated: "...and it seems that economism influenced this non-humanistic way of stating the issue before the materialist philosophical system did." Now the insidious force is traced back to its origin. It was what the Pope called, "this practical error that struck a blow first and foremost against human labor, against the working man;" and it is "[T]he same error, which is now part of history, and which was connected with the period of primitive capitalism and liberalism." What is more, we are warned that it "can nevertheless be repeated in other circumstances of time and place, if people's thinking starts from the same theoretical or practical premises." The corrective is: "overcoming this error...through adequate changes both in theory and in practice, changes in line with the definite conviction of the primacy of the person over things, and of human labor over capital as a whole collection of means of production" (62).

It is important to note that the juxtaposition established by the Pope is not between human labor and the other human persons, the capitalists, but between human labor and the "whole collection of means of production." As a factor of production, however, human labor is superior on what he refers to here with the unusual term, "the ontic level." In other words, on the level of being, or ontologically, man is superior to material. That has already been established earlier on the grounds that "labor is always a primary *efficient cause,* while capital remains a mere *instrument* or instrumental cause" (62). And since efficient causes are ontologically at a higher level than instrumental causes, one may conclude also that the persons who act as the former occupy a prior status in the economic process to those who merely supply the latter, unless they are also engaged in the *work* of actually managing the enterprises in which their capital is invested. Otherwise they are passive factors like absentee landlords; and like them, they are entitled to a fair return on what they own and make available to the productive process. It appears that no one would object to rentier landlords being placed at a lower level of economic priority than the actual cultivators who work the land. And capitalists, meaning the owners and providers of capital to enterprise, have come to occupy more and more a parallel position with regard to those who actually work at various capacities, including management, in the actual operation of the enterprises where their capital is used in production. Furthermore, it is possible to separate the material means, capital, from its owners, the capitalists; but it is not possible to separate labor or work from the persons who perform it. The latter are intrinsically associated with their services to the economic enterprise.

It is also noteworthy that the Pope once again used a qualifying adjective with "capitalism." He referred to it as *primitive* capitalism, which he linked with "liberalism." Previous pontiffs had already spared capitalism, as such, from being condemned as an intrinsic evil, like atheistic communism, for example. However, the liberal economic philosophy, which attached itself to capitalism in roughly the same period when the industrial age began to revolutionize economic life in the modern world, has always been declared to be a false philosophy. Thus, we have John Paul II here linking the two phenomena during a certain period in history that is now past. But he warned that it "can nevertheless be repeated in other circumstances of time and place..." This encyclical was issued in 1981 precisely at a time when the resurgence of free marketeering capitalism was becoming a high priority in various countries, including the United States.[8] The problem lay not so much in that capitalism, in itself not evil, was being restored to the status it enjoyed before the economic collapse of the 1930s, but in that the liberal economic philosophy of the 18th century was being refurbished and presented as the panacea for the economic problems which faced us.

John Paul II was well aware that the terms *labor* and *capital* as they are used in contemporary discussion do not refer simply to "'impersonal forces' operating in economic production.... Behind both concepts there are people, living actual people: on the one side are those who do the work without being the owners of the means of production, and on the other side those who act as entrepreneurs and who own these means or represent the owners" (63). That led him into reaffirming the traditional Church position on private ownership, and to a defense against the "program of collectivism as proclaimed by Marxism and put into practice in various countries." However, he also indicated: "At the same time it differs from the program of capitalism practiced by liberalism and by the political systems inspired by it." In other words, "Christian tradition has never upheld this right as absolute and untouchable," but as "subordinated to the right to common use." That "radical" doctrine as restated at this point in *Laborem Exercens* has always been a bitter pill to swallow for those who are, in effect, hopeful for a return to "primitive capitalism and liberalism." Yet, as the Pope indicated, the private ownership of capital was never intended "to practice exploitation of labor," or to "be *possessed against* labor," or even "*for possession's sake.*" Then comes what must be regarded as "heresy" by the devotees of the newly revived free market ideology. The private ownership of the means of production, i.e., of capital, "*should serve labor,* and thus...make possible the achievement of the first principle of this order, namely, the universal destination of goods and the right to common use of them." As if to compound the "heresy," the Pope went on to state that, "therefore...one cannot exclude the *socialization,* in suitable conditions, of certain means of production." Here there is no ambiguity or liberty in translation, as was the celebrated case concerning *Mater et Magistra.* John Paul II was talking about government ownership and operation in certain situations. It is useful to bear in mind that some of the most vigorous market economies at present take it for granted that, for example, airlines, railroads, and certain public utilities are owned and managed by national or local governments.

As if anticipating the inevitable remonstrance to such "socialist talk," the author of this encyclical reminded us that on this matter, "the position of 'rigid' capitalism continues to remain unacceptable, namely the position that defends the exclusive right to private ownership of the means of production as an untouchable 'dogma' of economic life." He was not talking now of the past. Otherwise there would not be this mandate: "The principle of respect for work demands that this right should undergo a constructive revision, both in theory and in practice." It is up to those who find such Christian teaching on private ownership hard to swallow, to examine their consciences in order to determine whether they are not still clinging to "rigid capitalism" whose position on this matter "continues to remain unacceptable."

The attempt by the Church to break out of that historical capitalistic mold included proposals for "*joint ownership of the means of work,* sharing by the workers in the management and/or profits of business, so-called shareholding by labor...[Italics in text]" (67). These date back to at least *Quadragesimo Anno* in 1931, and they have been repeated also in *Mater et Magistra.* Clearly, such programs are not prescribed infallibly by the *Magisterium.* They represent prudential hints for implementing the approach to private ownership of the means of production—an approach which is indeed magisterial. John Paul II indicated that by the statement: "Whether these various proposals can or cannot be applied concretely, it is clear that recognition of the proper position of labor and the worker in the production process demands various adaptations in the sphere of the right to ownership of the means of production." He offered the "escape" for those who still insist on espousing "rigid capitalism," by indicating that it "must undergo continual revision, in order to be reformed from the point of view of human rights." At the same time he made it clear again that "*a priori elimination of private ownership of the means of production*" is not an acceptable solution.

That leads only to "*monopoly of administration and disposal*" by another group which may easily end up "offending basic human rights." What real socialization means, as used in this encyclical, is a situation where "the subject character of society is ensured," i.e., "when on the basis of his work each person is fully entitled to consider himself a part-owner of the great workbench at which he is working with everyone else" (68-69).[9]

It is at this point, where John Paul II began to discuss "socializing" property in a manner which is acceptable that we find mention once again of the somewhat indeterminate concept: "intermediate bodies." We do not find the terms, "vocational orders" or "functional groups," as used by Pius XI in *Quadragesimo Anno*, let alone any reference to "guilds." But who is to say that the "vocational orders" proposed by the latter are not included in what the present Pope called "a wide range of intermediate bodies with economic, social and cultural purposes"(14)? Indeed, the medieval guilds, of which "vocational orders" were to be an updated version for modern industrial society, did indeed have "economic, social, and cultural purposes." Also, the author of *Laborem Exercens* envisioned the intermediate bodies mentioned here as, "enjoying real autonomy with regard to public powers"; and Pius XI asked that the vocational orders be "autonomous in character" (*Quadragesimo Anno*, par. 83). And just as John Paul II saw them operating "in subordination to the demands of the common good," Pius XI called for them to function in such a way "that both justice and the common good be taken into account" (*Quadragesimo Anno*, par. 86).[10]

In concluding this third part of the encyclical, its author returned to the "personalist" position that whatever form the economic structure may have taken historically, a worker must have the sense that "he is working for himself." Such awareness is, of course, hampered "in a system of excessive bureaucratic centralization where the worker feels like a cog in a huge machine moved from above." Whatever the social system, a man "wishes the fruit of this work to be used by himself and others; and he wishes to be able to take part in the very work process as a sharer in responsibility and creativity at the workbench to which he applies himself." Unfortunately, although the "excessive bureaucratic centralization" was endemic to socialist systems, and it played no small part in their universal demise a few years after this encyclical was issued, that can also be present in so-called market economies where business firms become excessively large and unwieldy. The result: "incalculable damage...throughout the economic process, not only economic damage, but first and foremost damage to man" (71).

IV. Rights of Workers

After the exalted status of the worker in the economic process was set forth in the third part of *Laborem Exercens,* John Paul II turned to the specific rights of workers which flow from that position. But in providing the setting for the discussion of worker rights, the duty incumbent on all is first established. "Work is, as has been said, an obligation, that is to say, a duty on the part of man" (73). It is a duty which flows from the mandate of the Creator, but also from man's own humanity "which requires work in order to be maintained and developed." But man is also a social being so that he "must work out of regard for others," which range from "his own family," to "the country of which he is a child, and the whole human family of which he is a member." It adds up to what the Pope called "the moral obligation to work, understood in its wide sense."

That leads into an interesting distinction, peculiar to this encyclical, between the *direct* and the *indirect* employer. The former is "the person or institution with whom the worker enters directly into a work contract." The latter includes all of the other "factors...that exercise a determining influence on the shaping both of the work contract and, consequently, of just or unjust relationships in the field of human labor" (76).

The "indirect employer" therefore includes "...every society and in the first place the State," inasmuch as these have it in their power to establish an *"ethically correct labor policy"* (78). What is implied here is the entire body of labor legislation and jurisprudence which establishes the framework within which the workers and employers must operate. That it extends beyond the individual state, however, is clear from mention of the impact which foreign trade conditions have on the workers' welfare. There is reference, for example, to the effect which "companies referred to as multinational or transnational" have by their power to "fix the highest possible prices for their products, while trying at the same time to fix the lowest possible prices for raw materials or semi-manufactured goods" (79). John Paul II took this opportunity to point out that the "gap between most of the richest countries and the poorest ones is not diminishing or being stabilized, but is increasing more and more, to the detriment, obviously of the poor countries." In other words, the social injustice which Paul VI made the central theme of an entire encyclical is far from resolved! Nor was John Paul II resigned to leaving resolution of this grave problem simply to the free forces of the market. It is the so-called "free market," after all, which brings about the problem, because the powerful control it and structure it in their favor: i.e., "to fix the highest possible prices for their products," while at the same time setting "the lowest possible prices for raw materials or semi-manufactured goods." Thus, the Pope once again disappointed the free marketeers by urging all of "the *International Organizations*...beginning with the United Nations Organization," and its Food and Agricultural Organization (FAO) to help in dealing with this problem. Such appeal to anything beyond the free market goes counter to the 18th century economic liberalism which has resurfaced in our time; but there is more such papal "irreverence" yet to come.

This "indirect employer" was also charged with helping to resolve the problem of unemployment; and "the question of finding work," or, "the issue of suitable employment for all who are capable of it" was listed here as "a fundamental issue," as the Pope began his discussion of workers' rights. And it is up to "the agents included under the title of indirect employer...to *act against unemployment*, which in all cases is an evil, and which when it reaches a certain level, can become a real social disaster" (82). It begins to appear as though the Pope's purpose for introducing this new category—the "indirect employer"—was to disarm the resurgent liberal ideology with its naive, if not self-serving, reliance on free market forces to make all things come out right in the economy. He went so far as to call on the "indirect employer" to "make provision for *overall planning* with regard to the different kinds of work by which not only economic life but also the cultural life of a given society is shaped." However, there is the precautionary statement that, although "this overall concern…in the final analysis…weighs on the shoulders of the State;" nevertheless, "it cannot mean one-sided centralization by the public authorities." Undoubtedly that reflects the principle of subsidiarity, even though it is not mentioned specifically at this point; but there is mention of "a just and rational *coordination*" involving "the *initiative* of individuals, free groups and local work centers and complexes." And the "enormous part" which international organizations have to play is mentioned again in the context of an appeal that "the living standard of the workers in the different societies will *less and less show those disturbing differences* which are unjust and are apt to provoke even violent reactions." The Pope returned to the theme of Paul VI, whose encyclical *Populorum Progressio* he cited at this point. He also referred to the "disconcerting fact of immense proportions…that, while conspicuous natural resources remain unused, there are huge numbers of people who are unemployed or under-employed and countless multitudes of people suffering from hunger" (87). It is the basic theme of *balance* within and among national economies which had preoccupied the thinking of Blessed John XXIII in *Mater et Magistra.*

Central to the resolution of the "social question" overall has been the just wage doctrine first presented in its modern form by Leo XIII in *Rerum Novarum.* At this point in *Laborem Exercens*, John Paul II stressed that centrality in a manner that is perhaps unprecedented in the modern social teachings of the Church. Turning now to the workers' rights, he indicated that these "in the final analysis are formed within the relationship between worker and direct employer" (88). Furthermore, "the key problem of social ethics in this case is that of just remuneration for work done"—in other words the just wage! The importance of the just wage is set forth now with spectacular emphasis by the statement that, "the justice of a socioeconomic system and…its just functioning, deserve in the final analysis to be evaluated by the way in which man's work is properly remunerated in the system." After recalling the "*principle of the common use of goods,*" and indicating that wages for their work are "still a *practical means* whereby the vast majority of people can have access to those goods which are intended for common use," the Pontiff repeated the thought, as if to emphasize its importance, that "a just wage is the concrete means of verifying the justice of the whole socioeconomic system and, in any case, of checking that it is functioning justly" (89). This repetition, within the same paragraph, of an idea that the Pope obviously regarded as critically important, should not be surprising in view of the basic theme of this encyclical which puts human work at the core of the entire economic process.

What follows is another interesting instance of further development in papal teaching on this important matter of the just wage. The Polish Pope offered two possible ways in which the just wage could be approached for the purpose of providing the adult worker with "remuneration which will suffice for establishing and properly maintaining a family and for providing security for its future." It may take the form of payment of "what is called a *family wage*—that is a single salary given to the head of the family for his work, sufficient for the needs of the family without the other spouse having to take up gainful employment outside the home..." That has become the more or less established way of looking at the just wage. However, it inevitably encounters the difficulty of family size. How large a family are we talking about when we try to determine the just wage? Therefore, we are now presented by John Paul II with another possibility. The just wage can be achieved by "*other social measures* such as family allowances or grants to mothers devoting themselves exclusively to their families" (90).[11]

Now the "family allowance" idea was already mentioned in previous social encyclicals beginning with *Rerum Novarum.* However, it was generally presented prudentially as a generous and useful extra benefit provided by some especially benevolent employers. The problem was and is, if employers were expected to pay higher wages to their workers on the basis of their family size, those with large families, precisely those who needed the supplements most, would soon find themselves discriminated against in employment, and in certain situations virtually unemployable. Obviously, such a program on anything but a limited voluntary basis would not suffice for implementing the just wage which the Pope was definitively establishing here as the criterion for evaluating the entire economic system. Therefore, we are talking about a program which would have to be undertaken by government, funded probably out of general revenue, or by specific payroll tax much like the present social security system in the United States. In fact, family allowances are already paid in most nations throughout the world, but not including the United States.[12] Therefore, since this is a system that is already in place throughout the world, it would not prove a wrenching experience to increase the allowances so as to bring them up to the level which the just wage principle requires.

The just wage discussion also provided John Paul II with another opportunity to make a bid for mothers to remain at home and provide the essential service of taking care of their children. He did so now in no uncertain terms, calling for no less than "*a social reevaluation of the mother's role* [italics in text] of the toil connected with it, and of the need that children have for care, love and affection in order that they may develop into responsible, morally and religiously mature and psychologically stable persons." Lest that statement would leave any doubt about what has always been the Church's position on this matter in its social teachings, we find also: "It will redound to the credit of society to make it possible for a mother—without inhibiting her freedom, without psychological or practical discrimination, and without penalizing her as compared with other women—to devote herself to taking care of her children and educating them in accordance with their needs, which vary with age." The Pope added that, "having to abandon these tasks in order to take up paid work outside the home is wrong from the point of view of the good of society and the family when it contradicts or hinders these primary goals of the mission of a mother." One might question whether this last statement leaves an escape for mothers to leave their homes to go out to work. There are undoubtedly exceptional cases where a mother occupies a position which is so sensitive and important, like being the ruler of a country, so that she must entrust the care of their children to trained, full-time, hired "nannies." But the operative word is, "exceptional." Few duties are so vital and non-transferable that they supersede the maternal care of one's own children.

While the principle that "the mother's place is in the home" remains substantially inviolate in Catholic social teaching, cultural changes do occur; so "in many societies women work in nearly every sector of life." Indeed, there have always been unmarried women who have served admirably in various occupations. John Paul II added his voice to the general consensus at large in our time that women should be able to "fulfill their tasks *in accordance with their own nature,* without being discriminated against and without being excluded from jobs for which they are capable." The words italicized in the text of the Encyclical suggest that not all jobs, even in our times, are "*in accordance with their own nature* [*sic*]." One wonders whether there have to be so many women working as policemen, firemen, soldiers, truck drivers, on "road gangs" as our culture is promoting in our time. Rather than emancipation, this would seem, in many cases, to be rather a crude exploitation of the feminine nature—a phenomenon of Soviet society which America used to look askance at not too many years ago! The question is all the more urgent at a time when there is a widespread abandonment of the "irreplaceable role" of women as mothers, to the detriment of the family.

Pope John Paul II turned next to the right of workers to form unions. Leo XIII had identified their right to organize as stemming from the natural right of people to form associations. And he indicated that, in the industrial age, the exercise of that right by workers had become necessary to aid them in securing the just wage among other benefits to which they were entitled. The *Solidarność* Pope also began his discussion of this right by referring to the more generic category—*the right of association.* He indicated that in the present context of society these "associations are called *labor or trade unions*" (91).

Leo XIII never went beyond use of the expression "workers associations" in his labor encyclical. It seems he was unwilling to rule out the possibility of eventually getting back to the kind of associations which included both employers and workers, since he did mention "the guilds of artisans" and societies...composed either of workers alone or of workers and employers together."[13] And now, John Paul II also suggested that "unions go back to the medieval guilds of artisans, insofar as those organizations brought together people belonging to the same craft and thus *on the basis of their work.*" But he immediately pointed to what he called "an essential" difference between guilds and unions as stemming from "the struggle of the workers...to protect their just rights vis-à-vis the entrepreneurs and the owners of the means of production." The Pope exempted the modern labor union from being, in principle, an organ of class struggle, by suggesting that it is "indeed *a mouthpiece for the struggle for social justice.*" He proposed, therefore, that union efforts should be "for" that justice, and "*not a struggle 'against' others.*" The Pontiff did however, provide what appears to be a subtle echo of the Church's hope, as articulated especially in *Quadragesimo Anno,* that people should again form also associations which transcend the workers vs. the employers approach. He based this on what he termed a "characteristic of work that it first and foremost unites people." Calling this "its social power: the power to build a community," he moved on to the proposal that eventually, "both those who work and those who manage the means of production or who own them must in some way be united in this community." That represents "a constructive factor of *social order* and *solidarity,* and it is impossible to ignore it" (96).

Other limitations on unions are indicated by the counsel that their demands "cannot be turned into a kind of *group or class 'egoism.'*" The admonition does not deny them the right to also enter "the field of politics, understood as *prudent concern for the common good.*" Nevertheless, they are cautioned against simply becoming organs of political powers, and to not "have too close links with them," because they then tend to "easily lose contact with their specific role…to secure the just rights of workers within the framework of the common good of the whole of society."[14] Praising also the role which unions often play in educating the workers, the Pope indicated that by such activities on the part of their unions, "workers will not only *have* more, but above all *be* more."

While the right to strike is upheld, what emanates next is somewhat parallel to the Church's just war doctrine. Since the strike is characterized as "an extreme means," and a "kind of ultimatum to the competent bodies," it is actually seen as a weapon of last resort. Thus, it is "a legitimate means," but the Pope indicated with italics that: "*It must not be abused.*" Also, where "essential community services are in question, they must in every case be ensured, if necessary by means of appropriate legislation."[15]

Following the pattern established by Blessed John XXIII, Pope John Paul II dedicated a section of this encyclical to agriculture, specifically, agricultural work. The status of farm work has suffered, perhaps ever since the onset of the Industrial Revolution and the supposed glamour that came with it and its ever more sophisticated aftermath. Indeed, the Pope indicated that agricultural work involves "a lack of appreciation on the part of society," and that farm people "feel that they are social outcasts" (101). This applies both in the developing nations where "millions of people are forced to cultivate the land belonging to others and are exploited by the big landowners, without any hope of ever being able to gain possession of even a small piece of land of their own." However, it is a problem also in "economically developed nations where farm workers are denied the possibility of sharing in decisions concerning their services, or when they are denied the right to free associations."[16]

Sometimes it takes a disaster of colossal dimensions, like a devastating major war where the normal economic processes are disrupted, and where perhaps even much of the economic infrastructure is destroyed, before modern man will again appreciate the importance of agriculture and farm work. Before all else, man must eat to sustain life and to engage in all other forms of economic activity. When the veneer of modern society is peeled off, therefore, a long lost sense of priorities may again emerge.

In the affluent, economically advanced United States, few workers experience so pathetic a fate as the so-called migratory farm workers. They are often deprived of any sense of belonging to some community; their youngsters, who often work long hours alongside their parents in the fields of vast, profit-oriented "agribusinesses," frequently are unable to get the consistent schooling to which they have a right. Occasionally an awareness of the plight of these hapless victims of the "free" market for their products and also for their labor gains a brief glimmer of publicity; but soon they are again simply taken for granted, and a festering social injustice remains unresolved. Pope John Paul concluded that "it is necessary to proclaim and promote the dignity of work, of all work but especially of agricultural work, in which man so eloquently 'subdues' the earth he has received as a gift from God and affirms his 'dominion' in the visible world" (103).

A positive indicator, a sign of social progress in a world otherwise marked by harshness and pessimism, is afforded by measures taken in some countries on behalf of handicapped persons, also in this matter of work. Valiant efforts have been made in recent times to reduce their isolation from the rest of society, so that many of them have been able not only to move about among their fellow citizens, but also to perform useful work. John Paul II noted that with approval, since "disabled people are subjects with all their rights (and) should be helped to participate in the life of society in all its aspects and at all levels accessible to their capacities" (105). In fact, to do otherwise would be "*a serious form of discrimination*, that of the strong and healthy against the weak and sick." Indeed, the urgency of that kind of support for the handicapped is such that it is the "dignity of man...the subject of work and not...economic advantage" which must be taken into account. What this means is, once again, that profitability is not the highest goal of life in society, including the economic process. In other words, such people are not simply to be exploited as cheap labor, but entitled to "their just remuneration, to the possibility of their promotion, and to the elimination of various obstacles" (106).

Another type of worker who operates, as it were, along the fringes of society, and who is liable to be subjected to out-of-the ordinary difficulties if not outright discrimination, is the emigrant in search of work. The papal statement here, while upholding the right to immigrate and emigrate "for various motives," makes a strong and significant case for creating conditions in the homeland which will not make such movement necessary. Aside from the obvious difficulties involved, emigration "constitutes a loss for the country...left behind" (107). The national community is losing a "member" who must then "begin life in the midst of another society united by a different culture and very often by a different language." Also there is "the loss of a subject of work, whose efforts of mind and body could contribute to the common good of his own country, but these efforts...are instead offered to another society which in a sense has less right to them than the person's country of origin." Clearly then, the Pope was viewing emigration as a course of last resort. In fact, he called it "a necessary evil." "Loss" is involved, not to mention difficulties! What is left to be done, then, is damage control. Emigrants are to be protected, where necessary, also by legislation; and they "should not be *placed at a disadvantage* in comparison with the other workers....in the matter of working rights." The emigrant worker is in a certain sense also "handicapped"; and like the physically handicapped person, he or she too "*should not be exploited.*" Ultimately, we come back to the same underlying principle, which John Paul II repeated here: "...the hierarchy of values and the profound meaning of work itself requires that capital should be at the service of labor and not labor at the service of capital" (109).

V. Elements for a Spirituality of Work

Returning to the more specifically spiritual elements underlying this discussion of human work, the Polish Pope concluded his "theology of work." He began by announcing that the Church "sees it as her particular duty *to form a spirituality of work* which will help all people come closer, through work, to God, the Creator and Redeemer, to participate in His salvific plan for man and the world and to deepen their friendship with Christ in their lives" (111). Referring again to the mandate and example of the Creator Himself, the Pope called the first chapter of the book of Genesis, "also, *in a sense the first gospel of work*" (114). It was there that God showed by word and example the need to work, and also to rest.

In our time, the Sabbath has increasingly become just another day. Businesses, especially stores, which are by no means of a nature that they must do so, remain open. People shop and do things which could as well be done on the other six days of the week. It is the concept of profitability once again gone out of control, which has led to this abuse. It is misguided because there is extra gain only if the occasional business remains open while most others are closed on a Sunday. Ironically, even the profitability factor becomes dubious once the practice becomes widespread, as it has in many of our cities and suburbs. The extra day of operation simply means, for the most part, that the available, finite amount of spending power in a community is spread over a seven-day rather than a six-day period. Accordingly, the wages and other costs required for the seventh day of operation end up being a loss rather than a profit factor. Therefore profit-at-all-costs actually ends up being profit-at-extra costs. Not considered at all is the burden placed on employees who must find a way to reconcile their obligation to worship and the need to rest on Sunday, with the demands of their employers that they make it a regular day of work. The only way to curb this abuse and to restore the integrity of the Sabbath as required in God's commandments is by a consensus among businessmen that all of them will observe the Sunday closing. While the guilds and their regulations have been much ridiculed for the restrictions which they placed on competition, a guild-like consensus among shopkeepers would make possible a restoration of the observance of the Sabbath. That is precisely an example of how action by "intermediate" social bodies can prevent excessive intervention by the state, thereby facilitating the operation of the principle of subsidiarity. Meanwhile, Christians could help the process along by simply showing their respect for the Sabbath by refusing to shop on Sunday.

Turning from the Creator to His Son, Pope John Paul II indicated how man's participation "in the activity of God Himself, his Creator, was *given particular prominence by Jesus Christ*...the carpenter" (118). Christ established once and for all the dignity of work—ordinary work like that of the carpenter—by His own example of many years in the shop of his foster father, Joseph. Lest there be any doubt, the Pope referred to no less than 26 examples of different occupations, most of them humble, in the Old and New Testaments. Then there was the example of St. Paul who "boasts of working at his trade (he was probably a tent-maker)." It was also that Apostle to the Gentiles who said: "If any one will not work, let him not eat."[17]

Pope John Paul II then moved beyond Sacred Scripture to recount a significant statement on human work in Second Vatican Council's *Pastoral Constitution on the Church in the Modern World*:

> Just as human activity proceeds from man, so it is ordered towards man. For when a man works he not only alters things and society, he develops himself as well. He learns much, he cultivates his resources, he goes outside of himself and beyond himself. Rightly understood, this kind of growth is of greater value than any external riches which can be garnered...Hence, the norm of human activity is this: that in accord with the divine plan and will, it should harmonize with the genuine good of the human race, and allow people as individuals and as members of society to pursue their total vocation and fulfill it (*Gaudium et Spes*, 35).

It is that "*vision of the values of human work*, or in other words such a spirituality of work," which explains the "right meaning of progress: A person is more precious for what he is than for what he has..." The Pontiff indicated that only this kind of "vision" can bring to fulfillment all of the progress and development which "dominates present-day thought." Clearly that applies also to the emphasis on development in recent papal encyclicals.

To the very last section of *Laborem Exercens* is reserved the redemptive aspect of human work—toil. The Pope tells us here that "all *work*, whether manual or intellectual, is inevitably linked with *toil*." (125). There is no attempt to sugar-coat the prophetic announcement: "Cursed is the ground because of you; in toil you shall eat of it all the days of your life." (*Gen.* 3:17). It reflects not only the punitive aspect of work after the Fall, but also what the Pope referred to here as "*an announcement of death*" (his emphasis). Therefore, although the mandate to work—to "fill the earth and subdue it"—preceded the Fall, the Fall did occur, and subsequently work took on also its redemptive aspect. "Sweat and toil, which work necessarily involves in the present condition of the human race, present the Christian and everyone who is called to follow Christ with the possibility of sharing lovingly in the work that Christ came to do." Therefore, "By enduring the toil of work in union with Christ crucified for us, man in a way collaborates with the Son of God for the redemption of humanity." Christ, of course, provided the example for us, proceeding all of the way to His own death on the cross. Thus, the "Christian finds in human work a small part of the Cross of Christ and accepts it in the same spirit of redemption in which Christ accepted His Cross for us." But as with His Resurrection, we always find in work "a glimmer of new life, of the new good."

At the close of the encyclical, Pope John Paul II emphasized the link between earthly progress and "the expectation of a new earth" for which we are destined. We are told that, "the expectation of a new earth must not weaken but rather stimulate our concern for cultivating this one." That, because the body of the human family grows here; and it "even now is able to give some kind of foreshadowing of the new age." Also, earthly progress "can contribute to the better ordering of human society" so that, "it is of vital concern for the Kingdom of God" (131). That finally and definitively refutes again, as previous popes have done in earlier encyclicals, the primordial Marxian accusation that Christianity somehow dampens concern for a just order in the present world.

"Let the Christian who listens to the word of the living God, uniting work with prayer, know the place that his work has not only in *earthly progress* but also in *the development of the Kingdom of God*." (131).

Notes

1. The other two are: *Sollicitudo Rei Socialis* (1987) and *Centesimus Annus* (1991).

2. Heinrich Pesch, S. J., *Lehrbuch der Nationalökonomie* (Freiburg: Herder, 1925), 2: 214ff.. Cf. the Rupert J. Ederer translation: Pesch/Ederer, *Lehrbuch der Nationalökonomie/Teaching Guide to Economics* (Lewiston: The Edwin Mellen Press, 2002), vol II, bk.1, 236ff. The system outlined by Pesch is designated alternately as the "social" and the "solidaristic system of human work."

3. Pesch, 1: 1-73. The entire first chapter develops the theme under successive section headings: man as lord of the world according to God's ordinance; man as exercising that dominance by means of his work; and such dominion is accomplished in the context of society.

4. The words "economism," and "economistic" are rare and unusual. The only other place where I have found them previously is in Pesch's writings. It refers to exclusive emphasis on purely economic considerations.

5. There is great irony in the fact that it was the downtrodden working class in Poland which united against its Communist overlords and finally overthrew their regime.

6. Several renowned scholars drew attention to the growing gulf between an emergent managerial class which became increasingly dominant in the control of corporations, especially the larger ones. Cf. Adolf A. Berle, Jr. *Power Without Property* (New York: Harcourt, Brace & World, 1959); James Burnham, *The Managerial Revolution* (Bloomington: Indiana U. Press, 1941); Gardiner C. Means, *The Corporate Revolution in America* (New York: Crowell-Collier Press, 1961). The interesting parallel development in socialist society was noted by a former vice-president of Yugoslavia. He indicated how a managerial elite was becoming more and more dominant and privileged, albeit of a more

bureaucratic complexion than in the West. Cf. Milovan Djilas, *The New Class* (New York: Praeger, 1957).

7. Economists whose names moved into the forefront of public recognition were: George Gilder, Milton Friedman, and Arthur Laffer, along with older economists who had long espoused the free market ideology, like Ludwig von Mises and Friedrich Hayek. Actually, the designation "supply-side" economics was a revival in modernized form of the classical "Say's Law of Markets," by the classical French economist J. B. Say (1767-1832).

8. George Gilder, replying to a question about capitalism and self-interest during an interview, included the remark about Pope John Paul II: "It is the reason that the Pope persists in being a socialist." See "Jim Cook Interviews," *IRI Insights*, March-April 1981, 6.

9. Heinrich Pesch indicated at various points in his *Lehrbuch* that machinery or capital cannot be "socialized." Only people can and should socialize. Cf. Pesch, 2: 219, 246ff. Also, Pesch/Ederer, vol. II, bk. 1, 241, 268ff. Therefore, he preferred the term "*Verstaatlichung*" (literally, statification) for what we tend to refer to as "socialization" while referring to the material means of production, which cannot socialize or be socialized.

10. Oswald v. Nell-Breuning, alleged by some to be the "author" of *Quadragesimo Anno*, late in his lifetime stated that the principle of occupational organization as proposed in that encyclical was no longer a viable concept for our time. At various times in interviews and articles he declared it "dead." In fact, according to one report he declared the encyclical *Quadragesimo Anno* as "*tot*" (dead).

11. The possibility of using different approaches to the just wage was discussed by scholars back in the 1950s. Cf. Michael P. Fogarty, "The Catholic Theory of the Family Living Wage," *Review of Social Economy* XV (September 1957), 91.

12. This does not include the United States, where an obsessive preoccupation with an alleged "population explosion" would make such a program hard to promote in any case. What we have had is a program which favors those in the higher tax brackets, because it takes the form of a relatively insignificant tax exemption for each dependent.

13. Leo XIII, *Rerum Novarum* (68).

14. American labor unions, following in the tradition established by Samuel Gompers in the late 19th century, have leaned predominantly toward what has been called "business unionism," while avoiding "revolutionary unionism." The former is devoted to improving the wages and working conditions within the framework of the existing social system, not to its overthrow. Thus, it was generally in harmony with what Pope John Paul II is saying here. Also, political labor parties, which have been tried at various times in our history, usually were unsuccessful and short-lived.

15. Provisions for resolving labor disputes which are deemed to gravely affect the public interest have been included in American labor legislation starting with the Railway Labor Act in 1924. Later, in 1947, a similar provision was included in the Taft-Hartley Act, a law which was technically a lengthy amendment to the original (1935) National Labor Relations Act. Similar provisions are included in many of the state laws passed in more recent times to enable public employees to organize.

16. In the United States, for example, even though most classes of workers are now protected in their right to organize, farm workers are not. They may organize; but they do so at their own risk, so to speak, as was the case with all workers before their right was protected by labor legislation early in the 20th century.

17. Oddly, this quotation from his Second Epistle to the Thessalonians was quoted verbatim, without indicating the source, in the Constitution of the now dismembered Soviet Union. Cf. Article 12 of the *Constitution of the Union of Soviet Socialist Republics*.

Chapter 6
John Paul II
Sollicitudo Rei Socialis

The encyclical *Sollicitudo Rei Socialis* (1987) usually bears the English title: *On Social Concerns.* It was issued to commemorate the twentieth anniversary of the encyclical *Populorum Progressio* by Paul VI. Therefore, it is of a second generation of social encyclicals addressed to the worldwide dimensions of the "social question."

In its opening paragraph Pope John Paul II indicated that "successive contributions of the Magisterium have developed what "has now become and updated doctrinal 'corpus'" (1). He stated "*two objectives*" for issuing this encyclical: first, to pay homage to the "historic document of Paul VI and to its teachings"; second, "to reaffirm the *continuity* of the social doctrine as well as its constant renewal." That is a significant statement in view of a continuing search for novelty and radical new departures by some commentators on social encyclicals. Instead, the Pope makes it clear here that "continuity and renewal are proof of the perennial value of the teaching of the Church." "Continuity" suggests the "vital link with the Gospel of the Lord." And the "renewal" is necessary to adapt to changing "historical conditions" and the "unceasing flow of...events" (3).

The fourth paragraph contains the prophetic dimension which has emerged at various times in this Pope's statements. After indicating that what Paul VI had to say 20 years ago still retains all of its force now, John Paul II referred to the "eve of the third Christian millennium" and a widespread expectancy of a "'new Advent.'" The tone is similar to the "new Pentecost" of which John XXIII spoke, and the "new springtime in history," which Pius XII predicted shortly before his death.[1] Amid doom and gloom which has characterized actual events during the 20th century, such statements suggest a more positive course of developments for the future. But meanwhile, much still needs to be done!

Pope John Paul II alluded to the fact that the Pauline encyclical was the first social encyclical since the Second Vatican Council, that it was inspired by the Council, and that accordingly it takes into account certain important teachings by that Council. It refers frequently to *Gaudium et Spes*—indeed a hopeful title for a document which has to do with *The Church in the Modern World.*[2]

Yet, at the same time those opening words of the document are followed by the more somber words, "the griefs and the anxieties of the people of this age, especially those who are poor or in any way afflicted" (6). It is precisely the afflictions of the latter, which John Paul II termed "another name" for "*poverty and underdevelopment,*" that became the theme of *Populorum Progressio*. He then highlighted three points in that encyclical. The first is the way in which the Church, which Paul VI called "an expert in humanity," got involved and solicited "all people of good will" to get involved, in "a matter which at first sight is solely *economic* and *social*: the *development of peoples*" (8). Indeed, the rash of critical comment which followed *Populorum Progressio*, and also this encyclical commemorating it, stemmed precisely from a feeling that the Church was getting into something here which is beyond its depth—the same kind of objection which Leo XIII encountered more than a century earlier. The justification presented here by Pope John Paul II either went unnoticed, or it was deemed unacceptable. Indeed, "the term 'development' is taken from the vocabulary of the social and economic sciences." He pointed out that Paul VI "emphasized the *ethical* and cultural character of the problems connected with development," therefore, "the legitimacy and necessity of the Church's intervention in this field." Given therefore the "ethical" character of the problem, the Church considers that "the word of God" has "application…to people's lives and the life of society as well as to the earthly realities connected with them, offering 'principles for reflection,' 'criteria of judgment,' and 'directives for action.'" In other words, "these three elements" have "a prevalently practical orientation," meaning they are "directed toward *moral conduct*" (8). Those words are convincing enough unless someone does not choose to be convinced! We are operating here in the area of social virtues, specifically justice and charity, which have a profound bearing on the problem of "poverty and underdevelopment" and on the projected remedies.[3]

The "*second* point *of originality*" of *Populorum Progressio,* according to John Paul II (9), is the way in which it extends the application of the Church's social principles now to the worldwide problem of "poverty and underdevelopment." Admitting that Blessed John XXIII had opened the door to this kind of treatment and that Vatican II had carried on in the same tradition, the Pontiff was saying here, even if not in so many words, that the Paul VI encyclical really defined the issue in such clear terms that it must be regarded as the definitive Church document on it. This is not to say that the "social question," having "assumed a worldwide dimension," "has lost its incisiveness or its national and local importance" (9). Actually the problems facing workers and "the union movements of a particular country or region" are interrelated with "factors beyond regional boundaries and national frontiers." No economist with any vision would deny this. That inference of worldwide economic inter-relatedness provides access for Pope John Paul II to what is to become a dominant theme in his own encyclical—solidarity—and in this case, worldwide solidarity.

If *Sollicitudo Rei Socialis* were to be given a title based on its central theme rather than simply using its opening words, it could without stretching the point be called the encyclical *On Solidarity*.[4] That will become clear later. Here the term is used for the first time, indeed, as Paul VI had used it several times in *Populorum Progressio.* The latter was speaking specifically of the "duty of solidarity" as a manifestation of the interdependence in dealings between the developed and the underdeveloped nations of the world. The moral evaluation of the "universality of the social question" ultimately came down to this: "True development *cannot* consist in the simple accumulation of wealth and in the greater availability of goods and services, if this is gained at the expense of the development of the masses, and without due consideration for the social, cultural, and spiritual dimensions of the human being [Italics in text]" (9).

A third "original contribution" in *Populorum Progressio*, according to Pope John Paul II, is in its summary statement: "Development is the new name for peace" (10). The linkage is established once and for all between future peace in the world and a kind of economic development process, which recognizes that severe economic imbalance between the majority of nations that are poor and a minority of nations that are rich cannot persist without grave consequences for all. The alternative is violence, especially in the face of that most anomalous of all situations, where billions are spent for sophisticated weaponry, whereas a diminishing pittance manages to get itself channeled into productive, worldwide economic development. John Paul II added to the Paul VI statement that "development is the new name for peace," his own significant one that, "war and military preparations are the major enemy of the integral development of peoples" (10). And if the prospect of worldwide conflagration appears for the moment, and perhaps deceptively, to be somewhat diminished, the cruel fact is that before and while Paul VI issued his important encyclical, and in the years since, while people were looking skyward for the incoming missiles of World War III, many small-scale wars, some internecine, others across national boundaries were, and continue to be, waged within and among the developing nations. A most relevant scriptural quotation was included by Pope John Paul II at the conclusion of the second part of *Sollicitudo Rei Socialis*: "What causes wars, and what causes fighting among you? Is it not your passions that are at war in your members? You desire and do not have" (James 4:1-2).

Survey of the Contemporary World

This third part of *Sollicitudo* is based on the premise that the "social context in which we live today cannot be said to be completely *identical* to that of twenty years ago" (11). How does it differ? First, unhappily, because the "*hopes for development*, at that time so lively, today appear very far from being realized." Although Paul VI for his part never minimized the gravity of the problem, there was at large what John Paul II called "a *certain* widespread optimism," at the time (12). There were efforts by the United Nations and by individual nations to deal with the problem and to provide remedies.[5] Nevertheless, says the Polish Pope, the overall result "offers a *rather negative* impression" [Italics in text] ple—children, adults and the elderly—in other words, real and unique human persons, who are suffering under the intolerable burden of poverty." Indeed, specifically, there "is the persistence and often the widening of the *gap* between the areas of the so-called developed North and the developing South" (14). Nor is the pattern a uniform one, because "just as social inequalities down to the level of poverty exist in rich countries, so...in the less developed countries one often sees manifestations of selfishness and a flaunting of wealth which is as disconcerting as it is scandalous." Referring to the South, the Pope indicated that the problem is the more grave since "it is precisely in this geopolitical area that the major part of the human race lives." Pointing out that use of the word "gap" may create an impression that conditions are "stationary," he proposes instead that the "pace of progress" in recent years has been uneven in both the developed and the developing nations, so that the differences have widened. Current usage, therefore, has given rise to widespread use of the expressions: First World, Second World, Third World "and at times the Fourth World." The latter, somewhat less familiar, refers to the world of persons in the affluent nations who have been left behind and suffer poverty and humiliation equal to their fellow human beings in the Third World. John Paul II noted that the very use of such terms "undoubtedly conceals a *moral content*," which is precisely why the Church has a right and obligation to not "remain indifferent" (14).

However, the Mother and Teacher of nations is entitled to speak about elements affecting the cultural level which are also of vital concern, like "*illiteracy,* the difficulty or impossibility of obtaining *higher education,* the inability to share in the *building of one's own nation,* the *various forms of exploitation* and of economic, social, political and even religious *oppression* of the individual and his or her rights, *discrimination of every type* especially the exceptionally odious form based on difference in race" (15). Needless to say, these occur both in the North and in the South.

At this point there is a barbed reference to a situation in the socialist countries whereby their people end up being entrapped in a state of "almost absolute dependence, which is similar to the traditional dependence of the worker-proletarian in capitalism." The Pontiff was referring to the "passivity, dependence and submission to the bureaucratic apparatus" that ends up destroying the very important "*right of economic initiative*" which amounts to *the creative subjectivity of the citizens.*" Undisguised here, of course, is the inference of guilt shared by both economic systems: socialism and traditional capitalism [Italics in text].

What all of this adds up to is the fact that "in today's world there are many other *forms of poverty.*" These occur where other human rights are violated, like "the right to religious freedom, the right to share in the building of society, the freedom to organize and to form unions, or to take initiatives in economic matters." These, according to the Pope, constitute cultural deprivation and, accordingly, "underdevelopment (which) is not only economic but also cultural, political, and simply human." And it happens at least partly because there is at large "a *too narrow idea* of development...a mainly economic one" (15). Although the term, "economism," is not used at this point in the encyclical, it fits precisely as a description also of this state of affairs.

The glum outcome was stated frankly: "...conditions have become *notably worse*" (16). There is enough blame to go around! That extends also to "the developing nations themselves," and in them especially to "those holding economic and political power." And, of course, there are the developed nations "which have not always, at least in due measure, felt the duty to help countries separated from the affluent world to which they themselves belong."

Then there is an interesting reference to "economic, financial and social *mechanisms"* which, although they are "mechanisms," and "often function almost automatically," are nevertheless "manipulated by people." The outcome is "accentuating the situation of wealth for some and poverty for the rest." Apparently the Pope was referring here to market mechanisms behind which are manipulative marketeers, so that in reality the markets are anything but "free." Paul VI had already scored these "mechanisms" as working to increase the poverty of the poor while increasing the wealth of the rich, and he was roundly criticized for that. The critics are still at large, and they still would be the last to admit the *de facto* "interdependence" existing among the "four worlds," even given the severe plight at present facing in varying degrees also the First and the Second Worlds.

John Paul II, however, pointed out "specific signs of underdevelopment, which increasingly affect the developed countries also" (17). One is "the *housing crisis*"; and his encyclical appeared during the International Year of the Homeless "proclaimed by the United Nations." Thus we find "the sad spectacle of individuals and families literally struggling to survive, without a roof over their heads or with a roof *so inadequate* as to constitute no roof at all." Ironically, that problem is especially painful now in the United States, which is often identified as the "richest nation on earth."

A second problem afflicting also the "rich nations" is "*unemployment* and *underemployment*" (18). Probably the Pope was expressing a hope when he stated, "Everyone recognizes the *reality* and *growing seriousness* of this problem in the industrialized countries." That was in 1987, and the problem has persisted and gotten worse since. Yet, not "everyone" appears to recognize its seriousness, in particular some champions of what they perceive to be the best political, economic, and social system the world has ever seen! However, young people seeking to enter the work force for the first time are painfully aware that opportunities are not so widespread as they were some years back. In other words, what has happened is that worldwide imbalance in the distribution of opportunity and income is taking the same toll on economies throughout the world, as internal maldistribution did in the conditions culminating in the Great Depression, which Pius XI saw the need to address in 1931. This fact reflects back poignantly on the worldwide economic *interdependence* which Paul VI affirmed and which John Paul II was here reaffirming.

A "third phenomenon" is mentioned, "equally indicative of the interdependence between developed and less developed countries" (19). It is "the question of international debt." John Paul II stated, in what may indeed be seen as qualified terms, that loans from richer to poorer nations "can be considered a contribution to development, something desirable and legitimate in itself, even though perhaps imprudent and occasionally hasty." Are we entitled to infer from this that there should have been far more outright largesse, i.e., grants, in view of the Pope's statement that this device "has turned into a *counterproductive mechanism*," and that it has "turned into a *brake* upon development, and in some cases it has...even aggravated underdevelopment"? Also, the reader is reminded that "these observations should make us reflect on the *ethical character of the interdependence of peoples*" (19). What has happened is that the debt burden, where amortization is expected to occur on a set schedule, and where interest payments prove burdensome in varying degrees, has eroded the potential for the formation of capital needed to develop backward economies. Again, vindicating the affirmed interdependence among both the rich and the poor nations, banking systems in the former are sometimes severely afflicted by defaults on the part of the latter—a situation which may grow progressively worse and dangerous for the lender nations.

Getting into causes for the less than outstanding performance since *Populorum Progressio,* Pope John Paul II cited "especially...the *political* causes of today's situation." He referred to the "*political picture* since the Second World War" as "a fact which has considerable impact on the forward movement of the development of peoples" (20). We are talking about "the *existence of two opposing blocs,* commonly known as the East and the West." Here we find mentioned the system in the West, "which is historically inspired by the principles of the liberal capitalism which developed with industrialization during the nineteenth century." The other in "the East" is "inspired by *Marxist collectivism* which sprang from an interpretation of the condition of the proletarian classes made in the light of a particular reading of history." The Pope attributes to each "its own forms of propaganda and indoctrination," with a resultant "*ideological opposition.*" That developed into "a growing *military opposition*"; and herein lay the crux of the problem being addressed here: help from the developed to the developing nations. Although the dreaded "hot war" with its announced strategy of "mutually assured destruction" (M.A.D.) has not occurred, a prolonged "cold war" did persist; and it drained the vital economic resources of the two leading contenders, the United States and the Soviet Union. That hampered the good intentions expressed following World War II, when the rich nations appeared enthusiastic about helping the Third World into the 20th century, following the dissolution of colonial empires after that War. In addition, the same scarce, precious resources were drained off into numerous "wars by proxy" between the two rival blocs in the intervening years.

Time marches on! While Pope John Paul II, referring to the prospect of "*open and total* war," could observe in 1987 that "at the present time this danger seems to have receded," we now have the abysmal prospect of economic bankruptcy in both the Soviet Union, where it is already a fact and where it has led to political dissolution, and in the United States where it still represents a disguised, lurking menace defying any prospective solution.

What follows is the thinking which got the Pope into deep trouble with certain "conservative" commentators on this encyclical.[6] First he audaciously suggested that the contenders in the East-West confrontation proceed on the basis of "*concepts* of the development of individuals and peoples," both of which are "imperfect and in need of radical correction" (21). The fact that this antagonistic behavior has helped "to widen the gap already existing on the economic level between *North and South*" is just "one of the reasons why the Church's social doctrine adopts a critical attitude towards both liberal capitalism and Marxist collectivism." Nor are the developing nations, caught in the middle of the antagonism, unaware of what is happening. Indeed, they have remonstrated against what many see as "a form of neo-colonialism" by going so far as to establish "the *International Movement of Non-Aligned Nations*" (21). They are in varying degrees resentful of becoming merely what the Pope called here, "parts of a machine, cogs on a gigantic wheel" (22).

Once again, we have a suggestion that guilt falls on *both* ideological shoulders. "Each of the two *blocs* harbors in its own way a tendency towards imperialism, as it is usually called, or towards forms of new-colonialism." In any case, the continuing contention "deadens the impulse toward united cooperation by all for the common good of the human race, to the detriment especially of peaceful peoples who are impeded from their rightful access to the goods meant for all." This encyclical was issued in 1987, commemorating one issued 20 years previously; and we are now in a position to see the magnitude of the danger caused by the failure to attend to the worldwide imbalance between North and South, as aggravated by the ongoing ideological confrontation between East and West.

In 1989 the leader of the Soviet Union, Mikhail Gorbachev, made a historic visit to Pope John Paul II at the Vatican. Presumably he was there, among other things, to begin healing a then-72 year old rupture of relations with the foremost religious leader in the world. Since then, the Soviet empire crumbled into near chaos. Meanwhile the other ideological contender, while presumptuously declaring its triumph in the "cold war," does not yet fully appreciate the Pyrrhic dimensions of the "victory," as it wallows in an economic morass whose dimensions approximate conditions leading up to the Great Depression. One wonders when these former, long-time antagonists will begin to appreciate the reality of what popes since John XXIII have been calling the worldwide common good, and the imperative nature of solidarity among all nations. What Pope John Paul II said here appears almost as a trite truism in view of what has happened since *Sollicitudo Rei Socialis* was issued in 1987. "The statement in the Encyclical *Populorum Progressio* that the resources and investments devoted to arms production ought to be used to alleviate the misery of impoverished peoples makes more urgent the appeal to overcome the opposition between the two blocs" (23). Until then (1987) those resources were "used to enable each of the two blocs to overtake the other..." And based on "this fundamentally flawed distortion," they are prevented from "adequately fulfilling their duty of solidarity for the benefit of peoples which aspire to full development" (23). The paragraph ends with a serious indictment: "When the West gives the impression of abandoning itself to forms of growing and selfish isolation, and the East in its turn seems to ignore for questionable reasons its duty to cooperate in the task of alleviating human misery, then we are up against not only a betrayal of humanity's legitimate expectations—a betrayal that is a harbinger of unforeseeable consequences—but also a real desertion of a moral obligation" (23). Again, neither of the rival blocs is spared—both are at fault in different ways and perhaps also to different degrees—but there is enough guilt to go around.

What follows addresses the cynicism which goes along with the lucrative arms trade around the world. John Paul II pointed out that for some reason this trade transcends and overcomes all ideological barriers. He called it "a trade without frontiers, capable of crossing even the barriers of the blocs" (24). That occurs then while, oddly enough, "economic aid and development plans meet with the obstacle of insuperable ideological barriers." Thus, we are faced with a "picture which…leads us more quickly *towards death,* rather than…to true development," and to "a 'more human life' as envisaged by the Encyclical *Populorum Progressio.*" The result, among other things, is a flood of "millions of refugees whom war, natural calamities, persecution and discrimination of every kind have deprived of home, employment, family and homeland." "Terrorism" is another result, defined here as, "the intention to kill people and destroy property indiscriminately." The Pope went on record here by saying, "acts of terrorism are never justifiable," whatever the alleged reasons.

The 25th paragraph addresses the "*demographic problem.*" Several important points are made here. First, John Paul II acknowledged that there is a problem, "especially in the southern hemisphere," and that it "creates difficulties for development." However, he pointed out "immediately" that in the northern hemisphere "this problem is reversed." Here "the cause for concern is the *drop in the birthrate,*" to the extent that many countries face "aging of the populations," and that their population is often even "unable even to renew itself biologically." Less is heard of the latter problem, even while pension and health insurance systems are faced with staggering financial problems, given the onrush of a geriatric society.

What follows these statements of fact needs to be weighed carefully. Referring to the aging populations, the Pope indicated that "this is a phenomenon capable of hindering development." Obviously, a country which must begin to put an increasing percentage of its resources into funding infirmaries for the aged, and health insurance which the older population must make far greater use of than younger persons, along with a system of pensions which begins to bear down inequitably on the younger working population, is headed toward economic decline, not development. At the same time, the Pontiff indicated that the difficulties commonly attributed to demographic growth are not due solely to these. Furthermore, it is not even a proven fact "that *all* demographic growth is incompatible with orderly development." As indicated earlier, reputable economists have come forward to suggest that just the opposite is true: population growth exerts a pressure for economic development to nurture the growing number of people.[7] Also, a younger population is at the same time likely to be healthier and more productive, and to present less of a drain on the resources and fiscal mechanism of an economy than a senescent one. Therefore, needless to say, the Church of Paul VI and of Pope John Paul II has no tolerance for "systematic campaigns against birth, contrary not only to the cultural and religious identity of the countries themselves, but also contrary to the nature of true development" (25). The Pope took a dim view of pressure placed on recipient nations where the acceptance of such programs against new life are made a "condition for the granting of financial and economic aid and assistance." That "freedom of choice," which has become the war cry of those who demand for women the right to abort their offspring, is thus denied to the unfortunate persons in developing nations who desperately need economic assistance. Instead, they find themselves "often subjected to intolerable pressures…to force them to submit to this new form of oppression."

What must be said about all of the demographic hysteria which has infested modern society since the post-World War II era is now presented in the light of day! Namely, much of the motivation behind this anti-natalist propaganda is simply racism, thinly disguised: racism in another form, now that the older, crasser form has become unacceptable in polite society. The Pope called it by that name. Since the "poorest populations" which he sees as subjected to population control pressures (such as aid with strings attached) are generally the yellow and black races, we have here "a tendency towards a form of racism, or the promotion of certain equally racist forms of eugenics." Since the majority of the white populations on earth, most of them in the northern hemisphere, have long ago begun traveling down the road to demographic decline, the complexion of our world is destined to become "darker" in the generations ahead. Thus, such persons apparently feel a need, even a desperate need, to get the darker ("inferior") peoples to follow their example on the path toward demographic atrophy—and if it is not reversed—even to eventual extinction!

The third section of this encyclical is concluded on an upbeat note. Pope John Paul presented certain "positive aspects" amid an otherwise bleak prospect. They include the "full awareness among large numbers of men and women of their own dignity and of that of every human being" (26). One bit of evidence is the international effort to defend human rights and to monitor abuses. This involves both "private associations" and also the United Nations and its *Declaration of Human Rights*, now over 40 years old. Such actions reflect a growing appreciation of the "radical independence and consequently of the need for a solidarity which will take up interdependence and transfer it to the moral plane."

The Pope mentioned also the growth of a "respect for life" implicit in the widespread "*concern* for peace." It is an ambivalent respect for life, because it persists, "despite all temptations to destroy it by abortion and euthanasia."

Finally, there is the "*ecological concern*," which involves "a greater realization of the limits of available resources, and the need to respect the integrity and cycles of nature." The young people of today who have grown up with this movement cannot appreciate that a generation ago "ecology" was an arcane word, little used outside the scientific community. Now they express shock at how industrialists, for example, disposed of wastes, polluting air, soil and water, and how consumers used resources without any second thought about the finite nature of this globe on which we live. Even now, there is little appreciation of how the two World Wars probably deserve to be ranked among the most disastrous events of all times in terms of ecological depredation. Yet, the seemingly inevitable pendulum effect has made its presence felt here too. Some have erected ecological concern into a cult— a kind of *ersatz* religion. Accordingly, we find extremes which threaten to become as unconscionable as was the indifference toward legitimate ecological considerations on the part of past generations. Man is still the "lord" of creation, by the Creator's own ordinance, even though that dominion comes with a grave responsibility to exercise it with sensitive concern also for the rights of others, including generations yet unborn.[8] Previously the latter aspect was ignored; now the former is often lost sight of. *In medio stat virtus.*

The Pope closed this section with an acknowledgment of the many persons who have devoted themselves to this important effort on behalf of the poor nations of the world. By their efforts and those of "great *international organizations*...some countries...have succeeded in reaching a *certain self-sufficiency in food,* or a degree of industrialization." The vast and populous nation, India, comes to mind. Despite all of the predictions of gloom and disaster for it, India now is able to feed itself and even to export food. While it still faces some big problems, we have here another example of the pressure for economic development, referred to above, which population growth can exert on nations. "Thus," as the Pope said in concluding this section: "all is not negative in the contemporary world, nor could it be, for the Heavenly Father's providence lovingly watches over even our daily cares" (cf. Mt. 6:25-32; 10:23-31; Lk. 12:6-7, 22-30).

Authentic Human Development

After some brief respite from the generally somber tone of this encyclical, this fourth part starts off with an indication of how humanity has moved from the naive prediction of continuing progress stemming from the Enlightenment, to a less optimistic view of the future. That is based on greater reliance on actual economic and social reflection, "particularly since the experience of the two world wars, the planned and partly achieved destruction of whole peoples, and the looming atomic peril" (27). Moreover, even the economic aspects of development have receded somewhat in view of a growing awareness that economic progress itself "is not enough for the realization of human happiness." So we have descended from the promise of continuing and unending progress, to a preoccupation with the economic aspects of such progress, and finally to a perhaps still dim perception that even this, including "the many *real benefits* provided in recent times by science and technology, does not make men free "from every form of slavery." What is needed is "a moral understanding" and, "an orientation toward the true good of the human race."

It is at this point in the encyclical that the term "consumerism" occurs for the first time in papal social teachings, along with a denunciation of its implications. Again, it is not surprising that those who live in comfortable circumstance were not pleased with what Pope John Paul II had to say. He used the term, "*superdevelopment*," which he stated is "equally inadmissible" as underdevelopment. He is talking about the "so-called civilization of 'consumption' or 'consumerism,' which involves so much 'throwing away' and 'waste.'" Specifically: "An object already owned but now superseded by something better, is discarded, with no thought of its possible lasting value in itself, nor of some other human being who is poorer." In this surrealistic world of exaggerated affluence, we have what Pope John Paul II called here "precisely...one of the greatest injustices in the contemporary world." It is the fact "that the ones who possess much are relatively *few,* and those who possess almost nothing are *many.* It is the injustice of the poor distribution of the goods and services originally intended for all." We live in a world where "having" becomes so much more important than "being," so that people are esteemed more for what they have than for what they are.

From this discussion of a dichotomy between "having" and "being," the Pope arrived at the point where he alluded to concern also for the "*quality* and the *ordered hierarchy* of the goods one has." That has to do with the "subordination of goods and their availability to man's being and his true vocation." Thus, without denying the "*necessary economic dimension*" in the development discussion, development "is not limited to that dimension." If it is, "then it turns against those whom it is meant to benefit" (28).

All of that is not intended to lead us into some false asceticism. So long as the "*interior dimension*" is not lost sight of, we are not to disdain economic goods, or to lament the fact that industry "is constantly being enriched by scientific and technological progress" (29). Instead we are encouraged to use them and to "see them as a gift from God." That leads into a statement explaining man's "dominion over things." It involves not the "*indiscriminate* possession of created things and the products of human industry, but rather...*subordinating* the possession, dominion and use to man's divine likeness and to his vocation to immortality" (29). And when he disobeys God by refusing to submit to that rule "nature rebels against him as its 'master,' for he has tarnished the divine image in himself."

At this point, Pope John Paul II reaffirmed and developed further the "theology of work," set forth in his previous social encyclical, *Laborem Exercens.* The process and the challenge of continuing economic development is defended on scriptural grounds. There is the division of labor into several crafts in Genesis (4:17-26). And there is the stern admonition to put to work effectively the gifts received from God (Mt. 25:26-28). Indeed, God's plan for man eventually gives rise again to the "dream of 'unlimited progress'" (31). However, it is a "radically transformed dream," transformed "by the *new outlook* created by Christian faith, assuring us that progress is possible only because God the Father has decided from the beginning to make man a sharer of his glory in Jesus Christ risen from the dead." That offers a significant theological perspective; it is applicable to work, to ecological concern, and also to our view of the directions which history may take in the future! Indeed, the Pope made specific reference to certain Fathers of the Church who developed "in original ways a concept of the *meaning of history* and of *human work*" which is "an optimistic vision of history and work, that is to say of the perennial value of authentic human achievements inasmuch as they are redeemed by Christ and destined for the promised Kingdom" (31).

Here we find a discomforting reference to a possible conflict between the spectacle of "superfluous church ornaments and costly furnishings for divine worship," and the need "to provide food, drink, clothing and shelter for those who lack these things." The Pope stated boldly that "it could be obligatory to sell these goods" in order to provide those basic needs.

This part concludes in an exhortatory style, with an admonition that the development of peoples is not an individual "and still less an *individualistic* one, as if it were possible to achieve such development through the isolated efforts of each individual" (32). Just as that statement concludes this part, it also opens the way toward the dominant theme of the next part of the encyclical: solidarity. The problem of development is so massive and so fraught with both promise and danger that all—individuals, societies and nations, the Catholic Church and all churches, separately and in common efforts—must answer the challenge. It is a "duty *of all towards all*," extending to all parts of the world mentioned often in this encyclical: East and West, North and South. Yet, development must be "full development," meaning that it not only involves the "economic and social aspects," but that it also takes full account of "individual cultural identity and openness to the transcendent."

Connected to this we find a succinct and unambivalent statement of the Catholic Church's position on religious freedom: "Not even the need for development can be used as an excuse for imposing on others one's own way of life or own religious belief." Some, who were scandalized by the Vatican II *Declaration on Religious Liberty*, may find this difficult to accept, forgetting that religion, even the true religion, is not something which one is authorized to force down people's throats. And a discriminating intellect will appreciate that this is still a far cry from stating or even suggesting that one religion is as good as the next.

Once again, then, the two rival ideological blocs are both put in their places. Speaking about the "*intrinsic contradiction*" in "a development limited *only* to its economic element," Pope John Paul II indicated that such an approach to development "easily subjects the human person and his deepest needs to the demands of economic planning and selfish profit" (33). Clearly, the socialist system leaned toward the former, and liberal capitalism toward the latter. What follows may be seen as retrospective prophecy. If "the moral, cultural, and spiritual requirements" are lost sight of, "then all the rest—availability of goods, abundance of technical resources applied to daily life, a certain level of material well-being—will prove unsatisfying and in the end contemptible." Within each nation this translates, among other things, to the need for "respect for all rights...especially: the right to life at every stage of its existence, the rights of the family, as the basic social community...justice in employment relationships." And at the international level "between the different 'worlds'" it means "complete respect for the identity of each people, with its own historical and cultural characteristics." Specifically, each nation has the equal right "'to be seated at the table of the common banquet' instead of lying outside the door like Lazarus while 'the dogs come and lick his sores.'" That is a trenchant scriptural reference applied here to the central theme of this encyclical, and the one by Paul VI which it commemorates: the glaring gap between rich nations and poor ones in our present world. We are back to the basic problem which Leo XIII first addressed in *Rerum Novarum*: too many possessing too little, while too few enjoy too much. Now that "social question" persists on a world scale.

It is important to note that we are not dealing with a situation where the nations which are poor now were once rich. It comes down instead to the fact that today, given the genuine underlying blessings of the Industrial Revolution and the explosion in scientific and technological knowledge which is the ongoing phenomenon characterizing the history of the human race ever since that Revolution, the means to combat grinding poverty are readily at hand. But they have thus far been applied for the benefit of too few.

The conclusion of this part should please those who are rightly concerned about "ecology." It demands "respect *for the beings which constitute* the natural world" (34). The Pope included in such "respect" responsible use of "the different categories of beings, whether living or inanimate," an appreciation that "*natural resources* are limited," and that some are indeed not "renewable," and respect for "*the quality of life*" which has not always been in evidence, especially "in the industrialized zones." In other words, the dominion of man over nature is not "*absolute dominion*." The same restriction which Leo XIII established on the use of private property in general applies also to the use of the largesse of nature. Accordingly, it does not include "a freedom to 'use and misuse.'" All of this comes down again to the fact that in this problem of development too there is a "*moral dimension*"; and that is what entitles the Mother and Teacher of nations to make her voice heard on the matter.

A Theological Reading of Modern Problems

Since the Catholic Church has a moral theology of its own, its entry into these problems, having a "moral dimension," provides it with the opportunity to extend its moral theology so as to make that applicable to "the social question" with its various, attendant ramifications.[9] Indeed, before Pope John Paul II finished with this section, he made it clear that this is precisely what the social teachings by-and-large are all about.

He began this fifth section, referring again to the "moral character" of the development issue, and stating that if since the time of *Populorum Progressio*, "there has been no development, or very little, irregular, or even contradictory development," the reasons are not simply economic. They have to do with justice and "conformity with the common good of humanity." Nor is it the business of popes to involve themselves in what are solely economic or political problems. Pope John Paul II, like Paul VI before him, was involved in this development problem because there are "*moral causes* which...interfere in such a way as to slow down the course of development and hinder its full achievement" (35). Thus, since the "scientific and technical resources" are now available to resolve the problem, "the main obstacles to development will be overcome only by means of *essentially moral decisions.*"

The heart of the problem, according to John Paul II, is to be found in the ongoing division and contention in a world "divided into blocs," and "sustained by rigid ideologies" (36). What is needed instead of "different forms of imperialism" is "interdependence and solidarity." That brings up the concept which proved to be an affront to certain critics: "structures of sin." Not surprising, given that the very notion, "sin," evokes a tongue-in-cheek reaction on the part of sophisticated, post-Christian modern man. To then go on and imply that the social structure to which one is dedicated is "sinful" triggers a predictable response. The Pope was well aware of this, pointing out how he had in a previous statement made it clear that when structures are sinful, this is "rooted in personal sin, and thus always linked to the *concrete acts* of individuals who introduce these structures, consolidate them and make them difficult to remove."[10] And if the "sin" concept is unacceptable in modern parlance, he indicated that we are still entitled to speak of "selfishness," "shortsightedness" "mistaken political calculations," and "imprudent decisions." But are these not simply echoes of "an ethical and moral nature"? There follows what may be a deliberate play on words. After proposing that a more profound analysis of individuals' actions and omissions cannot be achieved without implying, in one way or another, judgments or references of an ethical nature, the Pope suggested that such an "evaluation is in itself *positive,* especially if it is completely consistent and if it is based on faith in God and on his law, which commands what is good and forbids evil." The prevailing sentiment in social science is positivistic, meaning precisely that it pretends to avoid "judgments...of an ethical nature." Here we are told that such "evaluation" is itself "*positive*"!

Following a "*general analysis,* which is religious in nature," come "*particular considerations*" intended to demonstrate that two "structures" embodying "actions and attitudes opposed to the will of God" and "the good of neighbor" are "very typical" (37). One involves "the *all-consuming desire for profit,*" and the other, "*the thirst for power*" with the intention of imposing one's will upon others. The first of these ensouls liberal capitalism, and the second, Marxian communism, although these terms are not introduced at this point in the encyclical. And in today's world, we are told that one or the other predominates. What is more, "nations and blocs" as well as individuals can "fall victim to this double attitude of sin." Peering behind the economic and political facade, the Pope identified "real forms of idolatry: of money, ideology, class, technology." This is a powerful indictment of the rival ideologies which were tragically propelling our world in opposite directions ever since World War II ended. And he minced no words, indicating that, "I have wished to introduce this type of analysis above all in order to point out the true *nature* of the evil which faces us with respect to the development of peoples." He told us, "it is a question of a *moral evil, the fruit of* many sins which lead to 'structures of sin.'" But the diagnosis suggests the possible cure, and it is made for that purpose. "To diagnose the evil in this way is to identify precisely...*the path to be followed* in order to *overcome it*" (37).

While that path is recognized as "*long and complex*" (38), the Pope invited all to summon up the courage to embark on it. Here the ecumenical thrust of this encyclical, like all social encyclicals since John XXIII addressed to "All People of Good Will," comes to bear once again. While the faithful recognize "a *moral* value" in what must be done, which is furthermore a "demand of God's will," "also men and women without an explicit faith," are invited to join in removing "obstacles to integral development" recognizing that such obstacles are "not only economic but rest on *more profound attitudes* which human beings can make into absolute values." For Christians that kind of change in "profound attitudes" is "called conversion." That such "conversion" is, so to speak, already in the wind, is marked by a "growing awareness of *interdependence* among individuals and nations."

At this point the author of the encyclical proceeded into developing an important theological insight which scholars who labor at updating theology should certainly take into account in their efforts. He now went on to identify the meaning of the kind of "interdependence" in question here, along with the virtue which corresponds to it. We have what appears to be the apogee of the entire encyclical which, as this writer suggested earlier, could be entitled: *On Solidarity*.

First, the interdependence at issue here is identified as "a *system determining* relationships in the contemporary world, in its economic, cultural, political and religious elements, and accepted as a *moral category*. Recognition of such interdependence, and action in accordance with it "as a moral and social attitude, as a 'virtue,' is *solidarity*" (38). We now have this important concept, mentioned repeatedly and increasingly in the Church's social teachings since the time of Pius XII, declared to be a "virtue." While the Pope used it here in quotation marks, that changed subsequently, in paragraph 40, which he commenced with the statement: "*Solidarity* is undoubtedly a *Christian virtue*" [Italics, as always, in the encyclical)].

However, before he told us what it is, John Paul II explained what solidarity is not. It is "not a feeling of vague compassion or shallow distress at the misfortunes of so many people, both near and far." It is, instead, "a *firm and persevering determination* to commit oneself to the common good; that is to say to the good of all and of each individual, because we are *all* really responsible *for all.* And it is applicable both "*within each society,*" and "in international relationships" (39).[11]

Within each society, solidarity involves recognition of "one another as persons, with those who are "more influential, because they have a greater share of goods," feeling "*responsible* for the weaker." But, once again, it is more than merely a "feeling of vague compassion or shallow distress," that is involved here. It is also a readiness "to share with them all they possess"—a radical doctrine indeed, as radical as Christianity itself when it first made its appearance 2000 years ago. The concomitant obligation on the part of those who are "weaker" involves also action on their part to resolve their plight. They are admonished to not "adopt a purely *passive attitude.*" But they are also warned not to adopt an attitude "that is *destructive* of the social fabric, but to "do what they can for the good of all," while also "claiming their legitimate rights." At this point Pope John Paul II included once again the "intermediate groups" which have been mentioned in social encyclicals since *Mater et Magistra.* Whatever forms these may take—and they may certainly include the "vocational groups" mentioned by Pius XI and suggested by Leo XIII—they too "should not selfishly insist on their particular interests but respect the interests of others" (39).

At the international level, "interdependence must be transformed into *solidarity*" because, "the goods of creation *are meant for all.*" It is here, then, that the various forms of "*imperialism* and determination to preserve their *own hegemony*" among the "stronger and richer nations" must be converted into "a sense of moral *responsibility* for the other nations" in recognition of the basic "*equality of all peoples*" Nor are the economically weaker countries to be forever recipients of assistance. By actualizing this awareness of interdependence into active solidarity, they "must be enabled... to make a contribution of their own to the common good with their treasures of *humanity and culture*" (39).

Clearly, all of this involves a kind of "conversion." Otherwise the Pope would not have felt free to stress "the importance of reawakening the *religious awareness* of individuals and peoples." He obviously felt that only such *awareness* will give rise to the *solidarity* which "helps us to see the 'other'—whether a person, people or nation," as not merely "some kind of instrument, with a work capacity and physical strength to be exploited at low cost and then discarded when no longer useful." This means that "the exploitation, oppression and annihilation of others are excluded." We are told that only in this way will peace at last be possible. Promoting it means getting rid of "structures of sin" which of themselves and by the "sins which they produce" are "radically opposed to peace and development."

What follows offers a dramatic example of the role of the papal magisterium as a continuing explication and application of Divine Revelation. John Paul II was doing no less here than presenting an addition to the traditional Old Testament wisdom. First he stated that "the solidarity which we propose is the *path to peace and at the same time to development,*" because "world peace is inconceivable unless the world's leaders come to recognize that *interdependence* in itself demands the abandonment of the politics of blocs, the sacrifice of all forms of economic, military or political imperialism, and the transformation of mutual distrust into *collaboration.*" That recognition and the proper actions based on it are "precisely the *act proper* to solidarity among individuals and nations." The conclusion which John Paul II drew from all of this is quite remarkable. As Pius XII used as his motto the passage from Isaiah: "*Opus iustitiae pax* (Peace is the fruit of justice)" (Is. 32:17), this Pope now stated: "Today one could say with the same exactness and the same power of biblical inspiration: *Opus solidaritatis pax,* peace as the fruit of solidarity."[12]

Small wonder then that Pope John Paul II felt entitled to declare that "*Solidarity* is undoubtedly a *Christian virtue*" (40). He claimed it as specifically *Christian,* because of its relationship with charity. Accordingly, as a Christian virtue solidarity "seeks to go beyond itself, to take on the *specifically Christian* dimension of total gratuity, forgiveness and reconciliation." It is a dimension which involves all of that for the simple reason that one's neighbor is more than just another human being "with his or her own rights and a fundamental equality with everyone else." The neighbor is "the *living image* of God the Father, redeemed by the blood of Jesus Christ and placed under the permanent action of the Holy Spirit." That involves the truly radical dimension of Christianity: love even for one's enemies—a love which therefore implies a willingness to forgive past transgressions. Conversion to that view of life and of who is one's neighbor, both within each community and among the nations which make up our world, would make possible at last the miracle—peace—which our sorry world is so much in need of now, certainly so much as at any time in its history. Radical problems require radical solutions: not radical as Karl Marx and Adolf Hitler proposed these, but as Jesus Christ proposed originally, and now again, two millennia afterwards, through his vicars on earth.

This critical, and one could say, climactic part of *Sollicitudo Rei Socialis,* ends, therefore, with talk of "a new criterion for interpreting "our vision of the world." It is this Christian vision of "the common fatherhood of God, of the brotherhood of all in Christ—'children in the Son'—and of the presence and life-giving action of the Holy Spirit" that is proposed to us as "the supreme *model of unity,*" which should "inspire our *solidarity.*" Returning to the "structures of sin," we are told that they can only be overcome "through the exercise of the human and Christian solidarity to which the Church calls us and which she tirelessly promotes."

The Pope closed this important section by recommending as models of "such solidarity," two canonized saints. They are St. Peter Claver "who served the slaves at Cartagena de Indias, and St Maximilian Maria Kolbe who offered his life in place of a prisoner unknown to him in the concentration camp at Auschwitz" (40).

Some Particular Guidelines

Declaring something to be "undoubtedly a Christian virtue" which has not been recognized as such in that specific form constitutes a contribution to the Church's moral theology. It by no means amounts to presenting "*technical solutions*" for the "problem of underdevelopment" (41). Indeed, John Paul II felt compelled to state in this encyclical that "the Church does not propose economic and political systems or programs, nor does she show preference for one or the other." Perhaps this disclaimer relates to his alleged identification with the organized movement, *Solidarność*, which later became a governing element in his native Poland. In any case, declaring something to be a virtue, thus involving moral conduct, is a venture in moral theology. Therefore the Pontiff stated now that the Church's social doctrine does not constitute an "*ideology*," but "theology and particularly moral theology."

Since the Church has the obligation to evangelize—to spread its doctrine among all of humanity—its social doctrine which involves moral conduct as applied to various levels and organs of society is also clearly an object of its evangelization efforts. That involves sometimes becoming quite specific with regard to abuses in human behavior, and also with regard to proposed remedies. It is such specificity which has exposed the Church to the charge that she has actually been proposing an ideology, and even a "'third way' between *liberal capitalism* and *Marxist collectivism*." Not so, and this particular encyclical offers an explicit disclaimer. What its social doctrine constitutes is instead, "the *accurate formulation* of the results of a careful reflection on the complex realities of human existence, in society and in the international order, in the light of faith and of the Church's tradition." One might add that the Church asserts the right to make such a "formulation" by virtue of its position as, in the words of Paul VI, an "expert in humanity."[13] And in view of the prevailing positivistic bias still at large in our times, especially among social scientists, John Paul II was not boring us by repeating once again that the "social question" in general and the problem of economic development under investigation here "cannot be reduced to a 'technical' problem." We are dealing with "guiding *people's behavior*," and specifically with a "commitment to justice"; and the *condemnation* of evils and injustices is also a part of that ministry of evangelization in the social field which is an aspect of the Church's *prophetic role*." But "proclamation is always more important than *condemnation*, and the latter cannot ignore the former" (41).

What followed then was a kind of recapitulation of how the Church has been fulfilling that prophetic role in this and recent papal proclamations, along with those of the Second Vatican Council. It involves an opening "to an *international outlook*" (4). Specifically there has been a leading emphasis on "the *option* or *love of preference* for the poor"—the so-called "preferential option for the poor." While this preference may have affronted some among the wealthy, it is not new in social teachings. Indeed, it first surfaced in *Rerum Novarum* where Leo XIII was taking up the defense of those who were, unlike the rich, not in a good position to defend their own legitimate interests. It is an option which is binding on all, including "the *leaders* of nations and the heads of *international bodies*." And it binds us now, as when Leo XIII spoke and when Blessed John XXIII and Pope Paul VI began applying it also to the economic imbalance among the nations of the world. That is because: "...instead of becoming fewer the poor are becoming more numerous, not only in less developed countries but—and this seems no less scandalous—in the more developed ones too." This unpleasant fact leads the present pope to repeat the basic Church position on private property as "*originally meant for all*," and therefore under a kind of "social mortgage" based on that "original destination of goods" (42).

Pope John Paul II then became quite specific in indicating how this doctrine applies on the level of "international imbalance." He called for "*reform of the international trade system* which is mortgaged to protectionism and increasing bilateralism; *reform of the world monetary and financial system*...the *question of technological exchanges* and their proper use; the *need* for a *review of the structure of the existing international organizations*, in the framework of an international juridical order" (43). All of these are clearly problems of a quite "technical nature," which may seem surprising in view of the prior disclaimer that the "Church does not have *technical solutions* to offer..."(41). But a closer examination indicates that it is still pointing out problems, and not offering technical solutions which indeed represent a task for specialists.

To head off criticism that the poor countries themselves are being relieved of responsibility for self-help, while the entire burden of guilt and of finding the remedy is placed on the richer nations, we find this:

> Development demands above all a spirit of initiative on the part of the countries which need it. Each of them must act in accordance with its own responsibilities, *not expecting everything* from the more favored countries, and acting in collaboration with others in the same situation...Each must make itself capable of initiatives responding to its own needs as a society. Each must likewise realize its true needs, as well as the rights and duties which oblige it to respond to them. The development of peoples begins and is most appropriately accomplished in the dedication of each people to its own development, in collaboration with others (44).[14]

That, again, is followed by a host of quite specific initiatives to be taken by the poor countries themselves, like promoting "*literacy* and *basic education*," and increasing their own food production in imitation "of not particularly developed nations which have nevertheless achieved the goal of *food self-sufficiency* and have even become food exporters." They are also urged to deal with what has become a sore point even for some who are well-disposed toward the whole program of international development aid: "to reform certain unjust structures, and in particular their *political institutions,* in order to replace corrupt, dictatorial and authoritarian forms of government by *democratic* and *participatory* ones" (44).

Having admonished the poor nations to also do all in their own power to help themselves, the Pope returned to his favored theme. He stated that all such measures cannot be achieved "*without the collaboration of all*—especially the international community—in the framework of a solidarity which includes everyone." However, he repeated the previous motif that "the developing nations themselves have the duty to practice *solidarity among themselves* and with the neediest countries of the world." That is because: "*interdependence* is already a reality in many of these countries"; and "[T]o acknowledge it, in such a way as to make it more operative, represents an alternative to excessive dependence on richer and more powerful nations." (45). All of this should certainly satisfy and silence those critics who suggest that in developing their case for international assistance between rich and poor nations, Pope John Paul II, and Paul VI and John XXIII, were simply advocating the establishment of a kind of "international welfare system."

Conclusion

The final part of this very important encyclical contains just four sections. The first draws attention to the "liberation theology" movement at large "especially in Latin America" (46). Zealous reformers have taken the reform of the social order in a direction which was unintended by all popes since Leo XIII who have addressed the problem. Various initiatives have included the call for armed insurrection to overcome injustices which are indeed real; and these have unfortunately been orchestrated according to the Marxian tune of class conflict. In the process, the priceless heritage of Catholic social teachings, extending back over an entire century, has often been shelved as too tame. Thus "the positive values, as well as the deviations and risks of deviation, which are damaging to the faith and are connected with this form of theological reflection and method have been appropriately pointed out by the Church's Magisterium."[15] Basically, the persons involved have either lost patience with, or been ignorant of, the social teachings which are a part of the Magisterium. Therefore, such misguided zealots were admonished again in this encyclical. Since liberation theology appeared, its enthusiasts have also been chastened by the dramatic course of events in the countries where the Marxian solution, having been tried, demonstrated its total inadequacy. The unfolding of history has shown unmistakably that, "Development which is merely economic is incapable of setting man free; on the contrary, it will end by enslaving him further" (46). Time will tell whether the devotees of "liberation theology" will return humbly and with greater patience to their Mother and Teacher to learn what the true remedies are.

There is a message also for persons reacting in other ways to the Church's proposals, in the warning that, "just as one may sin through selfishness and the desire for excessive profit and power, one may also be found wanting with regard to the urgent needs of multitudes of human beings...through *fear, indecision* and, basically, *through cowardice*" (47). This comes with a prophetic reminder that "we are *all* called, indeed *obliged,* to face the tremendous challenge of the last decade of the second Millennium..." And with that comes also the warning of "...a world economic crisis, a war without frontiers, without winners or losers."

The solution of these grave problems, however, implies a "peaceful campaign, a campaign to be conducted by *peaceful* means." No one should deceive himself about the relevance and validity of that assertion. We are completing a century rife with wars which were supposed to bring peace—"to end all wars," "to make the world safe for democracy," or "to guarantee the four freedoms." Then remarkably, the greatest single threat to peace and democracy and freedom appeared to wilt away almost without bloodshed before our eyes in just a few months' time! Is it perhaps time now to reconsider the question whether we can really establish peace by making war and by crushing enemies?

The anguished appeal by Paul VI, therefore, went out anew from the Polish Pope who knew something about war and peace, and about both Nazism and Communism. He summoned all Christians, also Jews, Muslims, and "followers of *the world's great religions*." Specifically he indicated that reforming the social order is the "preeminent role that belongs to the *laity,* because it is up to them "to animate temporal realities with Christian commitment by which they show that they are witnesses and agents of peace and justice." One may assume that it would not be improper for the laity to attempt what the Church avoids doing—to devise and implement where possible and feasible a "'third way' between liberalism and Marxist collectivism," or simply to formulate "an ideology" which is more in conformity with the Church's social teachings.

At the end, there is—as is characteristic of social encyclicals—the return to the spiritual theme. "The Kingdom of God becomes *present* above all in the celebration of the *sacrament of the Eucharist,* which is the Lord's Sacrifice" (48).

Then Pope John Paul II—who chose as the motto of his papacy *Totus Tuus,* indicating his total dedication to the Mother of God—concluded *Sollicitudo Rei Socialis* by doing something unique and distinctive. He dedicated the contents of the entire encyclical and its purpose to Mary. It was she who said to her son at Cana, "They have no more wine" (John 2:3). And it is she who praises God because, "he has put down the mighty from their thrones and exalted those of low degree; he has filled the hungry with good things, and the rich he has sent empty away" (Luke 1:52-53). Finally, it is she to whom we pray: "Holy Mother of God, despise not our petitions in our necessities, but deliver us always from all dangers, O glorious and blessed Virgin" (49).

Sollicitudo Rei Socialis ends with another prayer. It is taken from the Collect of the Mass; and it asks the Father that we may be inspired with the love needed to "share the good things" given to us by Him, so that we may finally "secure justice and equality for every human being, an end to all division and a human society built on love and peace" (49).

Notes

1. Pius XII, "The Springtime of History," *The Pope Speaks* 4,4 (Spring, 1958) 427-430.

2. The usual title in English is: *The Church in the Modern World.*

3. As *Mater et Magistra* by John XXIII and *Populorum Progressio* by Paul VI were criticized editorially in the *National Review* and the *Wall Street Journal* respectively, *Sollicitudo Rei Socialis* suffered the same fate at the hands of the *New York Times* conservative writer William Safire. Among other things, Safire, who is Jewish, commented that Pope John Paul II "risks becoming known as the foremost political-moral relativist of our time." Rather interesting is the fact that a number of conservative Catholic commentators promptly and enthusiastically adopted and parroted the criticisms.

4. Earlier encyclicals like *Rerum Novarum, Divini Redemptoris*, and *Mater et Mag-*

istra were given English titles descriptive of their main themes.

5. Special courses on development economics began appearing in university economics curricula, along with the usual proliferation of textbooks on the topic.

6. See footnote 3, above.

7. Colin Clark and Heinrich Pesch, for example, as already referred to in the chapter on *Mater et Magistra.*

8. As part of the "ecological concern" movement, one hears of "animal rights activists." Strictly speaking animals have no rights. Only God and human beings created in His image have rights. In a derivative sense one may perhaps speak of "rights" in animals which simply reflect the equal claims of others to whatever benefits animals provide as food, as pets, etc. Like all property, animals too may not be used wantonly without regard for the claims of other people specifically and generally.

9. Particularly since Vatican II, certain theologians have devoted great energy to discrediting the so-called "old" theology. There is much positive work to be done by competent theologians to adapt the many recent teachings of the Church, and to incorporate these into updated theological works and texts. Ecumenical councils, for example, occur but rarely in the Church's long history. Also, in modern times, the Church has been especially gifted with several outstanding popes who may one day rank as doctors of the Church. Leo XIII was one such great teacher, as was also Pius XII, along with Pope John Paul II and Pope Bénedict XVI.

10. The expression was first used by Pope John Paul II in his Apostolic Exhortation, *Reconciliatio et Paenitentia* (1984). He quotes extensively from that in a footnote to this encyclical.

11. Heinrich Pesch, who devised a system of economics built around the principle of solidarity, liked the motto: "One for all, and all for one," to express what that system was about. This comes close to what John Paul II is saying here.

12. One could venture to say that if he had not chosen the *Totus Tuus* motto for his pontificate to express his total devotion to Mary, the Mother of God, this pope could well have selected as his motto: *Opus Solidaritatis Pax.*

13. This expression was used first by Paul VI in *Populorum Progressio.*

14. One work contained essays, most of them critical in various degrees, commemorating a century of social teachings by the Church. It includes also the suggestion that the poor nations are not expected to contribute sufficiently to their own development. Cf. esp. Robert Royal, "*Populorum Progressio*," in *A Century of Catholic Social Thought,* ed. George Weigel & Robert Royal (Washington, DC.: Ethics and Public Policy Center, 1991), 115-130.

15. Two definitive *Instructions* have been issued on "liberation theology" by the Sacred Congregation for the Doctrine of the Faith, and both were approved and ordered published by Pope John Paul II. They are: *Certain Aspects of the "Theology of Liberation"* (August 6, 1984), and *Christian Freedom and Liberation* (March 22, 1986).

Chapter 7
John Paul II
Centesimus Annus

This third social encyclical by Pope John Paul II commemorated the 100th anniversary of *Rerum Novarum.* But as its author indicated, it also "honors those encyclicals and other documents of my predecessors which have helped to make Pope Leo's encyclical present and alive in history, thus constituting what would come to be called the church's 'social doctrine,' 'social teaching' or even 'social magisterium'" (2). He invited us to a "rereading" of *Rerum Novarum* "to discover anew the richness of the fundamental principles which it formulated." (3). But there is also the prospect of "the third millennium of the Christian era," so often alluded to by Pope John Paul II, which is "so filled with uncertainties but also with promises." Thus, we are asked to "look around" at the "'new things'" which surround us and in which we find ourselves "'caught up.'" Like all of the recent generation of social encyclicals since Blessed John XXIII, this one too is addressed to "All Men and Women of Good Will."

Chapter 1. Characteristics of "Rerum Novarum"

The first of the six parts which make up *Centesimus Annus* recapitulates the "old things" which were "new things" when Leo XIII issued *Rerum Novarum.* Although it is proposed that the new era was characterized by a great increase in political liberty, it actually brought the "threat of new forms of injustice and servitude" (4). That new "servitude" made itself felt especially in the economic order, what with labor becoming "a commodity to be freely bought and sold on the market, its price determined by the law of supply and demand without taking into account the bare minimum required for the support of the individual and his family." Therefore, the worker, enfranchised politically, was now held in bondage by so-called economic laws. Critical in this development was a "new form of property... capital; and a new form of labor—labor for wages."

Significantly, the author of *Centesimus Annus* referred us at this point to the largely forgotten Leo XIII encyclical on liberty, *Libertas Praestantissimum* (1888). There is a footnote reference to three other Leo XIII encyclicals addressed to the political order, which are unfortunately no longer widely known or read, even though they are prophetic documents, highly relevant to the conditions the world faced both in 1891 and at present. Here, the Pope is emphasizing the link between freedom and truth, at a time when there is so much talk of freedom without reference to the truth, or indeed with outright rejection of it and the possibility of attaining it. Therefore, we "end up submitting...to the vilest of passions to the point of self-destruction." Specifically, what Leo XIII was dealing with here was that deracinated concept of freedom as applied in the area of economic life. The result? "The 'new things' to which that pope devoted his attention were anything but positive" (5). And the end is not yet, as becomes clear in the course of the present encyclical.

An increasingly bitter conflict developed between "labor and capital," which came to be called "the worker question." The conflict, identified and goaded on by the socialists as the "class struggle," "set man against man, almost as if they were 'wolves,' a conflict between the extremes of mere physical survival on the one side and opulence on the other." Since the Church opposed the conflict as a destructive concept, it had no choice but to intervene; but it was not enough to declaim against it. Root causes had to be dealt with, and that meant identifying and coming to grips with the rampant social injustice, because "Peace is the work of justice." And since the root causes of the conflict both with and among countries are still very much at work, the Church now as then is entitled—in fact, compelled—to address "the social question" in the light of the Gospel and of the "'new evangelization,' which the modern world urgently needs." Indeed, the next paragraph refers specifically to an anomaly in present-day society: "...increasing instances of poverty or, more precisely, of hindrances to private ownership in many parts of the world, including those where systems predominate which are based on an affirmation of the right to private property" (6). And after recounting the various specific injustices addressed by Leo XIII, which were inflicted on workers in the name of "freedom of contract," Pope John Paul II commented: "Would that these words, written at a time when what has been called 'unbridled capitalism' was pressing forward, should not have to be repeated today with the same severity" (8). The implication is obvious.

Significant new matter appears in the tenth paragraph. It builds on what Leo XIII had to say about the fallacy of the economic liberalism which called for the state to refrain from positive actions in the area of economic life, with the result that the rich prospered, while the majority of society was left in poverty. That led the Church to the position which is now called "the preferential option for the poor," based on the obvious fact that "the richer class has many ways of shielding itself and stands less in need of help from the state; whereas the mass of the poor have no resources of their own to fall back on and must chiefly depend on the assistance of the state" (10). Such an approach does not, by any means, add up to enhancement of class conflict or the "class struggle." It leads instead to a proper application of "what we nowadays call the principle of solidarity, the validity of which both in the internal order of each nation and in the international order I have discussed in the encyclical *Sollicitudo Rei Socialis...*"[1] What is new here is the Solidarity Pope's explanation of how this concept was already mentioned by previous pontiffs who used different expressions for it. "This principle is frequently stated by Pope Leo XIII, who uses the term *friendship,* a concept already found in Greek philosophy." And according to John Paul II, "Pope Pius XI refers to it with the equally meaningful term *social charity.*" Then, "Pope Paul VI, expanding the concept to cover the many modern aspects of the social question, speaks of a *civilization of love*" (10). (*Note*: italics here and throughout the text are as in the original translated text of the encyclical, unless specifically identified as the author's). That is indeed a splendid and specific reaffirmation of the important solidarity principle. It is also illustrative, in that it indicates a certain development of the concept in successive papal social pronouncements.[2]

Before turning to the "New Things of Today" in the second chapter, Pope John Paul II offered a restatement of the specific term, "preferential option for the poor" as, in his words, "an option which I defined as a 'special form of primacy in the exercise of Christian charity'" (11). And while the state is expected to help those who have difficulty in helping themselves, the precautionary reference to the principle of subsidiarity also recurs, without use of the actual term. Finally, there is also a restatement of the personalist position of the Church in her social teachings beginning with Leo XIII. We are reminded that "the main thread and in a certain sense the guiding principle of Pope Leo's encyclical and of all of the church's social doctrine is a correct view of the human person and of his unique value inasmuch as 'man...is the only creature on earth which God willed for itself'" (11).

Chapter 2. Toward the "New Things" of Today

The discussion of "new things" begins with appropriate praise for the accuracy of Leo XIII's prognosis of what lay ahead. In looking at things retrospectively, we tend to forget that when *Rerum Novarum* appeared, socialism was, as John Paul II stated here, "still only a social philosophy and not yet a fully structured movement" (12). Yet the warning about it was emphatic and precise in that pioneer social encyclical which was issued twenty-six years before the Bolshevik Revolution claimed the first actual territory for Marxian socialism.[3] The unfolding of actual events, the emergence of "real socialism," proved the prophetic accuracy of the warning that, "The remedy would prove worse than the sickness."

The Polish Pope now added his own keen insight that "the fundamental error of socialism is anthropological in nature" (13). This means:

> Socialism considers the individual person simply as an element, a molecule within the social organism, so that the good of the individual is completely subordinated to the functioning of the socioeconomic mechanism...that the

> good of the individual can be realized without reference to his free choice, to the unique and exclusive responsibility which he exercises in the face of good or evil.

The social doctrine of the Church, on the other hand, holds the view that "the social nature of man is not completely fulfilled in the state, but is realized in various intermediary groups, beginning with the family and including economic, social, political and cultural groups which stem from human nature itself and have their own autonomy, always with a view to the common good." It would be difficult to devise a more concise, yet precise, statement of the Church's view of society and social order.

Equally incisive is the revelation of where the contorted and perverse views of society and man's relation to it, which have come to predominate in the modern history of mankind, stem from: "its first cause is atheism." And "the atheism of which we are speaking is also closely connected with the rationalism of the Enlightenment which views human and social reality in a mechanistic way" (13). In dwelling on socialism and the present evils in society the profound impact which Enlightenment philosophy had and continues to have on the way people regard society, and also economic life specifically, tends to be lost from view. As indicated previously in this commentary, the modern economic science was born during and, one must say also, out of the Enlightenment. The French Physiocrats who originated the first rudiments of the science were creatures of the Enlightenment, as was Adam Smith and other leading figures in the development of so-called classical economics. It was they who came to formulate economics mechanistically, as if driven by the same kind of laws and necessity as propel the physical universe.[4] Even Karl Marx, who erected his own view of economics on an abhorrence of the social conditions which classical economics helped to produce, did not escape from the mechanistic trap. His socialism was termed "scientific" for the precise reason that he too offered "laws" and "necessity" to explain what happened in economic life and in society overall. Indeed, John Paul II acknowledged that "socialism also derives its choice of means...from the same atheistic source" (14).

The Pontiff may have been offering some consolation to the proponents of "liberation theology," when he recalled that Leo XIII "does not, of course, intend to condemn every possible form of social conflict." This is based on solid scriptural grounds: "My mission is to spread not peace but division" (Mt. 10:34). At the same time, there may be an implicit warning to those who, having derived a comfortable living from the status quo, get upset when anyone, including their Church, "rocks the boat." The problem—"the social question"—is there. It is a fact of life, and there is no denying the existence of a conflict—what the Pope called here a "'struggle for social justice,'" quoting his own words from *Laborem Exercens.* What is at issue is not the existence of the conflict or the struggle, but the "choice of means" which "socialism" derived from "the same atheistic source" referred to above. Therefore, "what is condemned in class struggle is the idea that conflict is not restrained by ethical or juridical considerations or by respect for the dignity of others (and consequently of oneself)." Lacking that restraint, the "doctrine of 'total war' which the militarism and imperialism of that time brought to bear on international relations" is transferred "to the sphere of internal conflict between social groups.... Therefore class struggle in the Marxist sense and militarism have the same root, namely, atheism and contempt for the human person, which place the principle of force above that of reason and law" (14).

The rejection of two opposing views of society and its upholding of the common good was recounted once again. "*Rerum Novarum* is opposed to state control of the means of production, which would reduce every citizen to being a 'cog' in the state machine" (15). However, "It is no less forceful in criticizing a concept of the state which completely excludes the economic sector from the state's range of interest and action." The former rules out socialist collectivism; the latter rejects liberalist capitalism. The former, because: "There is certainly a legitimate sphere of autonomy in economic life which the state should not enter." The latter, because: "The state...has the task of determining the juridical framework within which economic affairs are to be conducted and thus of safeguarding the prerequisites of a free economy which presumes a certain equality between the parties such that one party would not be so powerful as practically to reduce the other to subservience."

The kind of juridical framework referred to here has indeed emerged in many countries during the years following *Rerum Novarum*. That has bought significant gains for workers in areas like "unemployment insurance and retraining programs," and also, "in the areas of social security, pensions, health insurance and compensation in the case of accidents." However, the role also of "trade unions" is acknowledged here by the Pope. Although the existence of effective labor unions also calls, at least minimally, for some adjustment in the "juridical framework," once they are in place and operating, they can accomplish much which would otherwise involve direct state intervention, as is the case in socialistic societies. For example, the Pope indicated here, they were "decisive...in negotiating minimum salaries and working conditions." Also, they played "an important role in bringing about the social reforms mentioned above. Thus, sound labor unionism provides a valid example of the operation of the principle of subsidiarity which is mentioned explicitly in this context.

After *Rerum Novarum*, the United States too did, in fact, begin to provide the proper "juridical framework" for those kinds of social reforms, and also for making the existence and success of labor unions possible.[5] What could possibly be interpreted as an accolade for specifically the American type of labor unionism, is the Pope's statement that the "...movement, which began as a response of moral conscience to unjust and harmful situations, conducted a widespread campaign for reform far removed from vague ideology and closer to the daily needs of workers" (16). A Jewish immigrant cigar-maker, Samuel Gompers, set the course for the American labor movement according to what came to be called "business unionism," perhaps a poor choice of words. Nevertheless, it involved a sound trade union philosophy intent on improving the wages, hours, and working conditions within the existing social framework, precisely without deference to any "vague ideology." With just few and relatively brief deviations, that has been the pattern for the labor movement in the United States ever since. Indeed, Christian labor leaders like Philip Murray, George Meany and John L. Lewis persisted in that philosophy at the top echelons of the American labor movement. Other countries did not fare so well because labor movements there were sometimes "dominated to a certain extent by the Marxist ideology" (16).

Unfortunately, the "prophetic message" of Leo XIII "was not fully accepted by people at the time." In pinpointing the blame for this, Pope John Paul II went to the root of the problem. It is "an understanding of human freedom which detaches it from obedience to the truth and consequently from the duty to respect the rights of others." Therefore, the "essence of freedom...becomes self-love carried to the point of contempt for God and neighbor, a self-love which leads to an unbridled affirmation of self-interest and which refuses to be limited by any demand of justice" (17). The error had "extreme consequences," including "the wars which ravaged Europe and the world between 1914 and 1945." All of this involved ultimately "hatred and injustice...sanctioned and organized by ideologies based on them, rather than on the truth about man."

Nor did it all end with the second great World War! Since then we have had what Pope John II now called "a situation of non-war rather than genuine peace" (18). It was in this situation that an "insane arms race swallowed up the resources needed for the development of national economies and for assistance to the less-developed nations"—the problem already addressed in encyclicals by Paul VI and Pope John Paul II, following the lead of John XXIII. In view of the disastrous potential which modern science has provided, the present Pope questioned, as did his predecessors in various ways, the "logic" of whether in this context, "confrontation and war itself are factors of progress and historical advancement," and also the very concepts, "'total war'" and "'class struggle'" (17).

As if to make such reflection retroactive, John Paul II alluded to the disappointing outcome of World War II "which should have re-established freedom and restored the rights of nations," but which "ended without having attained these goals" (19). On a more positive note, however, he recounted how some countries try "to rebuild a democratic society inspired by social justice, so as to deprive communism of the revolutionary potential represented by masses of people subjected to exploitation and oppression." These efforts generally involve an "endeavor to preserve free-market mechanisms, ensuring by means of a stable currency and the harmony of social relations the conditions for steady and healthy economic growth in which people through their own work can build a better future for themselves and their families." In what, if it is not a specific reference to the "social market economy" initiated by post-war Germany during the Adenauer-Erhard regime, is at least applicable to it, the Pope added: "At the same time, these attempts try to avoid making market mechanisms the only point of reference for social life, and they tend to subject them to public control, which upholds the principle of the common destination of material goods." Unfortunately, what follows could also be a reference to the same country, after it enjoyed the remarkable economic recovery brought on by the aforementioned regime: "Another kind of response, practical in nature, is represented by the affluent society or the consumer society" which "seeks to defeat Marxism on the level of pure materialism by showing how a free-market society can achieve a greater satisfaction of material human needs than communism, while equally excluding spiritual values" (19). While that certainly does not apply exclusively to prosperous Germany, perhaps characteristically its people have been more thorough in their consumerism than others. The burden of having to bring its eastern, formerly Communist part up from the socialist ruins may have come in the nick of time to save the affluent West Germans from themselves. They are face-to-face once again with a challenge which goes beyond crass self-indulgence. Meanwhile, we in the United States are confronted with what is perhaps a more dire mission, to salvage our debt-ridden, nearly bankrupt economy from outright disaster.

This chapter ends with the Pope turning his attention to the "decolonization" which came with the end of the old 19th century empires. He recounted the attendant problems, the projected solutions, (some more promising than others), the handicaps posed by the "tribal groups not yet amalgamated into a genuine national community," and the lack of "a class of competent professional people capable of running the state apparatus in an honest and just way, nor are there qualified personnel for managing the economy in an efficient and responsible manner" (20). That is a remarkably astute and succinct statement of the problems of new, developing nations emerging in the period after World War II.

The Pontiff concluded with a deferential nod to the United Nations Organization, which embodies the developing awareness of the "right of nations" (21). He noted that whatever its successes, that Organization "has not yet succeeded in establishing as alternatives to war effective means for the resolution of international conflicts."

Chapter 3. The Year 1989

One would not expect a pope of the Roman Catholic Church to issue a social encyclical in 1991 which did not allude to the dramatic events of 1989 marking the breakup of the last great surviving colonial empire—the Soviet Empire. That is the theme of the third chapter of *Centesimus Annus*. It refers to the "unexpected and promising significance of the events of recent years," which "certainly reached their climax in 1989 in the countries of Central and Eastern Europe" (22). These events involve, among other things, "new forms of democracy" which emerged from situations "weighted down by a painful series of injustices and resentments, as well as by a heavily damaged economy and serious social conflicts."

Reference to the need for "dialogue and solidarity" for resolving difficult problems leads to specific mention of Poland. The Polish Pope was not willing to let it be forgotten that the wave of "revolutions" which swept Eastern Europe in 1989 "began with the great upheavals which took place in Poland in the name of solidarity" (23). Nor was he prepared to let the opportunity slip by to allude to the supreme historical irony in the fact that this development involved "the fundamental crisis of systems claiming to express the rule and indeed the dictatorship of the working class." And finally, John Paul II found it "worthy of emphasis...that the fall of this kind of 'bloc' or empire was accomplished almost everywhere by means of peaceful protest, using only the weapons of truth and justice." There is food for much meditation in those thoughts, because in our fast-paced world besieged with ever changing headlines we tend to lose sight of salient facts.

Indeed, many have forgotten the sad fact of the post-World War II agreements where, in the view of many, the Western allies, having won the War, lost the peace. The Pope referred specifically to the Yalta Agreements of which his beloved Poland, in particular, was a victim. Indeed, it appeared that the state of affairs in Europe established by those agreements "could only be overturned by another war" (23). "Instead, it has been overcome by the non-violent commitment of people who, while always refusing to yield to the force of power, succeeded time after time in finding effective ways of bearing witness to the truth." That is well-deserved praise for his own people, even though other Soviet satellite nations may also share in it. It inspires the prayer that "this example will prevail in other places and other circumstances" (23).

What follows is a reference to the inherent flaws in the Communist system, which were also inevitable factors in its dissolution. The Pope pointed out that this "is not to be considered as a technical problem, but rather a consequence of the violation of the human rights to private initiative, to ownership of property and to freedom in the economic sector" (24). Beyond the merely economic shortcomings, however, there was also the "cultural and national dimension." "Different cultures are basically different ways of facing the question of the meaning of personal existence." And finally,

> the true cause of the new developments was the spiritual void brought about by atheism, which deprived the younger generations of a sense of direction, and in many cases led them, in the irrepressible search for personal identity and for the meaning of life, to rediscover the religious roots of their national cultures and to rediscover the person of Christ himself as the existentially adequate response to the desire in every human heart for goodness, truth and life.

The subsequent paragraphs present what amounts to a solid theological perspective on how the transformation of 1989 and the years following became possible. Ultimately, "it would have been unthinkable without immense trust in God, the Lord of history, who carries the human heart in his hands" (25). Nevertheless, it also involved a great price. "It is by uniting his own sufferings for the sake of truth and freedom to the sufferings of Christ on the cross that man is able to accomplish the miracle of peace." In the final analysis, peace does not come by incantations and demonstrations, but by penitential actions. No nation in recent history has suffered more than the Russian people, in terms of duration, intensity, and bloodshed at the hands of its own leaders, but also from World War II. And the Poles, of course, were subjected to their own intense martyrdom beginning in 1939.

There is mention then of a kind of rapprochement between the Church with its social doctrine and the labor movement which the Marxists had endeavored to lure into their trap "in order to struggle effectively against oppression" (26). Instead, what happened "was an encounter in some countries between the church and the workers' movement which came about as a result of an ethical and explicitly Christian reaction against a widespread situation of injustice." Clearly that labor movement, *Solidarność,* in Poland was the result of such an "ethical and explicitly Christian reaction."

What followed then represents an admonition for the "liberation theology" movement, even while admitting what is valid about it. "To those who are searching today for a new and authentic theory and praxis of liberation, the church offers not only her social doctrine and, in general, her teaching about the human person redeemed in Christ, but also her concrete commitment and material assistance in the struggle against marginalization and suffering." Lest there be any doubt about whom the Pope was addressing this to, there is the following paragraph: "In the recent past, the sincere desire to be on the side of the oppressed and not to be cut off from the course of history has led many believers to seek in various ways an impossible compromise between Marxism and Christianity" (26). One cannot help but wonder whether those Catholics who were deluded by the "liberation theology" cult will now at last, upon seeing the abject failure of the false gospel of Karl Marx, turn to the treasure which their Church had provided for them over the past century, reflecting the gospels of Jesus Christ.

The author of *Centesimus Annus* did not take the time to gloat over the demise of the Marxist-Leninist system in Europe. Instead, he warned that people not be carried away by the "hatred and ill will [which] have accumulated" while people and nations were under the Communist yoke. "There is the danger that these will re-explode after the collapse of dictatorship, provoking serious conflicts and casualties" (27). Pope John Paul II indicated perspicaciously how "the most elementary economic relationships were distorted, and basic virtues of economic life such as truthfulness, trustworthiness and hard work were denigrated" (27). In other words, a gravely afflicted patient does not, as a rule, recover suddenly. Great care is required over a period of time. The Pope also demonstrated historical insight by the statement: "In a sense, for some countries of Europe the real postwar period is just beginning." It is as if they were transported off to an unreal existence over a period of some 45 years, so that they now face "problems and sacrifices comparable to those which the countries of Western Europe had to face in order to rebuild after the Second World War (28)."

Since the latter countries received significant assistance in their reconstruction efforts, those newly emancipated would appear to be no less entitled to such help. As he stressed in *Sollicitudo Rei Socialis,* and as Paul VI did in *Populorum Progressio,* whenever assistance from more fortunate to more hard-pressed nations was under discussion, here too John Paul II warned those in need of assistance that, "they themselves must be the primary agents of their own development" (28). At the same time there is a reminder that such help "represents a debt in justice" where "the countries of Europe which were part of that history and which bear responsibility for it" are concerned. Lest they may feel too sorry for themselves, however, the latter are reminded that assistance to their neighbor nations in trouble "also corresponds to the interest and welfare of Europe as a whole, since Europe cannot live in peace if the various conflicts which have arisen as a result of the past are to become more acute because of a situation of economic disorder, spiritual dissatisfaction and desperation" (28).

Lest the help needed by the newly liberated nations should side-track the still urgently needed assistance to the Third World, John Paul II returned to the same theme presented by Blessed John XXIII, Paul VI, and previously, himself. The resources for providing all of this help should come from "disarming the huge military machines...constructed for the conflict between East and West." The prospect of this happening could, of course, be enhanced tremendously if finally, "in place of war, reliable procedures for the resolution of conflicts could be set up with the resulting spread of the principle of arms control and arms reduction also in the Third World" (28).

The chapter ends with the warning that, despite all of the economic necessity involved, economics alone is not the only or even the ultimate end of all human endeavor. "It is not only a question of raising all peoples to the level currently enjoyed by the richest countries, but rather of building up a more decent life through united labor, of concretely enhancing every individual's dignity and creativity as well as his capacity to respond to his personal vocation and thus to God's call" (29). That is followed by a most significant magisterial statement: "The apex of development is the exercise of the right and duty to seek God, to know him and to live in accordance with that knowledge." All of this is still made difficult for various reasons including the survival of "old forms of totalitarianism and authoritarianism;" the "excessive promotion of purely utilitarian values with an appeal for the appetites and inclinations toward immediate gratification;" and the emergence of "new forms of religious fundamentalism...which covertly, or even openly, deny to citizens of faiths other than that of the majority the full exercise of their civil and religious rights" (29).

Chapter 4. Private Property and the Universal Destination of Material Goods

This chapter presents a recapitulation of the Church's teaching on private property. It also offers some basic lessons in economics and economic history, as well as in comparative economic systems. The economics lessons are related, needless to say, to the ethical implications involved in certain economic developments and structures.

First, then, we find reaffirmed the position of Leo XIII on private ownership—a right which is natural to man and therefore inviolable. But as with all rights, there are concomitant obligations. This one involves the duty to always use one's property with due regard for the equal rights of others and also for the common good. In other words, "the possession of material goods is not an absolute right" (30). Their use must be social, meaning that it "is subordinated to their original common destination as created goods." Ultimately, this teaching also reflects the "original source" of those goods, God, who "gave the earth to the whole human race for the sustenance of all its members, without excluding or favoring anyone" (31).

At this point Pope John Paul II was afforded an opening to review his own teaching on the centrality of human work. That is because "the earth does not yield its fruits without a particular human response to God's gift, that is to say, without work." The proportional relationship between God's material creation and human effort has not always been the same. At one time in history the natural fruitfulness of the earth appeared to be and was in fact the primary factor of wealth, while work was, as it were, the help and support for this fruitfulness." Such a relationship could never explain, for example, the prosperity of present-day Japan or Switzerland. If natural resources were the dominant basis for national wealth, these two nations, like some others, would be abysmally poor.[6] In the modern world, "the role of human work is becoming increasingly important as the productive factor both of non-material and of material wealth.... Moreover, it is becoming clearer how a person's work is naturally interrelated with the work of others." This expression of solidarity in working relationships is becoming more evident in our time than ever: "More than ever work is work with others and work for others." Far fewer persons work by themselves and for themselves than in earlier periods in history, such as on the virtually self-sufficient family farms of times past, and at handicrafts (31).

In a society where there is a high degree of division of labor, far more is produced for use by others than by oneself. Therefore the exchange process becomes even more important than in the past; and by the same token so does the "just price mutually agreed upon through free bargaining" (32). Now, the just price doctrine was already well developed in medieval thought.[7] Indeed, it is often looked upon among some modern commentators as little more than a kind of museum piece of medievalism. Here we find it reaffirmed for the modern context, along with the stipulation, already expressed by the Medieval Schoolmen, that the just price can be arrived at "mutually...through free bargaining" (32). This does not mean that any price, so long as it is arrived at "mutually," or that any kind of "bargaining" between buyers and sellers may be presumed to add up automatically to a just price. It assumes that there is real freedom of a kind which involves a basic equality in the bargaining positions between buyers and sellers.[8]

In addition to providing the Pope with an opportunity to affirm the continuing validity of the just price doctrine, this section also enabled him to set forth the importance of entrepreneurial skills—a special kind of very important work in the modern form of productive enterprise. Those who produce things for use by others than themselves are often involved in something which "cannot be adequately produced through the work of an isolated individual." This involves "the cooperation of many people in working toward a common goal." Enter the entrepreneur and his special skills, such as "the ability to foresee both the needs of others and the combinations of productive factors most adapted to satisfying those needs." They involve also "Organizing such a productive effort, planning its duration in time, making sure that it corresponds in a positive way to the demands which it must satisfy and taking the necessary risks." All of that is seen by John Paul II as "another important source of wealth in today's society." However, the importance of "initiative and entrepreneurial ability" simply enhances the central importance of human work in modern society, because it is "an essential part of that work" (32).

The Pope returned to the critical-nature-of-human-work theme in discussing the "positive aspects" of the "modern business economy." Stressing the need for "freedom exercised in the economic field" along with "the duty of making responsible use of freedom," he indicated that "there are specific differences between the trends of modern society and those of the past, even the recent past":

> Whereas at one time the decisive factor of production was the land and later capital—understood as a total complex of the instruments of production—today the decisive factor is increasingly man himself, that is his knowledge, especially his scientific knowledge, his capacity for interrelated and compact organization as well as his ability to perceive the needs of others and to satisfy him.

That statement contains a great deal of perspective on economic history—the shift from a predominantly land- (nature-) based economy throughout ancient times, to a predominantly capital-based one in the "recent past," to a man- (work-) based one in the society that is emerging in our own time. Once again, the importance of the special skills of the entrepreneur are mentioned under the general heading of human work. The predominance of the factor of production, capital, defined here as "a total complex of the instruments of production" has come with the more recent centuries which historians refer to as the modern age (32). And it was especially enhanced by the Industrial Revolution and the technological advances which have continued to set the tone for modern society, specifically its economic life, since that time. Yet, the dominance of human work in the economic process and in determining the wealth of nations is cited here, as it was established in *Laborem Exercens*. That is because the human person is the only factor of production which is also more than a mere factor of production. The worker is not only a means, but also the end purpose for which those means exist, just as he or she alone is an *active* factor, working among and on the other *passive*, material factors of production.

The shadow side of this kind of development in economic life is the fact that "many people, perhaps the majority...do not have the means which would enable them to take their place in an effective and humanly dignified way within a productive system in which work is truly central" (33). Given the significant repetition of the theme of the centrality of human work, it is especially regrettable that too many people do not have the equipment or the opportunity to assume their proper places in such an economy. The reasons: "no possibility of acquiring the basic knowledge which would enable them to express their creativity and develop their potential." The result: "they are, if not actually exploited...to a great extent marginalized," so that "economic development takes place over their heads...when it does not actually reduce the already narrow scope of their old subsistence economies." The Pope was talking here, first of all, about people in Third World countries who are, among other things, "unable to compete against the goods which are produced in ways which are new and which properly respond to needs, needs which they had previously been accustomed to meeting through traditional forms of organization" (33).

There are others too, however, who, "while not completely marginalized, live in situations in which the struggle for a bare minimum is uppermost." That is because, "the rules of the earliest period of capitalism still flourish in conditions of 'ruthlessness' in no way inferior to the darkest moments of the first phase of industrialization." Elsewhere, with "land...still the central element in the economic process... those who cultivate it are still excluded from ownership and...reduced to a state of quasi-servitude." Thus, "it is still possible today, as in the days of *Rerum Novarum,* to speak of inhuman exploitation. Included as partial causes are "the human inadequacies of capitalism and the domination of things over people..." And all of this does not apply exclusively in Third World countries, but also "in developed countries, where the constant transformation of the methods of production and consumption devalues certain acquired skills and professional expertise..." Marginalized, then, we find "the elderly, the young people who are incapable of finding their place in the life of society and in general those who are weakest or part of the so-called Fourth World." Significantly, Pope John Paul II mentioned the plight of women as being "far from easy in these conditions" (33).

In the paragraphs which follow, there was a significant discussion of what may be termed the area of comparative economic systems with regard to their ethical content. This portion of the encyclical was seized upon eagerly by some as an endorsement of a particular kind of ideology and system which they happened to favor.[9] The wording of the encyclical, however, was cautious and conditional throughout. For example, Pope John Paul II did not open the discussion by saying that the "free market is the most efficient instrument for utilizing resources and effectively responding to needs" (34). He said, instead: "It would appear that on the level of individual nations and of international relations the free market is the most efficient instrument...." Following that use of the subjunctive mode to indicate something that is conditional, there followed immediately a host of qualifications. For example, "...there are many human needs which find no place on the market." For these, "It is a strict duty of justice and truth not to allow fundamental human needs to remain unsatisfied and not to allow those burdened by such needs to perish." The discussion of the inaccessibility of adequate health care for millions of citizens in the supposedly affluent United States is just one such case in point. Health care is a basic human need—a public utility—and it should be available to all without regard to the standard market criteria which are used to determine whether one can or cannot purchase a Cadillac automobile. Therefore, transcending "the logic of a fair exchange of goods and the forms of justice appropriate to it, there exists something which is due to man because he is man, by reason of his lofty dignity." Conversely, we make massive social interpositions in such matters as the right to purchase narcotic drugs or handguns, setting aside the normal market mechanism. Also, many who are still living will remember well how the market mechanism was set aside radically during World War II. It is a fair statement that the War could not have been conducted successfully without that abolition of the free market mechanism by strict controls on wages, prices, and rents, along with allocation of materials throughout the war period. The Pope also mentioned in this discussion such objectives as "a sufficient wage for the support of the family, social insurance for old age and unemployment, and adequate protection for the conditions of employment" (34).

Clearly, Pope John Paul II used the term "free market" in a different sense than those whose economic ideology reflects the Ludwig von Mises–Milton Friedman school of free marketeering. The role of aggressive labor unionism is invariably a discomforting element. For those who champion "free markets" as the highest good of economic life, labor unionism is generally viewed as a distorting such "free markets." That is because the term "union" is obviously synonymous with monopoly, in this case, on the supply side of the labor market. Yet the Pope, commemorating what Leo XIII said about the condition of labor, found here "a wide range of opportunities for commitment and effort in the name of justice on the part of trade unions and other workers' organizations" (35).

All of this adds up to "a struggle against an economic system, if the latter is understood as a method of upholding the absolute predominance of capital, the possession of the means of production and of the land, in contrast to the free and personal nature of human work." That predominance, even if no longer so "absolute" as it was earlier, is still a hallmark of capitalism, hence its name. In fact, Pope John Paul inferred as much when he referred to the unacceptable alternative "socialist system" as "in fact...state capitalism." The socialist system as it came to exist in the Soviet Empire put intense emphasis on developing its capital structure. The succession of notorious five-year plans, which allocated labor and materials in each period, inflicted austerity if not outright suffering in forcing the postponement of consumption until sometime in the elusive future—and that was done for the precise purpose of speeding up capital formation. Thus there was what amounted to capitalism under state auspices—hence, "state capitalism." Pope John Paul II was suggesting instead "a society of free work, of enterprise and of participation." He was talking about a society which is "not directed against the market, but demands that the market be appropriately controlled by the forces of society and by the state so as to guarantee that the basic needs of the whole of society are satisfied" (35).

It bears repeating once again that there are countries with better social control of the markets than exists in the United States where, among other things, some 25 million citizens must subsist on "food stamps" and where homelessness has become a national scandal.[10] While the Church in its social teachings has always acknowledged the "legitimate role of profit as an indication that a business is functioning well," the qualifying word, "legitimate," makes the difference between a *social* market economy and a *free* market economy where the profit motive is allowed to run wild. "Profit is a regulator of the life of a business, but it is not the only one; other human and moral factors must also be considered which in the long term are at least equally important for the life of a business."[11] In the light of all of such qualifications, it is difficult to make the Pope out to be a recent "convert" to capitalism.[12] He seems to lay that to rest himself with the statement: "We have seen that it is unacceptable to say that the defeat of so-called 'real socialism' leaves capitalism as the only model of economic organization." That is especially so when there remain "barriers and monopolies which leave so many countries on the margins of development" (35).

Meanwhile, there are "specific problems and threats emerging within the more advanced economies...related to their particular characteristics" (36). There, although subsistence needs have been dealt with in large measure, we find something lacking in the area of quality: "the quality of the goods to be produced and consumed, the quality of the services to be enjoyed, the quality of the environment and of life in general." In dealing with that aspect of economic want-satisfaction, we get into "the phenomenon of consumerism." Abuse in this area means that "consumer attitudes and lifestyles can be created which are objectively improper and often damaging to...physical and spiritual health." Here the Pope mentioned specifically, "drugs" whose widespread use "is a sign of a serious malfunction in the social system...also...a materialistic and in a certain sense destructive 'reading' of human needs." We are told that drugs, "pornography and other forms of consumerism," among other things, distort "the innovative capacity of a free economy" (35).

Another obvious transgression which has encroached also in "more advanced economies" as an abuse of the free market, the profit motive, and the like, is long-standing and ongoing ecological depredation. Much of what has emerged in our time as "the ecological question," is precisely the result of the abuse of free markets and the profit motive. It is cheaper to create "Love Canals," to spoil rivers and lakes, and pollute the air with wastes than to seek and apply socially responsible ways to deal with disposal.[13] Such actions come under the heading of "free enterprise." The Pope indicated that the "ecological question accompanies the problem of consumerism and...is closely connected to it." He sees all of this as a reflection of "the poverty or narrowness of man's outlook, motivated as he is by a desire to possess things rather than to relate them to the truth" (37).

While concern about natural environment is legitimate and overdue, and now widespread, it is left to the head of the Roman Catholic Church to also draw attention to safeguarding "'human ecology'" (38). This involves many factors, including "the serious problems of modern organization," and also "a 'social ecology' of work." But it involves first of all, the "fundamental structure for 'human ecology,' the family, in which man receives his first formative ideas about truth and goodness, and learns what it means to love and to be loved, and thus what it actually means to be a person" (39). Here one finds the kinds of words, the "hard sayings" which are not a part of the common jargon of our post-Christian times.[14] Who among our popular champions of ecology speaks of "the family as the sanctuary of life...the place in which life—the gift of God—can be properly welcomed and protected against the many attacks to which it is exposed..."? And who still espouses "the family founded on marriage in which the mutual gift of self by husband and wife creates an environment in which children can be born and develop their potentialities..."? Instead, we find too often "people...discouraged from creating the proper conditions for human reproduction and...led to consider themselves and their lives as a series of sensations to be experienced rather than as a work to be accomplished..." The result is that they begin to consider also "children as one of the many 'things' which an individual can have or not have, according to taste, and which compete with other possibilities" (39). In other words, children and child-bearing too become a part of the consumerist cult!

It is here that Pope John Paul II spoke unabashedly about the "culture of death," where more effort is "directed...toward limiting, suppressing or destroying the sources of life—including recourse to abortion, which unfortunately is so widespread in the world." And he scored the "systematic anti-childbearing campaigns" based on "a distorted view of the demographic problem." All of that is, of course, not entirely the fault of some economic system but of "an ethical and cultural system" of which the "economy in fact is only one aspect." However, "If economic life is absolutized, if the production and consumption of goods become the center of social life and society's dominant value," then, "the entire sociocultural system...ends by limiting itself to the production of goods and services alone" (39).

Another limit on market freedom is the "defense and preservation of common goods such as the natural and human environments which cannot be safeguarded simply by market forces" (40). Such a limitation applies whether we are talking about "primitive capitalism" or "the new capitalism." After making this distinction, the Pope indicated that in "primitive capitalism the state had the duty of defending the basic rights of workers." Now in the "new capitalism...the state and all of society have the duty of defending those collective goods which...constitute the essential framework for the legitimate pursuit of personal goods on the part of the individual." Specifically, "There are collective and qualitative needs which cannot be satisfied by market mechanisms." And there are "important human needs which escape its logic." After listing some "secure advantages" offered by market mechanisms, the Pope warned that these "carry the risk of an 'idolatry' of the market, an idolatry which ignores the existence of goods which by their nature are not and cannot be mere commodities" (40). A case can be made that medical care, for example, should be excluded from the category of "mere commodities," just as Leo XIII excluded the labor of human beings a century ago.[15]

The concept usually identified with Marxian thought, "alienation" comes up for discussion next. Whereas Karl Marx made this out to be one of the demons of capitalism, the Polish Pope pointed out that this was a "mistaken and inadequate" notion, because it was based on "a materialistic foundation" which took into account solely "the sphere of relationships of production and ownership."

Therefore the cure, collectivism, does not "do away with alienation but rather increases it, adding to it a lack of basic necessities and economic inefficiency" (41). However, he indicated that "alienation—and the loss of the authentic meaning of life—is a reality in Western societies too." It is to be found in "consumerism, when people are ensnared in a web of false and superficial gratification rather than being helped to experience their personhood in an authentic and concrete way." But it is also found in one's daily work, "when it is organized so as to ensure maximum returns and profits without concern whether the worker, through his own labor, grows or diminishes as a person, either through increased sharing in a genuinely supportive community or through increased isolation in a maze of relationships marked by destructive competitiveness and estrangement, in which he is considered only a means and not an end." Anyone who has experienced the kind of calloused wholesale elimination of jobs and even of plants and whole industries, on which the continued prosperity of entire communities hinges, will appreciate the bitterness of such alienation. In the monopoly game played at the headquarters of giant corporations and vast conglomerates, neither the individual workers and their welfare, nor the destiny and even the survival of the involved communities is a relevant factor. Relevant are profitability, successful competition with rival corporations or conglomerates. The hapless "pawns" who are swept off the conglomerate "chessboards" know the meaning of "alienation." In coming to grips with such matters, it is not the Pope who is cut off from reality, as is suggested in some "enlightened" circles, when he speaks of a "maze of relationships" and "destructive competitiveness" (40). The urge to deregulate industries which of their nature require regulation has in recent times yielded bitter fruits for millions. One has only to reflect, for example, on the plight of the airline industry in America. The policy of all out dog-eat-dog competition has led to the destruction of prestigious and well-run companies whose histories extend back to the start of the industry.[16]

A person well advanced in age, in a career, and in tenure with a company, who suddenly finds himself cut off from his livelihood by cold-blooded decisions of planners high up in corporate hierarchies, feels every bit as alienated as the hapless pawns of state planners in a collectivist state. Ironically, the latter often provided a certain basic security which the victims of the so-called "market mechanism" do not enjoy. It all comes out the same if "man does not recognize in himself and in others the value and grandeur of the human person," and where he is deprived of "the possibility of benefiting from his humanity and of entering into that relationship of solidarity and communion with others for which God created him" (41).

The "bottom line" on this matter of alienation is set forth clearly by Pope John Paul II. "A man is alienated if he refuses to transcend himself and to live the experience of self-giving and of the formation of an authentic human community oriented toward his final destiny, which is God." As for society, it is "alienated if its forms of social organization, production and consumption make it more difficult to offer this gift of self and to establish this solidarity between people." Thus, we have the Pope of solidarity introducing this principle as pivotal to the establishment of a humane social order, as intended by God.

The Pope would not be the pope if he did not return to the theological theme that "obedience to the truth about God and man is the first condition of freedom." That holds for freedom whether it is applied to the personal and to the social order overall, or to markets, or to competition, or to enterprise, in other words, throughout the economic order. Freedom unhinged from the truth about man and about God "cannot be free." Witness the plight of persons "concerned solely or primarily with possessing and enjoying," and "no longer able to control…instincts and passions or to subordinate them by obedience to the truth" (41). Time and again we find repeated the sad spectacle of persons who have more wealth than they could use prudently in several lifetimes, risking their good reputations and even literally their freedom, by preposterous, shady schemes to gather in still more riches. They are not free, as they are driven by their boundless greed, even if they do not actually land in prison although they occasionally do.

The Pope was now ready to return to what he called the "the initial question" (42). "Can it perhaps be said that after the failure of communism, capitalism is the victorious social system and that capitalism should be the goal of the countries now making efforts to rebuild their economy and society?" First of all, as was indicated in his previous social encyclical, and as he also repeated in this one, "The church has no models to present," because, "models that are real and truly effective can only arise within the framework of different historical situations through the efforts of all those who responsibly confront concrete problems in all their social, economic, political and cultural aspects as these interact with one another" (43). However, reference to "concrete problems" in all of these aspects involves first some reflection on this sometimes murky and often ideologically charged term, "capitalism."

Indeed, we must recognize that for some capitalism has simply come to mean simplistically whatever communism is not. Accordingly, extracting what they perceive to be the essence of the communist system, such persons then identify capitalism with the economic order where property, including ownership of the means of production, is private. Taken in that sense, most economic systems throughout history would have to be reckoned as capitalistic as, for example, those in medieval European cities where most means of production were privately owned. Yet, the medieval urban structure is typically classed as a kind of opposite of capitalism.

Karl Marx, although he never reduced his *bête noire* to an "ism," did use the expressions, "capital" and "capitalist" and "capitalistic," in terms that clearly suggest what we now designate as capitalism. Furthermore, it was he who more than any other person made the concept a part of our common parlance. He meant by it a social order where those who owned and controlled the factor of production, capital, became the dominant class in society, with their dominance extending beyond the economy to include also the entire political, juridical, religious, ethical structure which he saw as being based on the economic order.[17]

Pope John Paul II was obviously more aware of the lack of precision in definition of the term than others, including some of his critics. Thus, for his own good reasons, he was not content to dodge the issue by simply repeating that the "church has no models to present" (43). First he indicated that capitalism does in fact mean different things to different people; and some features attributed to it would be reconcilable with the ethics and theology implicit in the Church's social teachings, while others would not. In examining what he had to say, however, it is important to bear in mind that even if capitalism is taken in its most benign sense, the fact remains that, once again, the "church has no models to present." Therefore, whether capitalism in the eyes of the Church is an acceptable "goal of the countries now making efforts to rebuild their economy and society," depends on what exactly we mean by capitalism:

> If by capitalism is meant an economic system which recognizes the fundamental and positive role of business, the market, private property and the resulting responsibility for the means of production as well as free human creativity in the economic sector, then the answer is certainly in the affirmative... But if by *capitalism* is meant a system in which freedom in the economic sector is not circumscribed within a strong juridical framework which places it at the service of human freedom in its totality and which sees it as a particular aspect of that freedom, the core of which is ethical and religious, then the reply is certainly negative (42).

In language which is certainly plain enough so as to not mislead any but those who *want* the Pope to be saying what they want him to say, we are being told that whether or not *capitalism* is an acceptable system in terms of the Church's social teachings, depends on what one means by capitalism. If one means one thing, then the answer "is certainly affirmative." But if one means another thing, the answer is just as "certainly negative." Clearly there is no cause for anyone to celebrate the Church's unqualified acceptance of capitalism here. And just as clearly, the Pope was not satisfied with the way that term has come to be used. Otherwise he would not have felt the need to qualify his acceptance or non-acceptance by proposing that "it would perhaps be more appropriate to speak of a *business economy, market economy* or simply *free economy*." Now it is also not the business of the Church to propose names for economic systems, which is why Pope John Paul II approached this matter quite gingerly, and why he inserted the word, "perhaps." However, if economists who have gone to ludicrous extremes to demonstrate how "scientific" economics is, have not yet been able to deliver a precise terminology in this important area, the field may indeed be wide open![18]

Capitalism in any authentic sense carries significant historical baggage, much of which is not acceptable in terms of the Church's moral theology. Specifically, well along into the course of its history, capitalism had grafted on to itself the liberal economic philosophy which stemmed from the Enlightenment.[19] Accordingly, it incorporated a view of economic life which interpreted that in the same naturalistic, mechanistic terms as were being applied to the then new, and eventually very successful, natural sciences. Thus, self-interest came to be accepted as the motor force of economic life, with competition its sole and adequate regulator. If these were destined to govern economic life and conduct through the working of ineluctable "natural laws," then it behooved the state and other social organs, like guilds, to leave hands off the appropriate mechanism. In that way *laissez faire* was to be the rule, and Adam Smith's "invisible hand" was to make things come out right. The trouble was that actual historical events proved otherwise. Things did not come out right for a majority of people, only for a privileged few—a class of economic royalists which came to replace a feudal aristocracy—hence capitalism in place of feudalism. Consequently, the significant blessings implicit in the Industrial Revolution were squandered in the sense that its results benefited far too few at the expense of far too many. It is this liberalistic ideology which popes throughout the modern social teachings of the Church have scored as unacceptable when they modified the term capitalism with such terms as "liberal," "primitive," and "unbridled." And that is certainly one reason why Pope John Paul II was uncomfortable with the prospect of calling capitalism the best possible successor to "real socialism" which in 1989 collapsed before our eyes because of its inherent flaws. Indeed, he was so uncomfortable about the idea that he proposed alternative names, because he was probably aware that the term, "capitalism," had become immensely unpopular, not only among Europeans who first gave birth to the system, but also among people in the Third World countries, who in the days when the colonial powers enriched themselves at the colonials' expense did not get to share proportionately in the newly gained riches. Accordingly, there is less talk in other nations, including the former colonial powers, about "capitalism," than in the United States, where ironically the "conservative" regimes dating back to the Carter administration have been busy restoring "primitive," "liberal," and "unbridled capitalism" of the 19th-century variety.

The Pope warned that "there is a risk that a radical capitalistic ideology could spread which refuses even to consider" certain glaring problems "in the *a priori* belief that any attempt to solve them is doomed to failure, and which blindly entrusts their solution to the free development of market forces." Those problems include, basically, "the realities of marginalization and exploitation [which] remain in the world, especially the Third World, as does the reality of human alienation especially in the more advanced countries" (42).

Marginalization and exploitation in the Third World has already been the dominant theme of two entire social encyclicals.[20] The "reality of human alienation" in "the more advanced countries" was addressed exhaustively in *Laborem Exercens,* as well as in the pioneer social encyclical *Rerum Novarum.* Lest anyone missed the point, John Paul II pointed out again here that, whereas there is a certain "positive value" in the market and in enterprise, these too "need to be oriented toward the common good" (43). And that involves also a recognition of "the legitimacy of workers' efforts to obtain full respect for their dignity and to gain broader areas of participation in the life of industrial enterprise so that, while cooperative with others and under the direction of others, they can in a certain sense 'work for themselves,' through the exercise of their intelligence and freedom" (43).

If such democracy in the shop and in economic life generally appears radical to some, it is already on the march among some of the most progressive of entrepreneurs and managers in the United States. It comes under the heading of various kinds of management-, profit- and ownership-sharing schemes, as have been proposed in papal social teachings from their beginnings. Where they appear, they invariably demonstrate how the "integral development of the human person through work does not impede but rather promotes the greater productivity and efficiency of work itself." This involves a change of heart and a willingness on all sides to shed the old warrior "adversary relationship" between workers and their employers. For employers it implies a recognition that "business cannot be considered only as a 'society of capital goods,'" because "it is also a 'society of persons' in which people participate in different ways and with specific responsibilities, whether they supply the necessary capital for the company's activities or take part in such activities through their labor." However, it is important to note that this does not mean the end of labor unions, which is unfortunately sometimes the dominant motive for introducing such otherwise enlightened initiatives as profit-sharing and management sharing. As Pope John Paul II indicated, "there is still need for a broad associated workers' movement directed toward the liberation and promotion of the whole person" (43). We may assume it does mean, however, that labor unions would no longer feel the need to be so aggressively militant. Also, they would probably be less busy defending the basic rights of workers than they have been in the past, when business enterprise was more a "society of capital goods" than "a society of persons" (43).

What interested the Pope more than any attempt to establish capitalism, especially the old capitalism, is the establishment of the principle of solidarity throughout society and economic life, specifically at the level where workers encounter their employers in their everyday working lives. He returned to that favorite theme of his again in closing the fourth chapter of this encyclical. There is solidarity in the fact that a man "works in order to provide for the needs of his family, his community, his nation and ultimately all humanity." Indeed, the Pope called man's collaboration in the work of his fellow employees as well as in the work of suppliers and in the customers' use of goods, a "progressively expanding chain of solidarity." And he termed "illegitimate" the ownership of the means of production "when it is not utilized or when it serves to impede the work of others in an effort to gain a profit which is not the result of the overall expansion of work and the wealth of society, but rather is the result of curbing them or of illicit exploitation, speculation or the breaking of solidarity among working people" (43).

Finally, if one is obliged to "earn one's bread by the sweat of one's brow," this also "presumes the right to do so." However one may wish to designate an economic system or a society, if "this right is systematically denied," and if "economic policies do not allow workers to reach satisfactory levels of employment," it "cannot be justified from an ethical point of view nor can that society attain social peace" (43).[21]

Chapter 5
State and Culture

This chapter takes *Centesimus Annus* beyond the economic order. It moves more into the tradition established by Leo XIII in encyclicals on the political order, some of which preceded *Rerum Novarum.*[22] Specifically, since democracy and certain democratic institutions, like Montesquieu's division of governmental powers into legislative, executive and judicial ones, are mentioned with approbation here, a quick rereading of the encyclical *Graves de Communi* (*On Christian Democracy*), issued by Leo XIII in 1901, might be appropriate. Two things are certain: first, here as in the area of economic systems, "The church has no models to present." Monarchy, provided the basic rights of people are effectively protected by an appropriate constitution, can be an acceptable form of government, as can democracy. The other point which emerges as certain is that totalitarianism—the state as, so to speak, the beginning and end of all things—is unacceptable, since it represents a "denial of the transcendent dignity of the human person who, as the visible image of the invisible God, is therefore by his very nature the subject of rights which no one may violate—no individual, group, class, nation or state" (44). Basically, it turns people into means rather than the ends for which the political process exists, just as liberal capitalism turned them into means, not the ends of the economic process.

But lest anyone should be tempted to imitate the Pharisee who thanked God that he was not like other mere mortals, Pope John Paul II adds a pointed reminder that, "Not even the majority of a social body may violate these rights by going against the minority, by isolating, oppressing or exploiting it or by attempting to annihilate it" (44).

It is entirely possible to find in alleged democracies "the formation of narrow ruling groups which usurp the power of the state for individual interests or for ideological ends" (46). Indeed, in the capitalistic order that is precisely what happened, so that Marx was able to promote the credibility of his theory about the entire social "superstructure" being subverted to the ends of the ruling capitalistic class. This is why the Pope indicates here that the democratic system is valued "inasmuch as it ensures the participation of citizens in making political choices, guarantees to the governed the possibility both of electing and holding accountable those who govern them and of replacing them through peaceful means when appropriate." However, if a democratic society becomes degraded to the point where the ritual elections are no longer cherished by the people because they do not offer a genuine choice, such democracy becomes little more than precisely a ritual. Then this powerful indictment becomes applicable: "As history demonstrates, a democracy without values easily turns into open or thinly disguised totalitarianism" (46).

At issue, once again, is true freedom in its legitimate meaning. As *Centesimus Annus* made reference in its early paragraphs to the Leo XIII encyclical *On Human Liberty,* where freedom was linked inextricably to the truth, that same theme resurfaces here as this encyclical moves toward its conclusion. "But freedom attains its full development only by accepting the truth." And, "In a world without truth, freedom loses its foundation and man is exposed to the violence of passion and to manipulation, both open and hidden" (46).

Let us reflect carefully therefore, before we surrender to the temptation to become righteous about American democracy and to propose it unreservedly to all other nations in the world, especially those recently emerging from Communist totalitarianism. Is it not the crassest kind of violation of even the most basic of human rights to allow the massive slaughter of the unborn? Or does this not qualify as an example of what the Pope had in mind in warning that, "Not even the majority of a social body may violate these rights" (44). He speaks plainly enough on this matter, so that there can be no doubt, when he refers to the tendency toward "the democratic ideal" following emergence from "communist totalitarianism..." "But for this very reason it is necessary for peoples in the process of reforming their systems to give democracy an authentic and solid foundation through the explicit recognition of those rights," including, "the right to life, an integral part of which is the right of the child to develop in the mother's womb from the moment of conception" (47). In case this is still not explicit enough, we find: "Even in countries with democratic forms of government these rights are not always fully respected." However, the Pope indicated that "we are referring not only to the scandal of abortion, but also to different aspects of the crisis within democracies themselves, which seem at times to have lost the ability to make decisions aimed at the common good." Does it not strike close to home when he states: "Certain demands which rise within society are sometimes not examined in accordance with criteria of justice and morality, but rather on the basis of the electoral or financial power of the groups promoting them." Should we not perhaps be examining our own consciences rather than the consciences of others, when we read that, "such distortions of political conduct create distrust and apathy, with a subsequent decline in the political participation and civic spirit of the general population which feels abused and disillusioned" (47)?

The recent tragic history, specifically of Europe, makes clear that the Church is also a prime victim of totalitarianism in all of its forms. It was forced to fight for its life under the short-lived Nazi regime, as it continued to do so under the more long-lived Communist one. However, less noticed, less harsh, but nevertheless glaring oppression occurred, and continues to do so, even under our prized American democratic system. Parents have always had to pay double taxes in the United States if they chose to exercise their parental prerogative to have their children educated in schools oriented according to their own religious beliefs. Little mention is made of this among those who praise and extol our particular form of democracy, promoting its "separation of Church and State" as some kind of model for others to imitate. Leo XIII, whose great teaching this encyclical commemorates, felt otherwise! He referred to the so-called separation of Church and State a "fatal theory," and again, as "that fatal principle."[23] And lest any may feel that encyclicals by popes like Leo XIII and Pius XI were out of step with modern realities, the Second Vatican Council (1962-1965) denounced as a violation of distributive justice the requirement of such double taxation.[24] This is not a system which Americans can look upon with pride, especially in the face of the fact that many other countries, both democracies and monarchies, find themselves able to support church schools along with secular (public) schools.[25]

Before returning to the role of the state in economic life, Pope John Paul II closed this discussion of forms of democracy with a reaffirmation of what has been the Church's traditional attitude on the matter. "The Church respects the legitimate autonomy of the democratic order and is not entitled to express preferences for this or that institutional or constitutional solution" (47).

It is, of course, blatant folly to pretend that the state can divorce itself from its vitally important economic sector. One may wonder why the Pope would feel compelled to say in this connection: "Economic activity, especially the activity of a market economy, cannot be conducted in an institutional, juridical or political vacuum" (48). In fact, it is precisely in market economies that the myth flourished about markets working at their "magical" best if the state absented itself completely: "*Laissez faire et laissez passer, le monde va de lui-même.*"[26] In any kind of controlled or "command" economy, this will present no problem, except in the sense that there is too much intervention, or even total state control over economic life of its citizens.

Only a disordered society would present a situation where a Roman pope would feel compelled to point out certain specific functions which a state should perform for its people. These include "guarantees of individual freedom and private property as well as a stable currency and efficient public services." There is also an appropriate denunciation of "the spread of improper sources of growing rich and of easy profits deriving from illegal or purely speculative activities." However, the principle of subsidiarity is alive and well in this Pope's teaching, which means that "primary responsibility in this area belongs not to the state, but to individuals and to the various groups and associations which make up society." Nevertheless, the state "has a duty to sustain business activities by creating conditions which will ensure job opportunities, by stimulating those activities where they are lacking or by supporting them in moments of crisis." In other words, the state plays the subsidiary role—moving to "support in case of need...the internal life of a community of a lower order" and helping "to coordinate its activity with the activities of the rest of society, always with a view to the common good." Once again, the state's role is a coordinating, supportive one—a supplementary and complementary one. It is not to become a "welfare state" or a "social assistance state" seeking to provide for all of the needs of everyone. That approach "leads to a loss of human energies and an inordinate increase of public agencies which are dominated more by bureaucratic ways of thinking than by concern for serving their clients, and which are accompanied by an enormous increase in spending" (48).

From this point on, the encyclical moves toward its conclusion, which, as always in social encyclicals, is theologically based. Preparatory to that final stage, Pope John Paul II returned to the mission which the Church "received from Christ, her founder" (49). He pointed out that it continues to do what it has always done for the needy, including "offering…material assistance in ways that neither humiliate nor reduce them to mere objects of assistance." We move inevitably, therefore, to the role of "active charity" and more! There is the specific need in our times, ravaged by centuries of rampant individualism, to affirm and inspire "a concrete commitment to solidarity and charity." Although solidarity begins with "the mutual support of husband and wife," making the family "a community of work and solidarity," in times when economic life becomes seriously disordered, the family sometimes "finds itself without the necessary support from the state and without sufficient resources" (49).

We have been suggesting throughout these commentaries that the proposal of Pius XI in *Quadragesimo Anno* for "vocational orders" is not by any means obsolete. As indicated previously, recent popes have used the broader, more comprehensive term, "intermediate bodies." Here we find again the message that "other intermediate communities exercise primary functions and give life to specific networks of solidarity." What forms such bodies may take is left up to people operating in particular historic and cultural contexts. But in order that states not be overburdened and end up being "welfare states" or "social assistance states," it is clear that there must be other social bodies in place between the individuals at the bottom, and the state at the top. Here the Pope made it clear that today, in the absence of such intermediate organizations, the "individual…is often suffocated between two poles represented by the state and the marketplace." Such organizations, instead, are "real communities of persons" which "strengthen the social fabric, preventing society from becoming an anonymous and impersonal mass as unfortunately often happens today." It should be clear from this that the Church has never abandoned the idea of intermediate social organs, which are autonomous and not simply organs of the state, but which are kept within the bounds marked out by the overall common good, by a vigilant, but not domineering, state. The Pope concluded these observations with a significant reminder: "People lose sight of the fact that life in society has neither the market nor the state as its final purpose, since life itself has a unique value which the state and the market must serve" (49).

What is to be done in this regard is suggested in the next paragraph. The "obsolete forms…can be usefully replaced by others more suited to the times" (50). Nevertheless, when the young challenge these old forms and patterns, they should not simply "destroy or reject (them) a priori." It is better to distinguish "the valid elements in the tradition from the false and erroneous ones." One may apply this to the old guild structure of the Middle Ages. The guilds involved an idea which is perennially valid: vocational or occupational solidarity. Their specific form has outlived its usefulness in modern industrial society. But the ongoing "adversarial relationship" between those who hire, own, and manage, with those who work and carry out the instructions of those who hire, own, and manage—all working in the same firm, industry, or occupation—has also certainly outlived its usefulness.

Ultimately, although systemic changes are in order after a long period of societal dissolution, personal conversion is critical. The individual person must exercise "his creativity, intelligence and knowledge of the world and people." Also he must display "his capacity for self-control, personal sacrifice, solidarity and readiness to promote the common good" (51). Therefore, it becomes clear that "the first and most important task is accomplished within man's heart." It is here that the Church has a vital role to play because it "promotes those aspects of human behavior which favor a true culture of peace, as opposed to models in which the individual is lost in the crowd, in which the role of his initiative and freedom is neglected and in which his greatness is posited in the arts of conflict and war." It accomplishes this by instilling "an active commitment to our neighbor and demands of us a shared responsibility for all of humanity" (51). Thus we have here reference back to the social virtues, justice and charity, as applied to our neighbors individually, and to the common good, even though those precise terms are not used here. More recently, these have been extended to include also the virtue of solidarity. As has been made clear in social teachings, especially since those by John XXIII, the common good extends precisely to "all of humanity."

Here Pope John Paul II referred back to what may appear like an unlikely source—Pope Benedict XV. Yet, it was that all-but-forgotten Pope who set forth sound principles for peace which would have shortened World War I before it reached the monstrous dimensions that it eventually did reach; and his ardent pleas and counsel would have averted the vindictive terms of the Versailles Treaty which set the stage for the second, even more deadly, World War. Pope John Paul II appealed to that benevolent pontiff's efforts in referring to his own attempts to prevent what he calls here "the recent tragic war in the Persian Gulf" (52).

He echoed the cry also of Paul VI before the United Nations: "Never again war!" Yet this is not the futile clamor of thoughtless pacifism, because we are told: "...it must not be forgotten that at the root of war there are usually real and serious grievances: injustices, suffered, legitimate aspirations frustrated, poverty and the exploitation of multitudes of desperate people who see no real possibility of improving their lot by peaceful means." Hence, since "another name for peace is development...as there is a collective responsibility for avoiding war, so there is a collective responsibility for promoting development" (52).

A significant parallel was drawn here between what goes on within individual states, and what should come to apply among states. "Just as the time has finally come when in individual states a system of private vendetta and reprisal has given way to the rule of law, so too a similar step forward is now urgently needed in the international community." The Pope continued this analogy. "Just as within individual societies it is possible and right to organize a solid economy which will direct the functioning of the market to the common good, so too there is similar need for adequate interventions on the international level." This represents a difficult but urgent agenda for the nations of the world as they progress through the third millennium of the Christian era. And sacrifice is involved, "sacrificing the positions of income and power enjoyed by the more developed economies." Specifically this could involve "making important changes in established lifestyles in order to limit the waste of environmental and human resources" (52).

Chapter 6
Man is the Way of the Church

This final chapter sums up once again the reason for the Church's involvement in what has always appeared to some as purely secular matters. Among these are persons who are discomforted by the social teachings because they seriously challenge the status quo which has been kind to them, sometimes out of any proportion to what they deserved. But there are also others who remonstrate on pietistic grounds. The Church has been accused of being excessively humanistic, indeed, in even a secularistic manner. All such "dissenters" might profit from reflecting on this final chapter which is an apology for Church intervention in "human affairs," and specifically in what may appear to be the most pedestrian of human affairs: economic matters.

Pope John Paul II made it clear that the Church was not getting involved in such matters "in order to recover former privileges or to impose her own vision" (53). Instead, "Her sole purpose has been care and responsibility for man, who has been entrusted to her by Christ himself." Nor does she deal "with man in the 'abstract,' "but with the real, 'concrete,' 'historical' man." And what is more, she is concerned about "*each individual*, since each one is included in the mystery of Redemption, and through this mystery Christ has united himself with each one forever." Referring to *Rerum Novarum*, of which this encyclical commemorated the centennial anniversary, the Polish Pope pronounced it "a valid contribution to socio-economic analysis at the end of the 19th century." However, more importantly from the standpoint of Catholics in particular, he proclaimed it a part "of the Magisterium...together with many other documents of this nature." That should lay to rest the cavalier attitude among some Catholics regarding the significance of their Church's social teachings, as though they are somehow extrinsic to the mainstream of its role as teacher. To further emphasize that point John Paul II stated: "Thus the Church's social teaching is itself a valid instrument of evangelization" (54). Indeed, in terms of its evangelizing mission, it is addressed also to "every human being."

There followed the interesting statement that "Christian anthropology...is really a chapter of theology" (55). That is why, once again, the Church's social doctrine which reflects Christian anthropology "belongs to the field of theology and particularly of moral theology." That repeats what this same Pope wrote in *Sollicitudo Rei Socialis*. It also reaffirms what Blessed John XXIII said when he proclaimed "that the social teachings proclaimed by the Catholic Church cannot be separated from her traditional teaching regarding man's life."[27]

It was the hope of Pope John Paul II that the Church's social teachings will reach especially "the countries which following the collapse of 'real socialism' are experiencing a serious lack of direction in the work of rebuilding." But there is reference also to two other kinds of nations. There are the "Western countries" which "run the risk of seeing this collapse as a one-sided victory of their own economic system and thereby failing to make necessary corrections in that system." Anyone who tends to see our "capitalistic" or "market economies" as representing completed and perfect societies might benefit by reflecting on that statement. And finally, the Pope mentioned also the Third World countries which "are experiencing more than ever the tragedy of underdevelopment, which is becoming more serious with each passing day" (56).[28]

There is a reminder that the Church, time and again accused of the many faults to be found in its individual members, also has done its share of putting the Gospel message into action. Thus, "...down the centuries monks tilled the land, men and women religious founded hospitals and shelters for the poor, confraternities as well as individual men and women of all states of life devoted themselves to the needy and to those on the margins of society, convinced as they were that Christ's words—'as you did it to one of the least of these my brethren, you did it to me' (Matt. 25:40)—were not intended to remain a pious wish, but were meant to become a concrete life commitment" (57).

And they do so still! The name of Blessed Mother Teresa of Calcutta has become a household word in our time. And her reputation proves what the Pope said in this concluding portion of *Centesimus Annus.* "Today more than ever, the church is aware that her social message will gain credibility more immediately from the witness of actions than as a result of its internal logic and consistency" (57). That "internal logic and consistency" all too often even becomes the object of much controversy so that, instead of clarification and acceptance, we end up with a confused Babel. Few will reject the work of a Francis of Assisi, or of Mother Teresa whose spirituality resembles his so remarkably.

Leo XIII, whose great encyclical this equally great encyclical commemorates, lamented "with sorrow that the ideologies of his time, especially liberalism and Marxism," opposed the kind of cooperation needed to solve the problems generated by "new things" at the end of the last century. Now Pope John Paul II, having witnessed remarkable events in most recent times, ends on what may be viewed as an optimistic note, because in the century since 1891, "many things have changed, especially in recent years" (60). "The world today is ever more aware that solving serious national and international problems is not just a matter of economic production or of juridical or social organization, but also calls for specific ethical and religious values as well as changes of mentality, behavior and structures." The Pontiff even allowed himself to express "a reasonable hope that the many people who profess no religion will also contribute to providing the social question with the necessary ethical foundation." And he anticipated that "the various religions, now and in the future will have a preeminent role in preserving peace and in building a society worthy of man" (60). All such hopes are the reason why this and recent social encyclicals since the time of John XXIII have been addressed also "To All Men and Women of Good Will."

Centesimus Annus concluded with what one may consider a "Lincolnesque" view of the contemporary condition—the "new things" of our own time. John Paul II alluded to the remark by Leo XIII that industrialized society brought with it "'a yoke little better than that of slavery itself'" (61). Now we have a situation, addressed by the Church in recent social encyclicals, where "too many people live, not in the prosperity of the Western world, but in the poverty of the developing countries amid conditions which are still 'a yoke little better than that of slavery itself.'" Thus, the condition which Leo XIII addressed a century ago has now been written large: it is a worldwide condition of virtual slavery existing side-by-side with "consumerism" and profligate extravagance on the part of the few. And the tragedy now is that we are no longer talking about slavery imposed by a system which has disintegrated before our eyes of its own inherent flaws. Instead there is "a yoke little better than that of slavery itself," resulting from inhumane treatment of fellow human beings in a world which has announced itself as dedicated to "humanity."

Since the beginning of recorded history, the start of a new millennium has been a supremely rare occasion. Following the birth of Christ which marked the start of the first Christian millennium, mankind has been privileged only once before to witness such a turning point in history. Perhaps that is why the millennial allusion recurs often in the teachings of Pope John Paul II. After indicating that *Centesimus Annus,* like *Rerum Novarum,* "comes almost at the threshold of a new century," he affirmed that God's church will provide light for humanity "on its journey toward its eternal destiny" also in "the third millennium." This Marian Pope did not conclude without reference to "Mary, the mother of the redeemer," whom he asked also to "accompany humanity toward the next millennium..." (62).

Notes

1. Significantly, the Pope referred here to "what we nowadays call the principle of solidarity." To this commentator's knowledge, the only two persons who make reference specifically to "the principle of solidarity" are Pope John Paul II who, in *Sollicitudo Rei Socialis,* declared solidarity to be also "undoubtedly a *Christian virtue,*" and the German Jesuit economist, Heinrich Pesch. Cf. Heinrich Pesch, *Lehrbuch der Nationalökonomie,* (Freiburg: Herder, 1924), 1: 33ff, 408ff. See also: the English translation of that work by *Lehrbuch der Nationalökonomie/Teaching Guide to Economics,* trans. Rupert J. Ederer (Lewiston, NY: Edwin Mellen Press, 2002), vol. 1, bk. 1, 36ff.; vol. 1, bk. 2, 196ff.

2. The term "solidarity" appeared with increasing frequency in the relevant sense especially in the allocutions and addresses of Pius XII. Also, we find Pius XI, before him, including social charity as a specific virtue along with social justice, in *Quadragesimo Anno,* without offering a specific definition of it. Now, in *Centesimus Annus,* Pope John Paul II equated the Christian virtue, solidarity, with social charity. Moral theologians would do a service to their Church by researching and including in their textbooks this important social virtue which popes have now for more than a half century included in their social teachings.

3. We must recall once again that in the first year of his pontificate (1878) Leo XIII issued an encyclical *On Socialism* (*Quod Apostolici Muneris*). Karl Marx was still alive then, and the first volume of *Das Kapital* had appeared just eleven years earlier. All but forgotten is the fact that Pius IX already condemned what he called "these most fatal errors of Socialism and Communism" when socialists were little more than a gaggle of

pamphleteering agitators. (Cf. *Quanta Cura*, 1864, and the accompanying *Syllabus of Errors*).

4. Auguste Comte, for example, who claimed to be the discoverer of the *solidarity* concept, saw that principle as deriving from the natural sciences. Cf. Pesch, 1: 410. (Pesch/Ederer, 1, 2, 197).

5. Early in Franklin D. Roosevelt's long tenure as President of the United States, much significant social legislation was passed providing for minimum wages, regulating hours of work, protecting the workers' right to organize, and establishing the present system of social security in old age, and unemployment insurance. Early in his administration, Roosevelt was probably influenced by two clergymen, Msgr. John A. Ryan, and Rev. Charles E. Coughlin, who later opposed the President. Also, Senator Robert Wagner of New York, eventually a convert to Catholicism, who steered much of that legislation, was knowledgeable about the Church's social teachings.

6. The prosperity of Great Britain, at its peak, could be explained to a considerable extent in terms of its immense colonial possessions with their abundance of raw materials.

7. For an excellent treatment of this matter, see B. W. Dempsey, S. J., *The Functional Economy*, (Englewood Cliffs: Prentice-Hall, 1958), chap. 21.

8. That is an eventuality which is less likely to occur in present-day market forms ranging from oligopoly to outright monopoly, and including only rarely something approaching what economic theorists call "perfect competition." The latter involves a large number of sellers on the supply side of the market, none of which, acting individually, can establish the market price for the product that is in no sense unique, but rather in textbook terms, "homogeneous." It is the market form which most economists regard as a rare if not virtually extinct form. Briefly, it is precisely some approximation to perfect competition which could give rise to the kind of "just price" that the medieval analysts saw as resulting from mutual agreement among buyers and sellers in "free bargaining." More often than not in our time, pricing is largely dictated by sellers who enjoy varying degrees of dominance in the market either individually or by some form of tacit agreement with other sellers. Thus, while a "just price" still may and ought to obtain in any market form, one cannot assume that it will result automatically, any more than a wage will be just simply because it was agreed upon between workers and their employers. There must be significant, conscious ethical input in the price determination process, especially on the part of the sellers where they represent the dominant force in the market. Ultimately, if necessary, and following the principle of subsidiarity, public authorities may intervene and should do so, all else failing. ("Vocational orders" as proposed by Pius XI could accomplish this, with public authorities exercising vigilant supervision and intervening where necessary).

9. Cf. for example, Michael Novak, "Capitalism Rightly Understood: The View of Christian Humanism," *Faith and Reason,* XVII, No. 4 (Winter 1991), 317-352. Novak, a theologian, was severely critical of earlier encyclicals including those by John Paul II. He is better disposed toward *Centesimus Annus,* because, in his view, the Pope came around to favoring capitalism and the market economy.

10. This was reported early in 1992 by the U. S. Food and Nutrition Service. No such scandalous, anomalous situation exists in the German and Japanese economies both of which are socially oriented market economies.

11. Milton Friedman, the economist who was a leading spokesman for free markets in the original, classical sense, for example, holds a directly contrasting view. Friedman responded, "No," to the question whether businesses have moral responsibilities. His reply appeared in an article entitled: "The Social Responsibility of Business is to Increase Its Profits." Cf. Thomas R. Swartz and Frank J. Bonello, ed., *Taking Sides: Clashing Views on Controversial Economic Issues,* (Guilford, CT: Dushkin Publ. Group, 1982),

29-34.

12. Rupert J. Ederer, "Is the Pope a Convert to Capitalism?," *Fidelity* XI (March 1992), 14–20.

13. Love Canal came to symbolize ecological depredation. It is an area in the city of Niagara Falls, NY, which is built at the site of the great natural wonders of the world. Love Canal was used for toxic waste disposal by a chemical firm. Later it was filled in and a housing development was built over it. Many years before this was discovered two professors, including this commentator, pointed out to students at a nearby college that ecologically irresponsible actions were violations of the virtue of social justice. That was several decades before "ecology" became common currency in our national vocabulary. Fr. Albert Beckwith, S. J. and I both studied at St. Louis University where we were privileged to learn about social teachings of the Church from the learned Jesuit, Bernard W. Dempsey.

14. John 6:60. "This is a hard saying. Who can listen to it?"

15. This adds up precisely to "economism," an uncommon expression used by Pope John Paul II in his social encyclicals, and by Heinrich Pesch, S. J. in his *Lehrbuch der Nationalökonomie.*

16. In the airline industry, for example, venerable firms which were pioneers in air passenger travel, like Eastern Airlines and Pan-American Airlines, among others, were destroyed by what may be termed "cut-throat competition," or perhaps more appropriately, given the industry in question, by "fly-by-night competitors," following the onset of the deregulation urge in the U. S. That policy began with the Carter administration and continued afterwards. For transportation and public utilities, regulation had long been recognized as necessary. Indeed, many of the same tactics which brought disorder to the airline industry were used in the railroad industry in its early years, leading to the passage of a succession of laws beginning with the Interstate Commerce Act of 1887.

17. Cf. Karl Marx, *A Contribution to the Critique of Political Economy* (Progress Publishers: Moscow, 1970), 20-21.

18. Starting in the 19th century and continuing until the present, economists have increasingly endeavored to represent the terms of their science mathematically, despite the fact that it is a social science, and that the human dimension can never be reduced to quantitative dimensions. Meanwhile even the most fundamental terms, like "capitalism," are left in imprecise form, so that when two or more economists enter into serious discussion they are frequently not talking about the same thing!

19. During the start of what historians call the modern era, absolute monarchies began to sponsor and to subsidize the emerging class of capitalists under an economic regimen known in economic history as mercantilism. Karl Marx marked the start of capitalism as the point in history when, in his words, "the *chevaliers d'industrie*...succeed in supplanting the *chevaliers* of the sword." Cf. Karl Marx, *Kapital* (Chicago: Charles H. Kerr & Co.,1918), 1: 787. According to Marx, "Although we come across the first beginnings of capitalist production as early as the 14th or 15th century, sporadically, in certain towns of the Mediterranean, the capitalistic era dates from the 16th century." (Ibid. 787).

20. Paul VI, *Populorum Progressio* and John Paul II, *Sollicitudo Rei Socialis.*

21. In this commentator's opinion, if Pope John Paul II could have stepped down from his official capacity as being the head of the Roman Catholic Church, he would probably have proposed Solidarism as a "third way" between socialism which has failed, and the surviving contender which is failing. Why he did not include that system among the "more appropriate" names which he proposed in this encyclical, only he knew. One could surmise that, among other things, the term was and remains too far out of the mainstream of present-day thinking, which is, if anything, recidivistic in this matter. Also,

Heinrich Pesch, S.J., who formulated solidarism specifically as an alternative economic system (a "third way") was a trained economist, and he was entitled to do so. Pesch (d. 1926) was alive during the early Weimar Republic years when Nazis and Communists were contending for control; and he wrote pamphlets in support of a solidaristic system for the opposing Catholic Center Party. However, one could imagine the reaction in a largely secularized world to having a pope propose as an alternate economic system one devised by a Jesuit! Nevertheless, Pesch's views on what economic life is all about, and specific concepts like the *principle of solidarity,* are found throughout *Laborem Exercens, Sollicitudo Rei Socialis,* and *Centesimus Annus.*

22. Some of these are referred to early on in this encyclical in a footnote reference. In addition to *Libertas Praestantissimum* (*On Human Liberty*, 1888) mentioned in the text of the encyclical, we find listed in the footnote also: *Arcanum Divinae Sapientiae* (*On Christian Citizenship*, 1880), *Diuturnum Illud* (*On Civil Government*, 1881), and *Graves de Communi* (*On Christian Democracy*, 1901). Not mentioned is *Immortale Dei* (*On the Christian Constitution of States*, 1885). All of these are addressed directly to the political order, and they are still relevant and helpful for dispelling the ongoing confusion about such matters in our own time, especially for gaining a sensible grasp of what true "democracy" is.

23. Cf. Leo XIII, *Libertas Praestantissimum,* pars. 18-39. We may apply here the scriptural quotation, "He who is not with me is against me" (Matt.12:30). How literally "fatal" such separation can be is evident now in the millions of innocent lives taken in the abortion holocaust!

24. It was Pius XI who first drew attention to the implications of distributive justice in this matter of equal opportunity for parents who exercise their prior right to be educators of their children by choosing schools where there is religious education. Cf. his encyclical, *Divini Illius Magistri* (*On the Christian Education of Youth*, 1929), par. 81. The Second Vatican Council reaffirmed that position both in its *Declaration on Christian Education,* par. 6, and in the *Declaration on Religious Liberty*, par. 5.

25. In Canada, for example, tax money paid by parents for their children's schooling is assigned to the schools of their choice, including church-run schools. The same applies in Germany, and even in countries where there is an established church, as in England.

26. This statement is attributed to Jacques Claude Vincent de Gournay (1712-1759), although it is not certain that he was actually its author. In any case, it bespeaks the consensus about government intervention in economic life among Physiocrats and those who adopted their liberal economic philosophy. Adam Smith used the expression, "the invisible hand" in defense of the same basic ideology.

27. John XXIII, *Mater et Magistra*, 222.

28. In the same week that I was completing this commentary on *Centesimus Annus,* the United Nations Development Program, in its third annual report, presented figures showing that the income disparities between rich and poor nations more than doubled over the past 30 years. (Reported in "The Wealth of Nations," *U.S. News and World Report,* 4 May 1992, 54).

Chapter 8
Benedict XVI
Caritas in Veritate

The social encyclical *Caritas in Veritate* by Pope Benedict XVI, the German scholar-pope, is dated for the *Solemnity of the Holy Apostles Peter and Paul*, 29 June 2009. It was not finally released until 7 July 2009. The delay was attributed to, among other things, the perceived need to factor in the implications of the banker-driven, speculation-based collapse of the financial system in the United States, which quickly spread to economies worldwide in the autumn of 2008.

It is the eighth papal encyclical addressed to the economic order, thus rounding out an extensive cycle of such teachings begun by Leo XIII in 1891. Overall, *Rerum Novarum* was about the cardinal virtue, justice, as were several subsequent social encyclicals. The title *Caritas in Veritate,* those being the first words of the original text, suggests a continuing shift in emphasis toward the theological virtue of charity. Clearly though, a recognition of the important role of the virtue of charity for the restoration of social order had not and could not ever have been absent from the Catholic Church's concern in that area. This was made clear by Pope John Paul II in *Centesimus Annus* (10), the last of his great trilogy of social encyclicals.[1] Speaking of what he termed the "principle of solidarity," he indicated that Leo XIII had used the term "friendship," while Pius XI employed, as the Polish Pope put it, "the equally meaningful term 'social charity.'" And he noted further that Pope Paul VI, whom Pope Benedict XVI was commemorating by *Caritas in Veritate*, had used the expression, "civilization of love."

To mention the virtue of social charity, indicating its importance, was one thing. It is a reflection of the particular genius of John Paul II that he had already undertaken to present an extended definition of it in the second of his trilogy of social encyclicals, *Sollicitudo Rei Socialis* (1987). There, after explaining its meaning, he declared: "*Solidarity* is undoubtedly a *Christian virtue* [Italics as in the text]" (40). Subsequently, in *Centesimus Annus* (10) he closed an important circle by identifying the "principle of solidarity" with what Pius XI had presented in *Quadragesimo Anno* (88) as "social charity."

The author of *Caritas in Veritate* does not pretend to have expertise in the economic science. The special competence of popes who have written encyclicals relating to the economy has to do with moral theology and the natural law as these apply to economic life. Since the Catholic Church has gotten intensely involved in this area over the past century, some understanding of how the economic science has both reflected and also to some degree given direction to the actual economy can be useful. Familiarity with the beginnings of the science and early economic history will show how the two virtues, justice and charity, as applied to the social order were deleted from it since its beginnings.

Economics began humbly but honorably, deriving its name from the two Greek words *oikos* and *nomos*. Taken together they translate freely as *management* or *governance of the household.* That, ultimately up to the level of the national household, is what economic activity is all about. Therefore, regardless of its present shortcomings, it is a valid science about a vital sector of human existence.[2] It is nevertheless a "work-in-progress" and not an ancient science as compared, for example, with theology or philosophy. That is notwithstanding the fact that two venerable ancient Greeks already provided some impressive original notions about economic matters: I refer to Plato's *Republic* and Aristotle's *Ethics* and *Politics.* As a science, i.e., as a systematized body of knowledge about how people organize human and material resources to satisfy their temporal wants, economics began to take shape in a much later period of history amid the growing importance of rival European national states. It was also a time, incidentally, when theology had been marginalized, and philosophy had become disoriented—a time which ironically has nevertheless been designated by historians as the Enlightenment.

Scandalized perhaps by the bickering and eventually some horrendous deadly Reformation–and post-Reformation–era conflicts over the message which God had entrusted to mankind through the ministry of his Son and a motley crew of twelve, including some Galilean fishermen and a tax collector, philosophers contrived an indifferent, even apathetic, god. For some this was a distant and disinterested deity which entrusted the operation of the universe, including economic life, to laws devised and placed into operation by it from the beginning. Men had only to "discover" these laws so as to avoid interfering with their free operation.

With theism relegated to the uneducated peasantry, the more "enlightened" folks came to be known as deists. They influenced a group of men in France called Physiocrats—the first ever to refer to themselves as *Les Économistes*—who ventured to explain certain "natural laws" which applied in economic life. (Present-day economists, most of them positivists, may be surprised to know that their science is a spin-off of what happened to theology during the Enlightenment). Relying on the secure basis of the universal instinct for self-preservation, they translated this into self-interest in economic activity, with the equally universal (i.e., natural) competitive instinct providing the necessary control mechanism. That gave rise to the expression: *Laissez faire, laissez passer, le monde va de lui-même;* Later there came the law of markets, "discovered" by Jean Baptiste Say (1767-1832), revealing that supply eventually gives rise to its own equivalent demand. Then, to the great relief of employers everywhere, there was what certain socialists would later designate as the iron law of wages. According to it, population would adjust automatically so as to keep the wages of workers at bare subsistence. Such economic theories provided a welcome prospect especially among the rising class of merchant-capitalists and later industrial-capitalists, who felt increasingly stifled by all manner of regulations imposed by governments as well as by remnants of the medieval guilds. During that period, which economic historians have termed the Mercantilist Era, there was a general obsession among rulers to make their respective states dominant among the rising and contending national states by hook or by crook. Hook-or-crook involved all manner of regulations to assure a positive balance of trade along with the influx of gold and silver to cover the negative balances incurred by the other trading partners.

The *laissez-faire* world-view reflected the emergent worship of the goddess *Liberty* that came with the French Revolution, involving among other things the eventual vile desecration of the great Notre Dame Cathedral in Paris. It persisted long after the worst excesses of that Revolution had given way to what, following the Napoleonic episode, appeared to be more sedate conditions. What is more, it shaped the economic science which was emerging at that time into what came to be known as free market- or liberal economics—the latter expression having since evolved widely in contemporary usage into its virtual opposite. With the growing political and economic power of Great Britain, the influence of figures like Adam Smith, Thomas Malthus, Jeremy Bentham, David Ricardo, and John Stuart Mill came to play a predominant role in the development of the young science. The kind of economics, now termed classical, forged by these brilliant but philosophically misguided men was what Thomas Carlyle characterized aptly as "the dismal science." The astute Scottish-born historian also termed as the "pig philosophy" Bentham's ingenuous theory that all human actions are geared solely to deriving pleasure and avoiding pain, with individuals, rather than governments, obviously being better judges of what is pleasurable for them. That led Bentham to "pearls of wisdom" like: "Nothing ought to be done or attempted by government." He had a great influence on John Stuart Mill whose libertarianism, among other things, eventually got his work placed on the Catholic Church's *Index of Forbidden Books*. Meanwhile in his *Christmas Carol* and elsewhere, the novelist Charles Dickens employed his great genius to depict the glum social conditions to which free market capitalism gave rise.

Adam Smith (1723-1790), a Scot, was perhaps the most illustrious and influential among the classical economists. In his worldwide best-selling *Inquiry Into the Nature and Causes of the Wealth of Nations,* he dealt a lethal blow to the critical notion of the common good for which the state is in principle the ultimate protector. The book appeared first in 1776 and was eventually translated into all major world languages. In a chapter dealing with "Restraints on Particular Imports," Smith entrusted the "public interest" to each person's pursuit of his own self-interest. In his words that meant leaving the welfare of the nation to "every individual" who "intends only his own gain," being "in this, as in so many other cases, led by an invisible hand to promote an end which was no part of his intention." Thus, the man who began his scholarly career as a moral philosopher—an ethician—affirmed that simplistic act of faith by a remark brimming with cynical disdain for purposeful individual actions on behalf of the common good: "I have never known much good done by those who affected to trade for the public good." He termed that: "…an affectation, indeed not very common among merchants, and very few words need to be employed in dissuading them from it."[3] Indeed, "very few words" were employed in the immediate period, and for many years to come, to dissuade men from curbing their swinish instincts in economic life. The quality which the first German pope in over a half millennium would term "gratuitousness" (*Caritas in Veritate*, 34) vanished more and more from economic life. In the meantime, British economics carried the day, along with the aggressive spread of the Empire which came to include eventually one fourth of the world's land area. The undeniable leadership of Great Britain in advancing the Industrial Revolution also played a part. The emerging class of capitalists and entrepreneurs who were shaping the economic structures of the era predictably preferred free market economics, and they came to apply it with full force. Thus the antics of the pigsty, where avarice predominated, became part and parcel of economic activity as reflected in the developing economic science—a science which, in keeping with emerging positivistic inclinations, often reflected events more than it guided them.

In the ensuing economic tumult, the rank-and-file workingmen became the new serfs, while lacking the minimum security enjoyed by the medieval serf class. Poor wages for service in the emerging capitalist plutocracy constituted the high price paid for being emancipated from feudal lords and the landed aristocracy. In the capitalistic system the worker came to be treated like merchandise on the market. Other industrial nations on the European continent and elsewhere had no choice but to conduct themselves in the same manner if they wished to remain afloat in the competitive struggle. The majority of mankind, including colonial subjects who provided an abundant supply of cheap labor in the imperial territories (which also provided cheap raw materials for the budding industries), emerged as the "down-trodden working class." Their plight eventually stimulated the awakening of certain revolutionary spirits on the European continent, notably in Germany and France. The continent that had given birth to the free market ideology now nurtured equally talented agitators who fancied the prospect of putting an end to capitalist hegemony.

Karl Marx, a German-born Jew-turned-Lutheran-turned-atheist (1818-1883), was one among many socialists; but he left his mark as the most methodical and allegedly "scientific" one in moving the ideological pendulum to the opposite end of its arc from liberal or free-market capitalism. Other socialists before and after him included the moderate Frenchmen Claude Saint Simon (1760-1825) and Charles Fourier (1772-1837) who were classed as "Utopian." More radical socialists followed, like Louis Blanc (1811-1882), and Pierre Proudhon (1809-1865) who proclaimed that "Property is theft." There were other German revolutionaries besides Marx, like Karl Rodbertus (1805-1875) who proclaimed an "iron law of wages" (subsistence), and Ferdinand Lassalle

(1825-1864) who first spoke of capital as "the dead instrument of past labor." Then there were figures after Marx, like Karl Kautsky (1854-1938), and the two practicing revolutionaries, Vladimir Lenin (1870-1924) and Leon Trotsky (1879-1940)—who began putting Marx's nightmarish scheme into operation in 1917. More faint-hearted followers emerged who were referred to as "Revisionists" because they envisioned a more evolutionary approach to the socialist vision, like Eduard Bernstein (1850-1932). Ultimately the world bears witness to the grim fact that the ideas promoted by Karl Marx eventually inspired a revolution which turned the world upside down in 1917; and it persists even now in somewhat bastardized form in the most populous nation on earth—China. While the rulers of modern China appear to have opted for what they perceive as the best in Marxian socialism, along with the best in Western capitalism, they ended up instead with the worst of each.

The appalling results as the world reshaped itself in the industrial era should come as no surprise. These included also the increasing abandonment of belief in God whom the Deists had sought to transform into an indolent caricature, now deemed preposterous and irrelevant by people like Marx, to name just one among a growing number of rebellious philosophers as well as economists. Perhaps it was that infringement on its domain which at last drew the active attention of the Catholic Church, in what Pope Benedict XVI himself characterized as a "slow" reaction.[4] Belated or not, it did at last come in 1891 in the dramatic format of the encyclical *Rerum Novarum* by Pope Leo XIII. The Catholic Church felt forced to make its voice heard first of all in opposition to the all-out socialist attack on the right of private ownership of the material means of production, along with the flagrant abuse of that right by the capitalists. Then there was the need to reverse the dismantling of the all-important notion of the common good by the free marketeers, while at the same time opposing the grotesque one-sided caricature of it introduced by the socialists in the form of their hate-driven exclusivist class concept. That was but the first of the several encyclicals addressed to the economic order by successive Roman Pontiffs up to the latest one—*Caritas in Veritate*.

The usual gaggle of speed-readers showed up early to critique this sometimes complex work by Benedict XVI. Not much of what the Pope, a brilliant and insightful scholar, writes is lacking in complexity. So the encyclical does not lend itself well to a quick read. For the unsympathetic and impatient, that can lead to all manner of inane and often ideologically based intimations like: social encyclicals are by no means infallible proclamations; they are prudential in nature; they suffer from the peculiar ideological bias of European popes along with their advisors and writers, and so forth. And, of course, there is the predictable litany of "the-pope-should-have"–type second-guessing by those who are handicapped by a conviction that they certainly know better. Lost in the frenzy is, among other things, the important lesson presented by Pope John Paul II in the second of his important trilogy of social encyclicals, *Sollicitudo Rei Socialis* (1987). There the Polish Pope, who held doctorates in both theology and philosophy (ethics), pointed out that the Church's social doctrine "belongs to the field, not of *ideology*, but of *theology* and particularly of moral theology" (41). In the area of faith and morals, the Pope by himself or in council with his bishops is accepted by Catholics as the sole divinely protected teacher.

The German Pope is by training, inclination, and long practice a theologian. This is reflected perhaps in the fact that all three of his encyclicals thus far, including the latest one, address the theological virtues: *Deus Caritas Est* (2005); *Spe Salvi* (2007); and *Caritas in Veritate* (2009). John Paul II had sought to emphasize that in its social doctrine the Church is teaching in the area of morals. The moral theology courses which I took as a young man in the seminary did indeed involve important tracts on the virtues. These included specifically the theological virtues of faith, hope, and charity, as well as the cardinal virtues: prudence, justice, temperance and fortitude. The early social encyclicals by Leo XIII and Pius XI placed great emphasis on justice and specifically social justice. Not that the virtue of charity was by any means omitted. Indeed the virtue of social charity was presented alongside the virtue of social justice in the landmark Pius XI social encyclical *Quadragesimo Anno* (1931) as the "[M]ore lofty and noble principles" needed to establish social order (*Quadragesimo Anno*, par. 88). Even then, a specific definition of the virtue of *social justice* was not offered until several years later (1937) in his encyclical on *Atheistic Communism* (*Divini Redemptoris*).[5] For a more detailed exposition about the virtue of social charity, many more years were to pass. This demonstrates among other things that the social teachings of the Catholic Church are a work-in-progress, and they cannot be treated simply as a discontinuous series of essays issued at the whim of various popes down through the ages.

Unfortunately Pius XII, the brilliant immediate successor of Pius XI, is neglected in matters relating to Catholic social teachings.[6] While he did not issue any social encyclicals as such, he did reaffirm, elucidate, and expand the teachings of his predecessors in his many allocutions, radio messages, and encyclicals.[7] For example, it was that great Pontiff who first used the concept "solidarity" with great and growing frequency in his masterful and eloquent *Christmas Messages,* as well as in other addresses on a wide variety of occasions. In fact the vernacular Spanish title given to his important first encyclical, *Summi Pontificatus* (1939), was *Solidaridad humana y estado totalitario.* Blessed John XXIII and Paul VI continued using the expression in the relevant sense throughout their own social encyclicals. Finally in 1987 John Paul II devoted an entire chapter (the fifth) in the second of his great trilogy of social encyclicals, *Sollicitudo Rei Socialis,* to explain the meaning and certain applications of the concept, *solidarity.* He ended up actually paraphrasing the "*Pax opus iustitia*" expression of the Old Testament Prophet Isaiah (Is. 32:17) by introducing the term, "*Opus solidaritatis pax*" (*Sollicitudo Rei Socialis*, par. 39). At that point, John Paul II had come to be known as the "Pope of Solidarity," initially because of his support of the Polish labor union, *Solidarność*, which was instrumental in making an end to the Soviet Empire—or perhaps even more so because he taught that "Solidarity is undoubtedly a Christian virtue" *(Sollicitudo Rei Socialis*, par. 40). The great Pope's trilogy was completed in 1991 in the third of his social encyclicals, *Centesimus Annus*. There he wrote, referring to "what we nowadays call the principle of solidarity," that "Pope Pius XI refers to it with the equally useful term 'social charity'" (*Centesimus Annus*, par. 10). It is the same principle that Benedict XVI cites now in his social encyclical *Caritas in Veritate* (58), where he mentions "solidarity" some forty times in the critical and relevant sense.

Caritas in Veritate is a wide-ranging social encyclical which deserves patient and careful study. An essay such as this cannot possibly do justice to all of the important elements contained in it. Certain of these stand out, and reflection on them can serve to orient and hopefully motivate further serious study. For example, one of the first things that may strike one about the Pope Benedict document is his decision to present it in commemoration of a now largely neglected social encyclical, *Populorum Progressio* (1967), by an often vilified Roman pontiff whom many among those who consider themselves to be Catholics prefer to forget. Paul VI (1963-1978) was and still is criticized by people who either blame him for the doctrinal and disciplinary tumult in the Catholic Church or for not having modernized faith and morals enough following the Second Vatican Council. That was a Council convoked by his predecessor, Blessed John XXIII, which Pope Paul then found himself in the position of seeing through to its completion. Actually it is now being gradually realized, perhaps after a more careful reading of the actual documents, that the doctrinal and liturgical chaos which followed the Council stemmed not from the conciliar decrees, but from what is termed the "spirit of Vatican II." Such dissonance is not atypical of what followed other major Councils in the Church's 2000-year history.

More specific to Pope Paul VI himself, it was he who overrode the consensus reached by the majority of the experts whom he appointed to study the moral implications of the evolving technology, especially the contraceptive pill, for the Catholic Church's teaching about birth control.[8] His prophetic encyclical *Humanae Vitae* (1968) provoked a reaction seldom equaled in intensity during the post-Reformation era. The repercussions of the ensuing virtual schism, as well as the *actual* schism stemming from liturgical changes activated in the Paul VI papacy, are grave and, at this writing, still ongoing for the Church and for the world. That being said, they are not directly relevant to what Pope Benedict XVI wished to deal with in *Caritas in Veritate.*

What is *directly* relevant here is the fact that Pope Benedict XVI is referencing this, his first strictly-speaking *social* encyclical, on the basis of ground broken by Paul VI in the encyclical *Populorum Progressio* in 1967. In fact it is in a certain sense its sequel. That is already noteworthy, since previous pontiffs have typically issued their social encyclicals to mark anniversaries of *Rerum Novarum* or some subsequent commemoration of it. One other noteworthy exception was the second social encyclical by Pope John Paul II, *Sollicitudo Rei Socialis,* which also commemorated *Populorum Progressio* in the twentieth year after its appearance. As indicated in an earlier chapter, what was distinctive about *Populorum Progressio* is that it was the first social encyclical addressing specifically the worldwide dimensions and applications of the principles, social justice and social charity—principles that Pius XI had presented for reestablishing "social order," in economic life (*Quadragesimo Anno*, par. 88). Not that the alert Pius XI (who had to deal with the three tempestuous dictatorships of Stalin, Hitler, and Mussolini) was unaware of the world-wide dimensions of the emerging situation! It is remarkable that directly after he established social justice and social charity as principles for restoring social order, he stated: "Further, it would be well if the various nations in common counsel and effort strove to promote a healthy economic cooperation by prudent pacts and institutions, since in economic matters they are largely dependent on one another, and need one another's help" (*Quadragesimo Anno*, par. 89). For 1931, that was a remarkably prescient statement, foreshadowing the intensification of the solidarity among nations. It clearly anticipated the kind of social teaching that Pope Paul VI would establish as the central theme of *Populorum Progressio*; and it would provide a continuum along with what Pius XII would have to say in his first encyclical *Summi Pontificatus* (1939). His successor, Blessed John XXIII, moved forthrightly into the worldwide dimension with both of his social encyclicals, *Mater et Magistra* (1961) and *Pacem in Terris* (1963), thus paving the way for Pope Paul VI and *Populorum Progressio* in 1967.

While the second of John Paul II's social encyclicals (*Sollicitudo Rei Socialis*) was for the most part dismissed in the United States with intense silence, *Populorum Progressio* (*On the Development of Peoples*) had aroused the ire of the kind of ideologues who were soon to become known as "neo-conservatives."[9] Aside from their bellicose political prepossessions in favor of preemptive wars deemed unjust by the leaders of the Catholic Church, in their economic ideology these folks are passionately devoted to the free market and to the kind of economic theory which inevitably comes with that, as the usury-based economic collapse in 2008 proved once again. Pope Paul VI, now hailed as "Venerable" by his Church, was treated harshly in the *Wall Street Journal* where his appeal for the global spread of social justice and social charity (solidarity) in *Populorum Progressio* was criticized editorially as "warmed over Marxism."[10] He did not endear himself to those whose thinking failed to progress beyond 18th century economics and its latter-day revival by two Jewish agnostics, Ludwig von Mises and Friedrich Hayek (a former socialist), joined later by the University of Chicago economist, Milton Friedman. It did not assuage the feelings of their disciples—many Catholics among them—that the gentle Pope, in his Apostolic Letter *Octogesima Adveniens* (35) warned in 1971 precisely against the "renewal of the liberal ideology." He was referring precisely to the revival of the archaic free market notions and the government-be-damned *laissez faire* economic philosophy of the 18th century, which beclouded the beginnings of the economic science.

Introduction

Long after the blood-drenched instrument for the "liberation" of the masses—Madame Guillotine—had faded into history, worship of the "Goddess of Liberty" persisted in later centuries specifically in the confused political and economic thinking of leaders and common folk alike.[11] As if to counter this ongoing cult, Pope Benedict devoted the Introduction to his first social encyclical to exorcising the distorted notion of liberty, which has caused such great tumult in the modern era. The critical scriptural reference in this regard is the passage from St. John's Gospel (8:32). It is cited as the first and also as the last such reference in the introductory chapter: "then you will know the truth and the truth will set you free."[12] That has little to do with the freedom which libertarians everywhere, before and since the French Revolution, have been fantasizing about as they dance freely but blindly around the edge of the abyss, time and again toppling to their doom. As its title indicates, that represents the keynote for this encyclical. Its author says here: "Fidelity to man requires fidelity to the truth, which alone is the guarantee of freedom," which paraphrases the important words of Jesus Christ as contained in the quotation from St. John's Gospel. Indeed, the fact that the scriptural quotation (John 8:32) is cited again near the close of the introduction suggests that it is the *leitmotif* of Pope Benedict's first social encyclical. He may have disappointed some by not getting involved in the more technical aspects of economics for which, as he states, he has neither the expertise nor the authority. He is not an economist or a business analyst, but the head of the largest and oldest Christian Church dating back to Jesus Christ and Peter, the Galilean fisherman. It is the same Church which Pope Paul VI had characterized as "an expert in humanity." To repeat again, it is as John Paul II pointed out in *Sollicitudo Rei Socialis* (41): the Church's social teachings have to do with theology, specifically *moral theology.* And aside from being the pope, in theology Benedict XVI, like his Polish predecessor, is a lifelong master. In the encyclical *Caritas in Veritate* he is presenting the truth specifically about charity and the gap its absence leaves, as he lays bare once again the moral causes underlying the ongoing deficiencies and encroaching breakdown of the economic order.

The present economic mayhem is related not merely to the widespread absence of charity, but also to our deficient grasp of the essential truths about human nature and human relationships specifically in the economic order. These include now, as in the time of Leo XIII, the true meaning of freedom; and it has little to do with what paleo-liberals like the French Physiocrats and the Anglo economists Adam Smith and John Stuart Mill, along with neo-liberals like Ludwig von Mises, Friedrich Hayek, and Milton Friedman have proposed for our belief. Therefore, this encyclical may be seen precisely and above all as itself a great act of charity in that its author is presenting certain important truths about man in our once again faltering socio-economic order. That is neatly summed up by what Pope Benedict affirms at the outset—that "the Church's social teaching…is *caritas in veritate in re sociali*: the proclamation of the truth of Christ's love in society" (5).

A major theme that persists throughout *Caritas in Veritate* is introduced in the last paragraph of the introduction. As it was to his predecessors, including Pope Paul VI, whom Pope Benedict is commemorating by this encyclical, the concept "solidarity" is crucial to his social teaching, directed as it is to the global "*de facto interdependence*" (9) that has become increasingly pertinent also for world peace since the era following World War II. *Populorum Progressio* was devoted in a distinctive manner to the grave implications that came with the start of the post-colonialism era. It was then that a huge gulf in living standards between the established industrialized nations and the many newly constituted independent nations—the so-called "Third World"—became an especially serious challenge to the harmony and peace of the world. Pope Benedict expressed his concern here, since interdependence which has long since become a critical fact of life "is not matched by ethical interactions of consciences and minds that would give rise to truly human development" (9). In other words, what the Benedict finds troubling here is the lack of progress in the area of social charity—the Christian virtue of solidarity proclaimed by John Paul II in *Sollicitudo Rei Socialis*, paragraph 40.[13] This becomes ever more apparent as he proceeds through the six chapters of the encyclical.

Chapter 1. The Message of *Populorum Progressio*

For a Church that still suffers from internal contention between those who felt that the Second Vatican Council provided a pretext for changing everything, including defined doctrines of faith and morals, and those who took scandal to the extent that they rejected the Council itself, Pope Benedict appropriately emphasizes here the link between the body of the Church's social doctrine and the Vatican II Pastoral Constitution *Gaudium et Spes*. The former includes *Populorum Progressio* which this encyclical commemorates explicitly, as well as *Sollicitudo Rei Socialis* issued by John Paul II twenty years later. Perhaps suggesting the reason why he is commemorating a largely overlooked encyclical by a man whose papacy was considered by some as disappointing, the German Pope tells us that "his social *magisterium*...was certainly a social teaching of great importance." He indicated the reason for this: "Paul VI clearly understood that the social question had become worldwide"; also: that "he grasped the ideal of a single family of peoples in solidarity and fraternity." Thus: "he proposed Christian charity as the principal force at the service of development" (13).

As if to assure a restoration of attention for an under-appreciated Pope, Pope Benedict draws attention to three other social documents by Pope Paul VI: first there was the *Apostolic Letter Octogesima Adveniens* (1971); and then there were two "without any direct link to social doctrine." They are the encyclical *Humanae Vitae* (1968), and the *Apostolic Letter Evangelii Nuntiandi* (1975). The first was certainly related to the body of social doctrine, as it opposed both the Marxist ideology as well as the "renewal of the liberal ideology" which in the United States is the neo-conservative (actually neo-liberal in the classic sense of the term) return to free market economics that played a large role in bringing on the economic collapse of 2008. It also warns against "the danger constituted by utopian and ideological visions that place its ethical and human dimensions in jeopardy." *Utopian* visions would seem to include the persistent and often recurring nostalgic distributism where, it seems, all would be resettled as owners of small parcels of land allowing space for agriculture with modest husbandry, or self-employment at some craft. As the saying goes: "That ship has sailed."[14] As Pope Benedict stated here: "The idea of a world without development indicates a lack of trust in man and in God." It is an opposite reaction to one of two opposing naive responses to resolving "the social question" which the Church has now been addressing seriously in its social teachings from 1891 to 2009. The Pope identifies the two here: "Idealizing technical progress or contemplating the utopia of a return to humanity's original state, are two contrasting ways of detaching progress from its moral evaluation and hence from our responsibility" (14).

While Pope Benedict states that *Humanae Vitae* and *Evangelii Nuntiandi* do not have a direct link to social doctrine, there is no denying a definite indirect link. Among other things, Thomas Malthus (1766-1834), the Anglican minister noted for his gloomy population theory, has been ranked among classical economists since long before demography emerged as a separate discipline. His theories in somewhat updated form—often characterized later as neo-Malthusianism—about an inveterate and irremediable disproportion between population growth and food supply, along with its depressing impact on wages and on economic development, continue to influence contemporary discussion until now. Indeed the population factor continues to play an important role in the economic policies of many nations.[15] It is in the widespread anti-natalist policies at large in today's world that we find the obvious link to the Church's social teaching.

As for *Evangelii Nuntiandi*, Pope Benedict indicates: "Between evangelization and human advancement—development and liberation—there are in fact profound links" (15). The Church is entitled to speak about this because it deals with "the meaning of man's pilgrimage through history in company with his fellow human beings" with reference to "the goal of that journey." That is what led Pope Paul VI to shed, as Benedict points out, "the light of the Gospel on the social questions of his time" (16). What makes *Populorum Progressio* "still timely in our day" is its vision of "development as a vocation." That "development" he informs us has to do not "with merely technical aspects of human life" but with "the meaning of man's pilgrimage through history in company with his fellow human beings...and with identifying the goal of that journey" (16).

Ultimately the notion of "development as a vocation" involves "the central place of charity within that development" (19). And since Pope Paul VI pointed out that "the causes of underdevelopment are not primarily of the material order...we are to search for them in other dimensions of the human person, first of all, in the will, which often neglects the duties of solidarity." It is worth recalling here that solidarity is the same as what Pius XI nearly a century ago referred to as "social charity." He established it then as one of the two "noble principles" (along with social justice) needed to reestablish social order! Pope Benedict now cites precisely "the lack of brotherhood among individuals and peoples as a major cause of underdevelopment; and he indicates the need for what Pope Paul VI had termed "the need for deep thought and reflection of wise men in search of a new humanism" (19). But that is not enough, Benedict continues, because reason "cannot establish fraternity.... This originates in a transcendent vocation from God the Father who loved us first, teaching us through the Son what fraternal charity is." Therein lies precisely the Christian vocation of which Pope Benedict speaks here.

Chapter 2. Human Development in Our Time

The second chapter provides the update to our own time with frequent references to the current "crisis." Basically there is an admission that, despite much economic growth, the vision of Pope Paul VI in *Populorum Progressio*—and that encyclical was already permeated by what seemed like a Cassandra-cry of desperation—remain unfulfilled. It resounds with a lament that basic flaws present in 1967 remain even now. The utility of profit as a valid concept is affirmed, so long as it remains as "a means toward an end," (21) and not as the overpowering "exclusive goal" itself that is generated by "improper means and without the common good as its ultimate end." That synopsizes in few words a quintessential element of the Catholic Church's social doctrine. Clearly the debacle of 2008 saw profit once again becoming the "exclusive goal" generated by "improper means," with the common good nowhere in sight either as a proximate goal or as its "ultimate end." At its core are financial institutions engaging in usurious transactions and speculation in real estate and other financial instruments so sophisticated that ordinary mortals cannot understand, let alone explain, what is going on. The notion of the common good is greeted by such operators even now with the same cynicism evident in Adam Smith's 18th century discussion of the public good mentioned earlier. Also, Smith's "invisible hand" is indeed at work extracting money from the citizens' pockets in order to pay the usurers. And those unscrupulous operators are basically no different from those Pope Leo XIII warned about when he spoke of the prevalence of "rapacious usury" back in 1891 (*Rerum Novarum*, par. 2). The instruments have changed. Now they include also high interest rate credit cards, and so-called adjustable-rate mortgages by which countless numbers of unenlightened citizens spent themselves into bankruptcy.

With admirable insight, Pope Benedict points out: "The world's wealth is growing in absolute terms, but inequalities are on the increase."[16] Furthermore, "In rich countries, new sectors of society are succumbing to poverty and new forms of poverty are emerging." At the same time: "In poorer areas some groups enjoy a sort of 'super-development' of a wasteful and consumerist kind which forms an unacceptable contrast with the ongoing situation of dehumanizing deprivation." And so, "'The scandal of glaring inequalities' continues" (22).

It is at this point in *Caritas in Veritate* that Pope Benedict begins to dwell on the plight of workers as a consequence of the unhealthy drift of economies into the situation leading up to the present crisis. In other words, he is back to the unfinished business of *Rerum Novarum* faced by Leo XIII. The pressure to "outsource production at low cost" leads among other things to "deregulation of the labor market." (25). That may lead, among other things, to "a downsizing of social security systems...with consequent grave danger for the rights of workers." Benedict then speaks of a resultant "powerlessness" on the part of workers' associations, and of "trade union organizations" experiencing "greater difficulty in carrying out their task of representing the interests of workers." In the United States, after the enactment of significant progressive labor legislation during the New Deal era in the 1930s, there followed an unprecedented growth in union membership and power. Soon after World War II a reverse reaction set in beginning with the passage of the Taft-Hartley Act in 1947. Today, American labor unions represent scarcely half as many workers as in 1945; that is aside from government employee unions. which developed as a relatively new concept starting in the 1960s (they represent in certain significant respects a different phenomenon). Since then "traditional networks of solidarity have more and more obstacles to overcome.... [T]he repeated calls issued within the Church's social doctrine beginning with *Rerum Novarum* for the promotion of workers' associations that can defend their rights must therefore be honored today even more than in the past" (25).

Pope Benedict XVI associates the growing "uncertainty over working conditions" with "a climate of deregulation" which definitely became a factor in countries like the United States where the neo-liberal mentality took increasing hold from the late 1970s onward. That was bolstered even more by the surge in globalism which led to protective tariff reductions worldwide. Largely forgotten was the fact that in the original European Common Market, nations were not admitted as new members until they had already reached a certain level of parity in basic labor standards so as to avoid unfair competition with the workers in the original founding nations. From that stem the conditions giving rise to his concern about "the new forms of psychological instability" which lead to "difficulty in forging coherent life-plans, including that of marriage." Being the head of his Church, Benedict XVI can do no less than deal with the whole man who is more than simply a factor of production. That leads the German Pope to a concern also about "the freedom and creativity of the person and his family and social relationships, causing great psychological and spiritual suffering" (25).

Those who operate on the erroneous assumption that later social teachings by the Church supercede prior ones, rendering them obsolete, are hereby put on notice that this is not so. Some among the privileged sectors of society have been breathing a sigh of relief for some time over the fact that the power of organized labor, which began to increase following the earlier social encyclicals, has since diminished with the vehement re-emergence of the self-righteous free market mentality. They forget that what genuinely works in the legitimate interests of the majority of the population can scarcely be regarded as opposed to the good of society overall, in other words, the common good. The working classes in any normally configured post-agricultural social economy constitute the preponderant majority of people who derive most of their income from their work. If they are not secure and prosperous, their society is not secure and prosperous. Pope Leo XIII emphasized that point in *Rerum Novarum* back in 1891, and it is no less true today. The "current crisis" of which the Pope speaks again here can only highlight this fact (34).

Pope Benedict has more to say with regard to "the mobility of labor associated with a climate of deregulation." He states that "uncertainty over working conditions caused by mobility and deregulation, when it becomes endemic, tends to create new forms of psychological instability, giving rise to difficulty in forging coherent life-plans including that of marriage." And "This leads to situations of human decline to say nothing of the waste of social resources." The Pope once again relates such problems to "new forms of economic marginalization," which "the current crisis can only make worse."

Why this concern about labor, long regarded among free marketeers in the same way as any other "merchandise" on the market? Because the Church in its social teachings never tolerated considering the labor of human beings as a commodity! Neither did the United States, at least in terms of legal formality, since passage of the Clayton Anti-Trust Act in 1914. In order to exempt labor unions from prosecution under the Sherman Anti-Trust Law (1890), Section 6 of the Clayton Act states: "The labor of a human being is not a commodity or article of commerce." Therefore, after pointing out "the great psychological and spiritual suffering" caused by unemployment, Pope Benedict takes the occasion here "to remind everyone, especially governments engaged in boosting the world's economic and social assets, that the primary capital to be safeguarded and valued is man, the human person in his or her integrity." He adds a statement from the Vatican II document, *The Church in the Modern World*, that is highly relevant also for economic life in our present crisis: "Man is the source, the focus and the aim of all economic and social life" (63).[17] That was reaffirmed with great emphasis in the second great labor encyclical—*Laborem Exercens*—where Pope John Paul II, the one-time stone-quarry worker, wrote: "We must emphasize the primacy of man in the production process, the primacy of man over things." As for capital: "Everything contained in the concept of capital in the strict sense is only a collection of things" (*Laborem Exercens*, par. 57). That is where John Paul II introduced the concept—economism—which has become more commonplace since his time. He defined the error of economism as: "that of considering human labor solely according to its economic purpose" (*Laborem Exercens*, par. 60).

That discussion led to the emphasis on "solidarity with poor countries in the process of development" which Pope Benedict felt "can point toward a solution of the current crisis" (27). How so?

> Through support for economically poor countries by means of financial plans inspired by solidarity—so that these countries can take steps to satisfy their own citizens' demand for consumer goods and for development—not only can true economic growth be generated, but a contribution can be made towards sustaining the productive capacities of rich countries that risk being compromised by the crisis (27).

There appears to be a suggestion of the kind of "pump-priming" activity as took shape also in the last great crisis during the 1930s. It is interesting that the Pope is offering this in the context where he is speaking of "*food and access to water as universal right of all human beings.*"

At this point Pope Benedict made what some may choose to regard as a digression from the purely economic aspects of the problem at hand, i.e., the economic crisis. He introduced the "question of respect for life," and the attendant denial of the right to religious freedom. He nevertheless insisted that "the important question of respect for life...cannot in any way be detached from questions concerning the development of peoples." Why? Because the notions of poverty and underdevelopment must be considered in association with "acceptance of life, especially in cases where it is impeded in a variety of ways" (28). One problem seems to be the widespread failure to regard the working human person as not only a consumer of food and other resources, but also as their main producer. It has been said: "With every mouth comes a pair of hands."

The noted British economist Colin Clark (1905-1989) sided with a minority of the experts with whom Pope Paul VI chose to consult about the population problem in terms of the food supply and the new technological breakthroughs in birth control (mainly "the pill"). Clark had drawn attention to the incentive that population pressure brought to bear for more intensive production and the wiser use of available resources, for example in countries like Japan and the Netherlands.[18] In the end, the Pope's decision coincided with Clark's thinking. But since then, even while food production increased dramatically in nations that had been considered economic "basket cases," birth control, including even government-enforced limitation of births (China), and euthanasia have spread widely. In fact we have reached the point where in much of Europe, as well as Japan, birth rates have fallen below the replacement level. Pope Benedict XVI points to what has transpired, with the warning, "When a society moves towards the denial or suppression of life, it ends up no longer finding the necessary motivation and energy to strive for man's true good" (28).

But what of "the denial of the right to religious freedom"? Given the daily headlines about terrorist bombings and countless deaths and destruction in some parts of the world in the name of religion, can there be any doubt but that, "Violence puts the brakes on authentic development and impedes the evolution of peoples toward greater socio-economic and spiritual well-being" (29)? The Pope, being the world's foremost religious leader, could not neglect mentioning at this point also how the impact of "the deliberate promotion of religious indifference or practical atheism on the part of many countries obstructs the development of peoples, depriving them of spiritual and human resources." That is because: "God is the guarantor of man's true development."

Returning to specifically economic measures toward the end of the chapter, there is the requirement that "economic choices do not cause disparities in wealth to increase in an excessive and morally unacceptable manner" (32). In addition, Pope Benedict restates the need "to prioritize the goal of access to steady employment for everyone." The reason given makes this one of the very significant, specifically economics-related proposals in the encyclical:

> Through the systemic increase in social inequality, both within a single country and between the populations of different countries (i.e., the massive increase in relative poverty), not only does social cohesion suffer, thereby placing democracy at risk, but so too does the economy, through the progressive erosion of "social capital'": the network of relationships of trust, dependability, and respect for rules, all of which are indispensable for any form of civil coexistence.

What is more: "Economic science tells us that structural insecurity generates anti-productive attitudes wasteful of human resources, inasmuch as workers tend to adapt passively to automatic mechanisms, rather than to release creativity." That leads to this incisive papal statement. "Human costs always include economic costs, and economic dysfunctions always involve human costs" (32).

In the forty years that have passed since *Populorum Progressio,* Benedict continues: "...its basic theme, namely progress, remains an open question." That is now aggravated by "the current economic and financial crisis." Problems like "high tariffs imposed by economically developed countries" persist; and these "still make it difficult for the products of poor countries to gain a foothold in the markets of the rich countries" (33).

The "principal new feature" since *Populorum Progressio* has been "the explosion of worldwide interdependence, commonly known as globalization." And that has progressed at what Pope Benedict refers to here as a "ferocious pace." What it implies is at one and the same time a "great opportunity" and the threat of "unprecedented damage and...great divisions within the human family." Perhaps the threat underlying the ominous prophetic tone throughout *Populorum Progressio* is coming to realization in our time. Obviously *de facto* interdependence, now more than ever on a global scale, implies the need for its recognition and acceptance in charity in the form that Pius XI termed it—social charity— or in its John Paul II expression, solidarity. Here Pope Benedict XVI reverts to the term—"civilization of love"—which his immediate predecessor attributed to the pope whom he is commemorating by this encyclical.

Chapter 3: Fraternity, Economic Development and Civil Society

The third chapter opens with a reminder of original sin along with an interesting new expression added to the Catholic Church's social teachings; and the two are not unrelated. It rearranges the premise for dealing with the social question by recalling that the human being is, after all, not "the sole author of himself, his life and society," and attitude which leads to him being "selfishly closed in on himself." That, Pope Benedict XVI reminds us, goes with "a purely consumerist and utilitarian view of life" which leads to the kind of crisis in which we once again find ourselves (34). Here he introduces a new term which nevertheless echoes an important concept that has been present throughout the social teachings of the Church since *Rerum Novarum.* Pope John Paul II indicated in *Centesimus Annus,* par. 10):

> In this way what we nowadays call the principle of solidarity, the validity of which both in the national order of each nation and in the international order I have discussed in the Encyclical *Sollicitudo Rei Socialis* (38-40), is clearly seen to be one of the fundamental principles of the Christian view of social and political organization. This principle is frequently stated by Pope Leo XIII, who uses the term "friendship," a concept already found in Greek philosophy. Pius XI refers to it with the equally meaningful term "social charity." Pope Paul VI, expanding the concept to cover the many modern aspects of the social question, speaks of a "civilization of love."

And now, Pope Benedict XVI appears to be expanding the concept once again to cover more recent "aspects of the social question." The term "*gratuitousness*" which he introduces (34) perhaps seems more awkward in English than in other languages, as for example, "*gratuità*" in the Italian edition of this encyclical.[19] Since social charity was linked with social justice by Pius XI in *Quadragesimo Anno*, par. 88, and since the Pius XI stated in *Divini Redemptoris,* par. 51, that "it is of the very essence of social justice to demand from each individual all that is necessary for the common good," it appears as though *gratuitousness* calls for giving over and above what is required by justice. It is "the astonishing experience of gift" which Pope Benedict XVI tells us "the human being is made for." And that is notwithstanding a widespread denial of that fact in modern economic life, "because of a purely consumerist and utilitarian way of life" (34).

That brings us back to the principle of solidarity. As one of the two social virtues, social justice and social charity, which Pius XI told us were required for rehabilitating the social order, social charity, unlike social justice, requires *a gift*. Justice, strictly speaking, and that includes social justice, does not involve gift or giving, but seeing to it that each and all render to society at its various levels "all that is necessary for the common good" (*Divini Redemptoris*, par. 51). The Jesuit Heinrich Pesch in outlining his solidaristic system established "the social virtues, justice and charity" as "the basic ethical principles for the objective regulation of social life," which "represent sacred obligations binding consciences of citizens and kings, of those subject to authority as well as those who are heads of state."[20] That appeared in the first edition of his *Lehrbuch* published in 1909, where he could still refer to the "expression social justice" as "relatively new."[21]

The one specific example of social justice which Pius XI presented in *Quadragesimo Anno* had to do with the just wage. He was not referring to the payment of that wage by each employer to each worker, which is strictly speaking a matter of commutative justice, i.e., giving to each what is his due. Pius XI was referring to the much broader problem of where the social order was so out-of-order that many, if not most individual employers, could not possibly pay the just wage as called for in *Quadragesimo Anno* (and previously in *Rerum Novarum*), while still remaining solvent. Referring to such a situation, Pius XI wrote: "If in the present state of society this is not always feasible, social justice demands that reforms be introduced without delay which will guarantee every workingman just such a wage" (*Quadragesimo Anno*, par. 71). That is because justice in wage payments affects the overall common good inasmuch as it involves the preponderant majority of citizens in every age and culture who must work for a living. Pope John Paul II highlighted that very important point in *Laborem Exercens*. How else can one interpret these crucial and largely overlooked words by the Polish Pope? "It should also be noted that the justice of a socioeconomic system and, in each case, its just functioning, deserve in the final analysis to be evaluated by the way in which man's work is properly remunerated in the system" (*Laborem Exercens*, par. 89). The Pius XI *mandatum* involves all who can play a role in bringing about the general prevalence of the just wage: the workers themselves along with their labor unions, the employers themselves and in their associations, and political leaders who may ultimately be in a position to put in place the conditions which assure that this minimum basic just wage can be paid to all full-time adult workers. In all probability that will eventually involve also generosity, or giving, i.e., *gratuitousness* on the part of all parties involved.[22] In the kind of dire circumstances envisioned here, such giving could even mean giving way or yielding, which may at times involve parties on either side, or both sides, of the bargaining table.

Now a willingness to give, i.e., gratuitousness, where the common good is at stake, is in fact evident elsewhere in society. It simply has not made it into the critical sector of economic life where the welfare of working class families is at stake and with them the common good of all of society. For example, in small towns throughout the United States and elsewhere there are fire departments staffed by volunteers who time and again, at great inconvenience and sometimes even grave personal risk, give of their time and effort to assure that their communities may have necessary protection in various kinds of emergencies. While assistance to individual persons and households in particular calamities still constitute acts of individual charity, the willingness of volunteers to stand by and be ready day and night to help one and all provides a general sense of security for the community overall which can only be defined as social charity or gratuitousness. Involved are actions directed toward the safety and well-being of all, i.e., the common good. In the economic area, the willingness of the CEO of a large business organization to limit his own salary below the exorbitant amounts that have become commonplace, thus allowing hundreds or even thousands of his rank-and-file employees to earn a more equitable and just wage, would be a good example of gratuitousness on his part. Such action would certainly serve the common good of the particular business and of the economy overall, thus substantiating what Pope Benedict is proposing here.

The attempt to exclude gratuitousness has long been at work in economic life. There we find the "conviction that the economy must be autonomous, that it must be shielded from influences of a moral character that has led man to abuse the economic process in a thoroughly destructive way" (34). Other elements of the free market cult stand in the way, like free competition, legitimate self-interest, etc., which smack of the old *laissez faire* cult, and of Adam Smith's "invisible hand" along with his disdain for those who, in his words, "affected to trade for the public good." In Benedict's words: "In the list of areas where the pernicious effects of sin are evident, the economy has been included for some time now." In fact, "We have clear proof of this at the present time." He concludes with a reminder that "the logic of gift does not exclude justice, nor does it merely sit alongside it as a second element added from without." At the close of this important paragraph (34), its author reaches the point where he can speak of "the principle of gratuitousness." In fact, he appears to be continuing a shift in emphasis from social justice, toward what Pius XI long ago introduced as its twin principle for social order—social charity. That is a transition for which Pope Paul VI certainly prepared the way, and which John Paul II articulated at a very high level—as the principle of solidarity (*Sollicitudo Rei Socialis,* part V). Now Benedict XVI appears to be reaffirming it as "the principle of gratuitousness" stated as such in italicized form later in this chapter (36). And it is at this point where he turns his attention to the market and what is required for it to function as it should to fulfill its legitimate purpose.

The concept market as such is basically neutral—it being an arrangement for buyers and sellers to meet in order to transact sales and purchases. A market economy therefore has come to be understood as one where exchanges by and large take place in accordance with demand expressed according to the needs and utility estimates of buyers, and with supply manifesting the scarcity and costs experienced by sellers who endeavor to accommodate them. Under the best of circumstances, exchange takes place in accordance with commutative justice so that each gets what is his due: the buyer his merchandise, and the seller his just price. The appropriate governing principle was termed by medieval theologians the principle of equivalence, or equal value in return for equal value.[23] As it has developed over time in today's complex and interdependent society, the parties on either side of the exchange process often evolved into unequal contenders. Thus one may have the advantage over the other by virtue of unequal knowledge of the market condition, or unequal power (e.g., monopoly, combination) in the transaction so that it is completed on the basis of power rather than justice. Principles other than equivalence have come to prevail, such as: "Let the buyer beware," and the even more nefarious approach: "Every man for himself, and let the devil take the hindmost!" So now Pope Benedict can state with assurance: "*Without internal forms of solidarity and mutual trust, the market cannot completely fulfill its proper economic function* [his italics]." He does not cite this as a possibility, but rather as a fact, with the statement: "And today it is this trust which has ceased to exist, and the loss of trust is a grave loss" (35).

That condition is not new to the 21st century! Among other things, it helps to explain why in the post-World War II Western sectors of Germany emerging from thirteen years of National Socialism, Konrad Adenauer, a model Catholic Christian statesman who became the war-devastated country's first chancellor, worked to establish, not a free market economy, but a social market economy. Among other things it incorporated important social teachings of the Catholic Church which have a long history of development in the German-speaking lands.[24] West Germany's remarkable recovery from the ruins of World War II—its *Wirtschaftswunder*—following 13 years of Nazi rule became legendary.[25]

Meanwhile, resurrecting alongside the social market economy, on "a mountain in Switzerland," as the Austrian-born Harvard economist Joseph Schumpeter remarked, not without some sarcasm, was the neo-liberal revival led by so-called "Austrian economists" notably Friedrich von Hayek and Ludwig von Mises.[26] They won supporters in other lands, including the United States, who captivated the minds of political leaders of both major parties: Ronald Reagan and the two Presidents George Bush, as well as Jimmy Carter and Bill Clinton.[27] Together such economists, who were strangers to Christian social principles, master-minded the restoration of the "free market economy." That involved deregulation in certain sectors of the economy, including the banking system, the abolition of protective tariffs in the interests of globalism, and tax reductions especially generous for the upper income groups. The earnest effort to restore the *laissez faire* conditions, which led up to the economic collapse culminating in the Great Depression in the 1930s, got underway; and it brought the world to the brink once again in 2008.

Pope Benedict now points out that the social teaching of the Catholic Church includes, but moves beyond, the "principles of so-called commutative justice" to which the market certainly remains subject. "But the social doctrine of the Church has unceasingly highlighted the importance of distributive justice and social justice for the market economy, not only because it belongs within a broader social and political context, but also because of the wider network of relations within which it operates." What is more, "if the market is governed solely by the principle of equivalence in the value of exchanged goods, it cannot produce the social cohesion that it requires in order to function well." That by itself implies more than simply a free market, but, for want of a better name, a *social* market. Why? Because "*Without internal forms of solidarity and mutual trust, the market cannot completely fulfill its proper economic function* [Benedict's italics]." The Pope was beyond a purely academic observation here, stating, as indicated previously, "And today it is this trust which has ceased to exist, and the loss of trust is a grave loss" (35).

By Pope Benedict's assertion that "economic activity…needs to be directed towards the pursuit of the common good for which the political community in particular must also take responsibility," (36) he made no converts among persistent free marketeers who fancy an absentee government. Indeed, oftentimes Catholic neo-liberals who pretend to have some awareness of their Church's social teachings will appeal shamelessly to the principle of subsidiarity, as if that hallowed principle provided a clear track for all government to vanish so that the strong can continue to oppress and cheat the weak. That ploy was in fact unmasked by Pope Benedict's statement about "when economic action conceived merely as an engine for wealth creation is detached from political action, conceived as a means for pursuing justice through redistribution." And that was followed by the provocative reminder intended for Darwinist free marketeers: "The Church has always held that economic action is not to be regarded as something opposed to society in and of itself." He added: "The market is not and must not become the place where the strong subdue the weak." The market as such is exonerated by the Pope indicating that it may "become a negative force not because it is so by nature, but because a certain ideology can make it so." That "ideology" is the false concept of freedom as applied to the market and to economic activity overall to which Pope Benedict is applying instead certain truths so as make it a true freedom which liberates; and that, we need to recall here, is the purpose of this encyclical. "Economy and finance" are neutral tools, but they can cause mayhem as they are doing now once again, "when those at the helm are motivated by purely selfish ends." (36).

It is necessary to recall at this point that in our time the term "market economy" itself has acquired significant ideological baggage so as to make it often appear identical with the familiar notion, "free market economy." The latter is proposed by its most extreme adherents as the absolute good in opposition to the absolute evil of socialism. Actually through most of human history, there was no totally free market economy. That would represent economic anarchy. The notion has become a kind of ideological bauble since the late 18th century when the goddess *Liberty* became the object of worship among *avant-garde* Europeans.[28] During the Middle Ages there were significant controls imposed on markets by craft and merchant guilds, as well as by local governments or ruling aristocrats. Also the concept of the just price and the ban against usury, carefully developed by theologians, were not dismissed lightly. During the Mercantilist era after the close of the medieval period, monarchs interfered often on a massive scale, throughout the market processes (including pricing), as they attempted to assure an influx of gold and silver by positive trade balances. In more recent times there have been various degrees of state intervention in the market for goods and services, as well as for the factors of production. These eventually ranged from the near total command economy in the erstwhile Union of Soviet Socialist Republics, to instances of less but still substantial state control over economic life as, for example in Nazi (National *Socialist*) Germany and Fascist Italy, or even as in Great Britain directly after World War II. Closer to home there are still woeful lamentations at large about all of the "socialist" measures enacted during the New Deal era in the United States during the Great Depression; and much energy has been expended in the years following it to rid our country of such "over-regulation" of our economy.[29] That being said, until now I am not aware of any public outcry during the present economic catastrophe about the bank deposit insurance system (FDIC) which was installed early during the New Deal period. It was designed to prevent large-scale bank failures like those which brought the economy to its knees after the stock market crash in 1929. Also, few would deny that during the deadliest of all wars that followed the Depression (and finally put a definitive end to it!), it was necessary in the United States to set aside the so-called free market throughout substantial sectors of the economy. This involved allocation and rationing of materials and commodities in short supply (like coffee, sugar, meat, gasoline), along with wage and price controls generally, in addition to excess profit taxes and taxes on incomes which ran as high as 90 percent at the top brackets. Attempts to circumvent price controls were labeled with the pejorative term, "black marketeering," and subject to severe penalties. Under the circumstances there was little outcry about "socialism."

Such extreme situations bring the overall common good into sharp relief where it is obvious and can be recognized for its overriding presence and importance in economic life. But in fact the common good is always important and present, politically and economically, as Pope Benedict is reaffirming in this encyclical, and as his predecessors have been affirming since 1891. He indicates here: "The economic sphere is neither ethically neutral, nor inherently inhuman and opposed to society" (36). And that brings us to the kinds of problems we face once again at present, because "Without internal forms of solidarity and mutual trust, the market economy cannot completely fulfill its proper economic function" (35).

There was another new term presented in this chapter of *Caritas in Veritate* that is not found in previous social encyclicals; and it is worth noting. It is the concept *stakeholder* as juxtaposed to the *stockholder*. Pope Benedict introduces it in the context of his bold observation that, with "today's international economic scene...marked by grave deviations and failures...a profoundly new way of understanding business enterprise is called for." With "(o)ld models...disappearing...promising new ones are taking shape on the horizon" (40). "Stakeholders" include "the workers, the suppliers, the consumers, the natural environment, and broader society..." In a word, the Pope is speaking of the broader *common good* that extends beyond the *particular* good of the stockholders or owners or even of the enterprise as a whole. Thus, the central theme of this and previous social encyclicals comes to the fore again. It is the common good and everyone's obligations to it in social justice and social charity (solidarity). This stands in contrast to what the Pope characterizes as "a new cosmopolitan class of managers...answerable only to the shareholders," and such practices as "a speculative use of financial resources which yields to the temptation of seeking only short-term profit without regard for the long term sustainability of the enterprise" (40). That sounds all too familiar amid the wreckage of economies worldwide in 2008 on a high tide of sub-prime mortgages and arcane speculative devices like hedge funds and derivatives. One indication of the tenuous condition and vulnerability of the present economy where such things still abound is the undue preoccupation at large with indices like the Dow-Jones, Standard and Poor, and the like. These reflect mainly the guesses and hopes of speculators who invest in securities and commodities, and who have far less interest in the real economy and "the public good" (which Adam Smith referred to with such disdain), than in their own immediate prospects for gain. For them the economy is a vast casino where people play more than they work. The welfare of the people who work for a living and who are the ultimate heart and soul of any economy, providing the goods and services needed by all, is abandoned to a scramble for the crumbs off the gaming table.

The chapter ends with a papal statement citing Pope John Paul II to the effect that globalization as such is "neither good or bad," depending on "what people make of it." (42). And it was Pope Paul VI who already opposed the benighted notion held by some that "poor people should remain at a fixed state of development." What is needed instead to avoid "great dangers and difficulties" is an "ethical spirit" that drives globalization "towards the humanizing goal of solidarity."

Chapter 4: The Development of Peoples; Rights and Duties; the Environment

The fourth chapter of *Caritas in Veritate* is about solidarity, ethics in economic life, population, and environmental concern. As the third chapter ends with an affirmation of solidarity, so chapter four opens with a quotation from the Pope Paul VI encyclical *Populorum Progressio*, par. 17: "The reality of human solidarity, which is a benefit for us, also imposes an obligation" (43). Thus it becomes apparent that the concept *solidarity,* which Heinrich Pesch established as the governing principle for an economic system opposed to both liberal capitalism and collectivist socialism, is intended to play a major role in this encyclical. Pesch identified it in the first volume of his *Lehrbuch* as "first of all social interdependence, the actual mutual dependence of people on one another," indicating that: "This mutual dependence on the well-being of other persons in society is therefore no mere *de facto* relationship." Instead: "Inasmuch as the reciprocity and the community of interests has its foundation in man's rational nature, solidarity also represents a moral relationship between man and his fellow man."[30]

Another significant concordance between the German Pope and the German Jesuit's thinking comes to the foreground here. The first chapter in the first volume of the *Lehrbuch* is entitled "Natur und Mensch" (Nature and Man). The first section of that chapter establishes the proper hierarchy between the two by its heading: "Man as Lord of the World According to God's Ordinance." It does so on the basis of "the will of God, who assigned it to the father of the human race by virtue of the fact that He bestowed a rational nature on man, elevating him to a status higher than that enjoyed by the world of matter and plants and animals."[31] That makes Pesch's *Lehrbuch* the only economics text that begins on the basis of Sacred Scripture (Genesis 1:26, also 2:15), as well as in accordance with common sense.

Since common sense is not always so common, Pope Benedict XVI uses this chapter to defuse the sometimes exaggerated ecological concern which in our time has followed an era when the environment was not of significant concern at all, so that it became the object of what was too often wanton depredation. He uses terms like "neo-paganism" and "a new pantheism" (48) to describe the pendulum swing to an opposite extreme where nature represents an "untouchable taboo" (48). The Pope warns that "human salvation cannot come from nature alone."

Now there can be no doubt that in our own time there is still much violation of nature and waste of its resources. The capitalist spirit which has prevailed in recent centuries, where profit at all costs and without limit was the dominant obsession, played a large role in that. It is often based on attitudes which reduce "nature merely to a collection of contingent data," and it ends up "doing violence to the environment and even encouraging activity that fails to respect human nature itself" (48). Regrettably, and perhaps predictably, the environment and problems associated with it have also provided another opening for the population controllers. In the face of facts like the so-called Green Revolution[32] which among other things enabled some of the "overpopulated" and "starving" nations to become food exporters, along with the failure of their prophecies about imminent massive worldwide famine, some population alarmists[33] have shifted their emphasis to environmental concerns about imminent shortages of finite resources, and to overpopulation as a cause of underdevelopment. In this chapter, Pope Benedict devoted attention to such matters.

Once again the facts refute the theory, as Pope Benedict points out. "Populous nations have been able to emerge from poverty thanks not least to the size of their population and the talents of their people" (44). This was true in the past in nations with the highest population densities like Great Britain, the Netherlands, Japan, Germany and, in more recent times, India. Its converse is true now when, "formerly prosperous nations are presently passing through a phase of uncertainty and in some cases decline precisely because of their falling birth rates." As the Pope points out, "this has become a crucial problem for highly affluent societies" (44). It is due in part to what he cites as a "decline in births, falling at times beneath the so-called 'replacement level,'" which puts a "strain on the social welfare systems, increases their costs and eats into savings and hence the financial resources needed for investment, reduces the availability of qualified labourers, and narrows the 'brain pool' upon which nations can draw for their needs." Once again, the importance of solidarity comes into the picture, since "smaller and at times miniscule families run the risk of impoverishing social relations and failing to ensure effective forms of solidarity." Some may judge that the Pope is stepping beyond the proper bounds of the principle of subsidiarity by insisting (as the Second Vatican Council did back in 1965) that: "States are called to enact policies promoting the centrality and integrity of the family founded on marriage between a man and a woman, the primary vital cell of society." But we need to recall that we live at a time when the state has long since moved toward an opposite position which ranges all of the way from condoning homosexual "marriages" (in Spain, Canada, and increasingly, the United States), to severe punishment of couples for having more than one child (China).

Pope Benedict is supported here not only by the concern expressed by leaders in various nations where declining population growth rates have led toward economic stagnation so as to jeopardize future economic growth and national vitality, as in Russia and Japan. There is also the opinion of competent economists far apart in time and orientation. Heinrich Pesch, while outlining an economic system based on the principle of solidarity during the first quarter of the 20th century, also proposed a principle for population policy stating: "Where care has been taken to safeguard the quality of a nation's people, generally there will be no need for concern about their quantity."[34] In his support, he cited other distinguished German economists of his time including Adolf Wagner (1835-1917) and Wilhelm Roscher (1817-1894). The latter wrote: "A relatively large and dense population...is of itself a productive force. A more numerous and dense population has at its disposal more brains as well as more arms which provide for more capacity in the national work force, and which because of the possibility of more division of labor and combination of labor also makes for more efficiency in the work force."[35]

Among more recent economic analysts who addressed this topic was the British-born economist Colin Clark, mentioned earlier, who served on the group which advised Pope Paul VI in the preparation of his encyclical *Humanae Vitae* (1968). Clark was noted for his work on food supply and population. Using appropriate up-to-date statistical techniques and data, he arrived at the conclusion: "But we do have historical evidence of a number of cases of the beneficial effect of substantial population growth in communities with a limited area of agricultural land." He supported the thesis that population density, rather than hampering national growth and prosperity, can serve as a stimulus to greater national productivity. His analysis ranged from ancient Greece to present-day Japan and India.[36]

Influenced by, among others, those who spread panic about inevitable worldwide famine due to a "population explosion," there is now an equivalent tendency to attribute underdevelopment as well as environmental depredation to overpopulation. Therefore Pope Benedict XVI, feeling the need to respond, wrote: "To consider population increase as the primary cause of underdevelopment is mistaken, even from an economic point of view." While he upheld concern about "responsible procreation," he negated the kind of sex education "aimed solely at protecting the interested parties from possible disease or the 'risk' of procreation" (44). In a world that is being reduced to absurdity in such matters, the Pope reminded one and all that: "States are called to enact policies promoting the centrality and the integrity of the family founded on marriage between a man and a woman, the primary vital cell of society" (44).

There was a papal warning also about ecological extremism, indicating that "human salvation cannot come from nature alone" (48). Traditional economic textbooks taught students that there are three primary factors of production: land, labor, and capital—the first two being original and the third, derived from the other two. Heinrich Pesch altered that somewhat, to man, nature and capital—a difference reflecting his philosophical training which called for sharp definition. Water and wind, to cite just two such important natural productive elements present throughout history, may be subsumed under the term, "land" in a casual discussion; but that is not appropriate for a scientific analysis of the three traditional primary factors of production in economics.

Pesch, given his solid philosophical foundation, also had much to say about the other topic which Pope Benedict XVI included in this chapter: ethics and its relationship to the economic science and economic life. In a short work published in 1918, as well as in various relevant sections of his *Lehrbuch*, Pesch retrieved economics from the drab positivistic mode into which it had drifted.[37]

Here the Pope states in a straightforward manner that, "The economy needs ethics in order to function correctl"; and he presents that with the qualification: "not any ethics whatsoever, but an ethics that is people-centered" (45). Being the head of the largest and oldest Christian Church, no one should be surprised when he specifies the "underlying system of morality" of "the Church's social doctrine...since it is based on man's creation in the image of God (Gen. 1:27)...which gives rise to the inviolable dignity of the human person and the transcendent value of natural moral norms."

Pesch, a trained economist and author of the longest, most detailed economics text ever written, would agree. He had this to say about the role of ethics in economics and in economic life:

> Only in a nation where people, by and large, have a highly developed sense of moral responsibility so that they are willing to dedicate themselves conscientiously to their work and professions, and to avoid the restless pursuit of unlimited or even unjust gain, and where people regularly have concern for the good of other citizens and for the well-being of the whole of society, there and only there will the national welfare have a firm and, in fact, the best guarantee. The economist has to recognize that. We ask no more of him. He does not have to become a moralist or a preacher, or to demand the good because it is good; and neither does he have to try to discover ethical principles and laws, or to develop them. They are provided for him. It is enough for him to take note of them and to observe them. But it remains of the greatest importance for cultural advancement in our time that we are reminded of how, precisely in economic matters, the material welfare of nations is essentially conditioned by the active dominion of the eternal and divine moral law. An economy which operates solely on the basis of positive law with a historically variable morality, and on the basis of moral systems which are allegedly developed by people, remains unable in the long run to safeguard the common good against libertine egotism, and the institution of private property against the onslaught of socialism.[38]

Chapter 5: The Cooperation of the Human Family

The human race stems from a common Divine Father, its Creator, and also from common human parents named Adam and Eve. It was therefore a family from its beginning. As it proceeded down through history, the human family has taken many centuries to more fully realize its capacity (and also its need) to actively cooperate. That process was extended and accelerated in a spectacular manner by the virtual erasure of time and distance with and following the World War II era. The Church which assumed the name Catholic (i.e., worldwide), and which since its beginning has been active throughout the known world, has now begun to speak about worldwide solidarity.[39] That is implicit in the first paragraph of the fifth chapter of *Caritas in Veritate* in the important italicized statement: "*The development of peoples depends, above all, on a recognition that the human race is a single family* working together in true communion, not simply a group of subjects who happen to live side-by-side." (53) Thus the principle of solidarity comes even more to the foreground in this chapter with its title, "The Cooperation of the Human Family."

Here Pope Benedict XVI, the master theologian, makes the important point that the kind of solidarity involved here goes beyond the social sciences. It relies on "the contribution of disciplines such as metaphysics and theology." Among recent generations of social scientists, including economists, any such "contribution" would be taboo. Heinrich Pesch had to deal with that in his time when he was accused of "theologizing" economics.[40] As for metaphysics, he did not hesitate to quote extensively from a work by his older brother, Tilmann Pesch, S. J., a noted and much-published philosopher. And that was precisely for arriving at his original formulation of "the principle of solidarity."[41]

Typically, social scientists, especially economists, rely routinely on mathematical formulations for expressing the "laws" of their sciences. Physicists, astronomers and other natural scientists need to rely on mathematical principles, and they do not regard that as demeaning to their own scientific endeavors. In fact they get and have gained in the modern era remarkable results leading to great technical accomplishments. Social scientists, on the other hand, need to rely on metaphysics, ethics, and moral theology; and they do so whether they realize it or are willing to acknowledge it or not. Their persistent tendency to employ mathematical formulations has by and large gained little for them.[42] Perhaps that is why their sciences have not gotten the enviable spectacular results enjoyed by natural scientists over the past two centuries. The reason why ethics and eventually moral theology are of great importance to economics is because it is a *practical* as distinct from a *speculative* science—terms employed in Aristotelian-Thomistic philosophy. This means that economics involves the *free* acts of human beings, not spontaneous reflexive actions which man has in common with animals: like respiration, heart-beat, and digestion. Therefore moral philosophers (ethicians) and moral theologians have something to say to economists whose science deals with human actions for satisfying temporal wants. Technically speaking, that can be accomplished by theft or pillage, as well as by hard work or honest purchase. Ethically speaking only the latter options are licit. The most recent economic calamity that is addressed in this encyclical appears to substantiate once again—tragically—that immoral economic actions also end up being poor economic actions. That is because human beings are not exclusively economic beings. Being human makes them subject to the moral law—which is precisely why Pope Benedict XVI and several of his predecessors have gotten involved in issuing social encyclicals, the latest of which is *Caritas in Veritate.*

An especially critical specific area where ethics is of special relevance to economics is one which Pope Benedict addresses precisely in this part of *Caritas in Veritate*. It involves the just wage. That links him and his teaching with the great tradition of social encyclicals dating back to Leo XIII who originated the modern just wage doctrine in *Rerum Novarum.* Pius XI followed with the most detailed development of that particular doctrine which subsequent popes, including Pius XII, Blessed John XXIII, and Paul VI, have reaffirmed in various ways. It remained for John Paul II, to establish the just wage as the "key means...for verifying the justice of the whole socioeconomic system" in his own great labor encyclical *Laborem Exercens*, par. 89). That happens to conform with good economic common sense in normal human society. In such a society the preponderant majority of mankind relies mainly on its work for sustaining its livelihood—a condition which is to apply until the end of time according to what was foretold in Genesis (3:17-19). Therefore, Pope Benedict now stresses again "especially the right to a just wage and the personal security of the worker and his family" at this point in his own social encyclical issued at a time of great economic crisis (63). The Pope points out that "problems associated with development...highlight the direct link between poverty and unemployment," and that often "poverty results from *a violation of the dignity of human work* [italics in text] either because work opportunities are limited (through unemployment or underemployment)," or, and here he quotes directly from *Laborem Exercens* (*Laborem Exercens*, par. 37), "because a low value is put on work and the rights that flow from it, especially the right to a just wage and the personal security of the worker and his or her family" (63).

The matter does not rest there with a simple reaffirmation of the right to a just wage. Perhaps more than in any social encyclical since *Quadragesimo Anno,* the German Pope elaborates on what the just wage implies. He does so by indicating what "decent" signifies, as that was expressed by Pope John Paul II in a May 1, 2000 appeal for "a global coalition in favor of decent work." The latter made the statement in support of an initiative by the International Labor Organization which is the leading world body entrusted with establishing and safeguarding fair labor standards on a worldwide basis. The role of the ILO, first founded in 1918, is especially vital in the present era involving the globalization of markets for labor and for its products. This passage is worth highlighting since it now involves the approbation of two successive pontiffs during the first decade of the 21st century:

> It means work that expresses the essential dignity of every man and woman in the context of their particular society; work that is freely chosen effectively associating workers, both men and women, with the development of their community; work that enables the worker to be respected and free from any form of discrimination; work that makes it possible for families to meet their needs and provide schooling for their children, without their children themselves being forced into labor; work that permits the workers to organize themselves freely, and to make their voices heard; work that leaves enough room for discovering one's roots at the personal, familial, and spiritual level; work that guarantees those who have retired a decent standard of living. (63)

All of that does not retreat one iota from specifications by earlier popes about the just wage and the various ways in which it may be complemented or enhanced. Nor does it support escapes proposed by enthusiasts at various times and in various social contexts involving retreats to a simpler past, or fanciful ventures into some dubious futuristic scheme. It accepts the basic context of contemporary society, complete with all of the dynamism and potential, along with the pitfalls, as made possible by the ongoing technological revolution that has especially marked the recent modern era.

As for labor unions, some persons still somehow stand opposed to labor unionism in principle; and that includes not a few Catholics—notwithstanding more than a century of social teachings by the Catholic Church in support of them precisely in principle. Such opposition persists even after the dramatic role which the Polish labor union *Solidarność* played, at great personal risk to its leaders, (and probably to Pope John Paul II himself!) in bringing down the Communist government in Poland and, along with it soon afterwards, the entire Soviet socialist enterprise. Pope Benedict reaffirms here that labor unions "have always been encouraged and supported by the Church" (64). That happens to apply also to the personal support and encouragement which Pope John Paul II gave to *Solidarność* and its Nobel Peace Prize-winning leader, Lech Wałęsa. Pope Benedict now encourages unions to widen their horizons in keeping with the broadening global dimensions of the modern world economy. He asks them to consider also the concerns of consumers who in certain situations have felt the need to take issue with positions adopted by the workers and their unions. He also calls for national unions to take into account in particular the problems of workers in developing countries, who have not yet attained the level of protection which they have, and to perhaps offer assistance where possible. All of that does not, because it cannot, add up to a change in the Catholic Church's position with regard to the workers' right to organize into unions in principle, or in the mode that they have reached at this point in time.

This encyclical was issued after certain delays. At one point Pope Benedict had indicated that the economic collapse which occurred late in 2008 prompted him to delay its release so that he could address issues related to the financial crisis which led to that collapse. This would involve walking on thin ice inasmuch as it involves an area replete with sophisticated matter that is highly technical in nature. He therefore had to confine himself to a more general approach to the problem. This did not prevent the Pope from referring to "renewed structures and operating methods that have to be designed after its misuse (finance) which wreaked such havoc on the real economy" (65). The scolding continued: "Financiers must rediscover the genuinely ethical foundation of their activity, so as not to abuse the sophisticated instruments which can serve to betray the interests of savers." Even the sub-prime mortgages which caused widespread havoc and distress often proved deceptive for ordinary citizens whose lives were upset, often seriously. The shock waves extended well beyond, also to the countless workers who ended up losing their jobs and their livelihoods. Expressions occur in the encyclical like "scandalous speculation" and "the risk of usury"—a phenomenon which the Church has encountered and addressed at least since the Middle Ages; and suggestions are made about "credit unions," even "pawnbroking" and other ventures in "micro-credit," along with "new ventures" for the benefit of "the weaker elements in society" (65). And there is also a reminder about cooperative purchasing "like the consumer cooperatives that have been in operation since the 19 th century, partly through the initiative of Catholics" (66).

That may be a hint that ordinary people should have avenues leading away from macro-banking where their humble interests are sometimes lost sight of.

The chapter concludes with a reminder about "the unrelenting growth of global interdependence," i.e., worldwide solidarity. In this context Pope Benedict calls for a "reform of the *United Nations Organization*," among other "international institutions and international finance." It is a timely proposal, since there are many critics also among American Catholics who harbor a strong ideological opposition to the UN concept—and the supranational vision and commitments it implies—that emerged following World War II. Their antagonism extends to the Church's endorsement of the UN in principle, even while ironically many of them are "hawkish" with regard to American involvement in a series of questionable wars in the Middle East—wars deemed unjust by both Pope John Paul II (cf. *Centesimus Annus*, par. 52) and Joseph Cardinal Ratzinger, who was then his leading theological advisor, and ultimately his papal successor. That already made such persons hostile to Pope Paul VI who was the first pontiff to personally address the UN in New York, and who upheld the concept as such in *Populorum Progressio,* as did Blessed John XXIII before him (cf. *Pacem in Terris*, pars. 142-145).[43] While generally unsympathetic to the Church's social teachings, they nevertheless often take recourse in one of its leading precepts—the principle of subsidiarity—intimating that international bodies like the UN of their very nature represent transgressions of that principle. Pope Benedict mentioned the principle twice in this final paragraph of the fifth chapter, perhaps to reassure one and all that he is familiar with how international bodies like the UN *can* operate properly within its context. To some, subsidiarity apparently means leaving every individual to his own resources no matter how meager those may be, having been shorn of them by the rich and powerful. That echoes once again the free marketeering principle: *Every man for himself, and let the Devil take the hindmost.* Accordingly the same ideologues are reflexively opposed to aid from rich nations to the poor nations of the world.[44] One must conclude that they stand opposed to the fact and concept of worldwide solidarity. That is unless they expect that it too will happen along by chance in some happy equilibrium brought about by an "invisible hand," or by the kinds of "natural laws" about which Adam Smith and the Physiocrats had long fantasized. These early economists were of course mistakenly equating economic "natural laws" with physical natural laws, not with the natural moral law which Pope Benedict mentions again in the next chapter. The fulfillment of that law does not take place automatically; it requires deliberate human action—an *actus humanus*.

Chapter 6: The Development of Peoples and Technology

Pope Benedict XVI devotes the final chapter of his social encyclical to what is in a certain sense the overwhelming impact of advancing technology on contemporary mankind. His tenure as a distinguished university professor and scholar comes to the fore again here, and that at times makes for some difficult reading. This is a matter, incidentally, which occupied the attention also of the brilliant Pope Pius XII at various times during his nineteen-year pontificate.[45] For example, his 1953 Christmas Message—*Modern Technology and Peace*—scores "the one-sided influence of that 'technological spirit' which only recognizes and reckons as real what can be expressed in mathematical formulas and utilitarian calculations."

The chapter opens with an interesting parallel that illustrates one of Pope Benedict's special talents—his ability to lay bare fundamental errors in human conduct in what may seem at first to be a merely parenthetical comment. Pope Benedict proposes here that "the development of peoples goes off course, if humanity thinks it can recreate itself through the 'wonders' of technology, just as economic development is exposed as a destructive sham if it relies on the 'wonders' of finance in order to sustain unnatural and consumerist growth." Instead, we are redirected to a recognition of "the fundamental norms of the natural moral law which God has written in our hearts" (68). That statement would serve to redirect the errant arrogant technocracy of our times, along with the naive reliance on the "natural laws" of classical economics and its recurrent insistence on an unhinged concept of freedom which persists from the paleo-liberalism of the 18th century to the neo-liberalism of our own time.[46] The real question, then as now, remains: *Freedom for what end?* And that is where the theme of this encyclical applies: providing the *true* answer as an act of charity at the cosmic level. The same holds for technological progress. Technology is good, and we are not entitled to spurn it or clamor for a return to some more primitive form of society. As Pope Paul VI stated in *Populorum Progressio:* "The human spirit, increasingly free of its bondage to creatures, can be more easily drawn to the worship and contemplation of the Creator (*Populorum Progressio*, par. 41). In fact, Pope Benedict indicates here, "Technology, in this sense, is a response to God's command to till and to keep the land" (Gen. 2:15). But it may not be regarded as "self-sufficient"—as an end in itself—like "absolute freedom" (70).

We are then asked to look at the results today when "Often the development of peoples is considered a matter of financial engineering, the freeing up of markets, the removal of tariffs, investment in production and institutional reforms—in other words, a purely technical matter." Pope Benedict warns that: "Development will never be fully guaranteed through automatic or impersonal forces whether from the market or from international politics." In other words, economics is not a *positive* or purely *speculative* science, i.e., involving simply the presentation of truths without directly implying rules for deliberate actions and choices by human subjects. It is a *practical* science involving precisely deliberate free human actions and choices by free human subjects whose actions are subject to the moral law. As indicated previously, one can charge a just price, or cheat the customer, just as one can pay a just wage or cheat the worker; and one can lend at a usurious rate or charge legitimate interest. The relevant punch-line follows: "*Development is impossible without upright men and women, without financiers and politicians whose consciences are finely attuned to the common good* [italics in text]" (71).

The common good is, of course, one of the oldest and basic important concepts in Catholic social teaching, being, as it is, the object of both key principles for the restoration of social order—social justice and social charity (*Quadragesimo Anno*, par. 88). Even then, it did not receive a specific definition until Blessed John XXIII provided one in *Mater et Magistra*, and repeated it in *Pacem in Terris*. Soon afterwards it was included in the Vatican II *Pastoral Constitution on the Church in the Modern World.*[47] Unfortunately, without clear definition, such important principles tend to drift into the category of vague generalities or slogans so that their real meaning may become obscure, even distorted. For example, the important virtue of social justice was misconstrued for so long and in so many ways, that it is even today used by some as a slur and others as justification for questionable ideologies and programs.

Bioethics is cited here by Pope Benedict as one area where advancing technology has had a frightening impact in the recent modern era. He deals with it near the end of the encyclical as an area "where the very possibility of integral human development is radically called into question" (74). That is because we have moved closer to "the brave new world" of, one must say, a dehumanized future. This involves knowledge about "not just how life is conceived, but also how it is manipulated, as bio-technology places it increasingly under man's control." Thus: "*In vitro* fertilization, embryo research, the possibility of manufacturing clones and human hybrids: all this is now emerging and being promoted in today's highly disillusioned culture, which believes it has mastered every mystery, because the origin of life is now within our grasp." The implications are the more frightening because the dominant "culture of death" also has all of this new technology at its disposal. Thus, what are we to expect "at the other end of the spectrum"? What use will the pro-euthanasia forces make of his new technology? And what will the impact be on "the mentality for development"?(75)

Following the portrayal of that bleak picture, Pope Benedict XVI ended with a presentation of what he has to offer as the head of the largest Christian denomination on earth. He proposed that "*Development needs Christians with their arms raised toward God* in prayer, Christians moved by the knowledge that truth-filled love, *caritas in veritate,* from which authentic development proceeds, is not produced by us but given unto us" (79).

Then as the leader of the oldest of the Christian denominations, Pope Benedict XVI closed with something specific to the Roman Catholic Church (77, 79). He included a prayer to the Virgin Mary who was proclaimed *Mater Ecclesiae* (Mother of the Church) by Pope Paul VI, asking for her help in the task of bringing about what that pope laid the groundwork for in his own encyclical *Populorum Progressio*: "the development of the whole man and all men."

Notes

1. That paragraph is in *Centesimus Annus*, an encyclical often cited by those who mistakenly seized upon it as an endorsement of the free market eco nomy.

2. A distinguished American Jesuit economist who was my mentor a St. Louis University characterized economics as an "unsatisfactory science." Cf. Bernard W. Dempsey, S. J., *The Functional Economy* (Englewood Cliffs, NJ: Prentice-Hall, Inc.,1958), 1-37.

3. Adam Smith, *The Wealth of Nations* (New York: Random House, 1937), 423.

4. Benedict XVI, *Deus Caritas Est* (2005), 27.

5. "Now it is of the very essence of social justice to demand from each individual all that is necessary for the common good."

6. I hope to make a start toward remedying this unfortunate lapse with the publication of my book entitled *Pope Pius XII On the Economic Order.*

7. Cf. the definitive three volume work in German: Arthur-Fridolin Utz, O.P. and Joseph-Fulko Groner, O.P., *Soziale Summe Pius XII* (Freiburg, Switzerland: Paulus Verlag, 1954-1961.

8. Many years ago I was privileged to serve with the noted British economist Colin Clark on a lecture panel in St. Louis, Missouri dealing with the so-called overpopulation problem. Clark, the father of nine, was one of the experts appointed to Pope Paul's commission of advisors for the encyclical *Humanae Vitae.* The Pope sided with the minority, which included Clark, in opposition to artificial birth control.

9. John Paul II used the expression "neoliberalism" in his Apostolic Constitution *Ecclesia in America* (cf. p. 56) in 1999; and Paul VI had referred to it in 1971 as "a renewal of the liberal ideology" (*Octogesima Adveniens,* par. 35).

10. *Wall Street Journal*, March 30, 1967, 14.

11. Much of United States coinage until recent years bore the *Liberty* image in various forms and poses.

12. It is most unfortunate and not without some irony that the Pope's proof-readers erred in posting this all-important very first scriptural reference in his encyclical as John 8:22. That passage in St. John's Gospel is totally irrelevant to the terms of the discussion. John 8:32, on the other hand, is of the utmost relevance in that it posits *truth* as the guarantee of true freedom to do what is right—i.e., what corresponds to both justice and charity.

13. For whatever reason, none of the popes who wrote social encyclicals have mentioned by name the great Jesuit economist Heinrich Pesch (1854-1926) who, in a five-volume work, developed the outline for an economic system which he called *Solidarism.* Its operative principle is solidarity, the application of which he extended throughout society from its cell unit—the family—to intermediate (occupational) groups, to citizens of the same country, and eventually to "the universal solidarity of all mankind." Cf. Heinrich Pesch, S.J., *Lehrbuch der Nationalökonomie/Teaching Guide to Economics,* trans. Rupert J. Ederer (Lewiston, NY: The Edwin Mellen Press, 2002), vol. 2, bk.1, 235–316.

14. One should consider the prospects of redeploying the millions of hyper-industrious inhabitants of Hong Kong, or for that matter the population of New York City or London to small shops or farms. This could imply perhaps a post-doomsday scenario which, pray God, will remain science-fiction, like the kind of economy it proposes.

15. Heinrich Pesch identified the pressure stemming from population growth as leading to greater productivity, i.e., to a wiser use of available resources. His conclusion about the relationship was summed up by his proposition: "...where care has been taken

to safeguard the quality of a nation's people, generally there will be no need for concern about their quantity." (Pesch/Ederer, 2, 2:193).

16. Depending on whose figures one uses, CEO compensation is now some 431 times that of non-management production workers as compared with 71 times their pay in 1965.

17. A most significant recent statement about human labor and its priority is the John Paul II social encyclical *Laborem Exercens*. It proves definitively that the status of human labor and the just wage to which it is entitled still holds top priority in the Church's social teachings. See paragraph 89.

18. Cf. Colin Clark, *Population Growth and Land Use* (New York: St. Martin's Press, 1968).

19. In English usage the word "gratuity" refers commonly to "tipping," where a satisfied customer gives something extra in appreciation for services performed well. Actually a *gratuity* in that sense is supposed to be something over and above what a waiter or a barber, for example, is entitled to in strict (commutative) justice. However it is one of the vagaries of the free market system that many, perhaps the majority of workers who work for wages plus tips, would not survive if they had to live on their wage alone. Thus such workers are abandoned by their employers to the mercy of their clientele.

20. Pesch/Ederer, 2, 1: 296-300.

21. Ibid., 298.

22. For example, this could involve *voluntary* yielding by CEOs on their claims for multi-million dollars in compensation. See note 14 above.

23. Cf. Bernard W. Dempsey, *The Functional Economy* (Englewood Cliffs, NJ: Prentice-Hall, 1958), 369-370.

24. This includes such notable persons as Bishop Wilhelm Emmanuel von Ketteler, Heinrich Pesch, S.J., Blessed Father Adolf Kolping, Father Franz Hitze, Msgr. Georg Ratzinger, Karl Vogelsang, Msgr. Johannes Messner. Also, there was Engelbert Dolfuss, the Chancellor of Austria, who was martyred by the Nazis, and who had planned to inaugurate a "*Quadragesimo Anno State*."

25. The Archbishop of Munich, Reinhard Marx, one of the advisors to Pope Benedict XVI in the preparation of *Caritas in Veritate,* has advocated a return to the principles of the social market economy, extending them now also to the global level. See: Reinhard Marx, *Das Kapital,* (Munich: Pattloch Verlag, 2008), 291ff.

26. This was included in an address entitled, "The March Into Socialism," delivered by Schumpeter before the American Economic Association in New York on December 30, 1949, shortly before his death.

27. Democrat President Jimmy Carter took the initiative in deregulating industries which had traditionally been regulated, starting with the airline industry. Democrat Clinton played a major role in getting the United States tied into the global free trade program.

28. The French Revolution and its Reign of Terror stemmed from the excesses of the aristocratic nobility of the time. We now have a growing popular outrage against worsening excesses committed by a capitalist plutocracy as symbolized by Wall Street.

29. In a science where a modicum of scientific precision applies, the term, "socialism," would not be applied so loosely and vaguely as is the case currently in economics.

30. Pesch/Ederer, 1, 1: 36-37.

31. Pesch/Ederer, 1, 1:2.

32. The term "Green Revolution" came to be associated with a dramatic transformation in grain culture, especially wheat and rice. An American agronomist, Dr. Norman Borlaug (1914-2009), began research on new strains of wheat in Mexico in 1943, when that country was suffering from severe food shortages. By 1952 Mexico was self-sufficient, becoming an exporter by 1964. Subsequently India and the Philippines also

applied his research and both went from famine conditions to becoming major food exporters. Borlaug, whose special field was plant pathology, was awarded the Nobel Peace Prize in 1970. He is acclaimed as "the man who saved a billion lives."

33. Dr. Paul Ehrlich, a biologist whose special field of expertise was butterflies, helped to shape the thinking of an entire generation with his book, *The Population Bomb* (1968). He predicted mass worldwide famine as even then irreversible, and urged strict population controls. China followed that path. His propaganda may by now have led to the loss of a billion lives!

34. Pesch/Ederer, 2, 2: 193.

35. Ibid., 78.

36. Clark, 272-273.

37. Heinrich Pesch, *Ethics and the National Economy*, trans. Rupert J. Ederer (Norfolk, VA: IHS Press, 2004). Original: *Ethik und Volkswirtschaft* (Freiburg: Herder, 1918).

38. Pesch/Ederer, *Lehrbuch/Teaching Guide*, 1, 2: 331.

39. Pius XII used the term "solidarity" in the relevant sense in his first encyclical *Summi Pontificatus* (20 October 1939) shortly after World War II broke out. As if to counter the xenophobic nationalism that underlay both World Wars, as well as the racism that drove the Nazi movement, he spoke for the first time in this encyclical of the "law of human solidarity and charity" (35). Later, in his discourses and *Christmas Messages* he used the expression, *solidarity,* countless times, as did his immediate successors Blessed John XXIII and Pope Paul VI, to whom this present encyclical is dedicated in a special way.

40. See: Pesch/Ederer, *Lehrbuch/Teaching Guide* 2, 1: ii-iv.

41. Ibid. 1, 1: 37.

42. John Maynard Keynes, who at times himself deferred to the penchant among economists for using mathematical formulations, did not have a high regard for their usefulness. He wrote in his major work, *The General Theory of Employment, Interest, and Money*: "Too large a proportion of recent 'mathematical' economics are mere concoctions, as imprecise as the initial assumptions they rest on which allow the author to lose sight of the complexities and interdependencies of the real world in a maze of pretentious and unhelpful symbols." Cf. John Maynard Keynes, *The General Theory of Employment, Interest, and Money* (New York: Harcourt, Brace and Co., 1935), 298.

43. Pope Pius XII already gave approval to the UN in principle very early in its development. In his 1948 *Christmas Message* he wrote: "May the United Nations Organization become the full and faultless expression of this international solidarity for peace, erasing from its institutions and its statutes every vestige of its origin which was of necessity a solidarity in war."

44. See, for example: Thomas E. Woods, Jr., *The Church and the Market Economy: A Catholic Defense of the Free Economy* (Lanham, MD: Lexington Books, 2005). Citing several experts in the field, the author of this book *Chapter Four* ("The Economics and Morality of Foreign Aid)" to showing how wrong the Catholic Church, specifically Pope Paul VI, was in proposing aid by rich nations to poor nations.

45. The 19 Pius XII *Christmas Messages* deserve careful study as part of the sum of the Catholic Church's social teachings. See Vincent A. Yzermans, ed., *The Major Addresses of Pope Pius XII* (St. Paul: North Central Publishing Co., 1961), 173ff.

46. Pope Paul VI challenged the return to the old classical liberalism in his Apostolic Letter, *Octogesima Adveniens* in 1971, where he referred to it as a "renewal of the liberal ideology" (35). Pope John Paul II warned against that more recently in an Apostolic Exhortation, *Ecclesia in America* (1999), noting that "...in many countries of America, a system known as 'neoliberalism' prevails, based on a purely economic conception

of man" which "considers profit and the law of the market as its only parameters, to the detriment of the dignity of and respect due individuals and peoples" (56).

47. In *Mater et Magistra* (65) we find: "This embraces the sum total of those conditions of social living, whereby men are enabled more fully and more readily to achieve their own integral perfection." It is cited in that form in *Pacem in Terris* (58). Subsequently we find it also in the Vatican II document *Gaudium et Spes* (*Pastoral Constitution on the Church in the Modern World*, par. 74).

Conclusion

A Perennially Relevant Corpus of Economic Social Teachings

After more than a century of teachings on social order generally and on also on the economic order specifically, we are in possession of a significant body of magisterial teachings, beginning with what Etienne Gilson called the "Leonine *Corpus.*"[1] That is now "an updated doctrinal *corpus*" in the words of Pope John Paul II,[2] according to whom it is also a part of the Church's "moral theology."[3] And for Catholics who are prepared to take seriously the words of Blessed John XXIII, this body of teaching on moral matters is certainly a part of the Church's *Ordinary Magisterium.*[4] It has been adapted over the past century to keep it relevant to the changing historical context (*res novae*), especially on anniversary dates of *Rerum Novarum.* Thus, we have here a splendid example of the development of doctrine in the legitimate sense of that term.[5]

Given the sheer volume of his teachings and the fact that no single authority is referred to more frequently in Vatican II documents overall, to not include the significant contributions of Pius XII to the Catholic Church's social doctrine may be regarded as one of the *lacunae* of this commentary.[6] Actually they are so extensive that they merit a separate study devoted to that brilliant pope, whom a characteristically enthusiastic John XIII already referred to unofficially as a "Doctor of the Church."[7]

Two other statements on social teaching are also not included, and that is by no means because they are insignificant. *Gaudium et Spes* is one of the sixteen documents which came out of the historic Second Vatican Council. Its English language title is *Pastoral Constitution on the Church in the Modern World*, and it was issued with papal approval on December 7, 1965. Then there is *Octogesima Adveniens* which, unlike the other documents in this commentary, is not an encyclical but an Apostolic Letter addressed by Pope Paul VI to Cardinal Maurice Roy, then President of the Council of the Laity and of the Pontifical Commission for Justice and Peace. It appeared on May 14, 1971 to commemorate the 80th anniversary of *Rerum Novarum.*

It is the purpose of this commentary to address the Church's teachings relating to the economic order of society. Both *Gaudium et Spes* and *Octogesima Adveniens* are, each in its own way, of a different genre than the others. They possess a broader dimension going well beyond the specifically economic aspects of the social order.

Gaudium et Spes is to a large extent a capsule summary of prior papal teachings on the social order. It has two parts, each with several chapters. These range across the entire spectrum of the social order, from the family to the international political community. The third chapter of Part II addresses the economic order. It is entitled "Socio-Economic Life," and it reaffirms basically what is found in the papal social encyclicals from *Rerum Novarum* until *Mater et Magistra*, which was the last one issued prior to the Second Vatican Council. Subsequent encyclicals nevertheless include many references to *Gaudium et Spes.*

Octogesima Adveniens is another matter. There are important sociological and political considerations like urbanization with all of its attendant problems, also problems faced by contemporary youth in that setting, the role of women in modern society, discrimination because of "race, origin, color, culture, sex or religion (16)," emigrants seeking employment far from home, the environment, the influential and often problematical role of the media. Two significant elements in this document concern economics more or less directly. One has to do with ideologies, the other with methodology.

On ideology, there is the precautionary note that, even while there has been "a retreat of ideologies" which could prove "favorable for an openness to the concrete transcendence of Christianity, there is also "a more accentuated sliding towards a new positivism" (29). While the Marxian ideology was still a more intense concern of the Church in 1981, dramatic changes of the more recent era, following the collapse of the Soviet Empire after 1989, have perhaps borne out what Paul VI called to mind in *Octogesima Adveniens*, par. 30, quoting John XXIII: "'Neither can false philosophical teachings regarding the nature, origin and destiny of the universe and of man be identified with historical movements that have economic, social, cultural or political ends, not even when these movements have originated from those teachings and have drawn and still draw inspiration therefrom.'" That statement caused considerable controversy when it first appeared in *Pacem in Terris* in 1963. Blessed John XXIII had proposed that "teachings, once they are drawn up and defined, remain always the same, while the movements being concerned with historical situations in constant evolution, cannot but be influenced by these latter and cannot avoid, therefore, being subject to changes, even of a profound nature."[8] Retrospectively, one can certainly affirm that the flow of events in the Communist world were indeed influenced by the actual historical situations in constant evolution" so that they became more and more detached from the original Marxian dogmas. Nevertheless, those words were originally written in 1963; and in 1971 Pope Paul VI still saw fit to warn that Christians should not permit themselves to be carried away by real or apparent changes in the Communist world.

At the same time, Pope Paul could also see and view with anxiety "a renewal of the liberal ideology"(35). He had already foreclosed on a Christian adopting that ideology, with the words:

> ...nor can he adhere to the liberal ideology which believes it exalts individual freedom by withdrawing it from every limitation, by stimulating it through exclusive seeking of interest and power, and by considering social solidarities as more or less automatic consequences of individual initiatives, not as an aim and a major criterion of the value of the social organization (26).[9]

The "renewal of the liberal ideology" came to some extent as a reaction against "the increasingly overwhelming hold of organizations, and...the totalitarian tendencies of political powers." One should note that so far as Americans were concerned, this warning came nearly a decade before the start of the Reagan administration (also the Thatcher era in England) which already constituted a backlash in the direction of precisely the so-called free market ideology that is still designated in encyclical language and in certain European circles as economic liberalism.[10] In a statement which needs to be taken far more seriously than it has until now, Pope Paul VI warned that "Christians who take this path tend to idealize liberalism in their turn, making it a proclamation in favor of freedom...forgetting that at the very root of philosophical liberalism is an erroneous affirmation of the autonomy of the individual, his motivation, and the exercise of his liberty" (35). The Christian is urged instead to "draw from the sources of his faith and the Church's teaching the necessary principles and suitable criteria to avoid permitting himself to be first attracted by and then imprisoned within a system." He should go "beyond every system, without however failing to commit himself concretely to serving his brothers" (36). Thus, he may avoid the "weaknesses of ideologies" then "trying to affirm themselves...in concrete systems" like "bureaucratic socialism, technocratic capitalism and authoritarian democracy" (37).

That led Pope Paul directly into a discussion of methodology in what he referred to here as the "human sciences." He saw a problem arising because our world is "dominated by scientific and technological change which threatens to drag it towards a new positivism" (38). A twofold problem arises in that ambience, because "man now finds that he himself is as it were imprisoned within his own rationality," so that "he in turn becomes the object of science." No one could deny Pope Paul's statement that "the 'human sciences' are today enjoying a significant flowering." They are usually referred to as "social sciences," and it is perhaps significant that Paul VI chose to refer to them as "human sciences." They subject to "critical and radical examination the hitherto accepted knowledge about man, on the grounds that this knowledge seems either too empirical or too theoretical." Yet, on the other hand, "methodological necessity and ideological presuppositions too often lead the human sciences to isolate, in the various situations, certain aspects of man, and yet to give these an explanation which claims to be complete or at least an interpretation which is meant to be all-embracing from a purely quantitative or phenomenological point of view."

This should raise the eyebrows of those social scientists, including economists, who have yielded to the temptation of positivistic denial of the legitimacy of value judgments in "true sciences," meanwhile trying to reduce all of the principles and dynamics of their sciences to mathematical terms. It may indeed seem odd that a pope, exercising his magisterial position, should have to lecture them on proper methodology. Paul VI did so, however, because he saw such "scientific reduction" as betraying "a dangerous presupposition." His concern was expressed in this urgent statement: "To give a privileged position in this way to such an aspect of analysis is to mutilate man and, under the pretext of scientific procedure, to make it impossible to understand man in his totality" (38). Eventually the human sciences can instigate action, "giving rise to the elaboration of models of society to be subsequently imposed on men as scientifically tested types of behavior." In other words, ultimately the "human sciences" are, in Aristotelian terms, practical, not merely speculative sciences. Thus, their object is something which can be done or left undone of man's free choice; and that makes them subject to the moral law—which is clearly an appropriate province of papal commentary and admonition. That is why Pope Paul VI saw in social science a "grave danger for societies of tomorrow and for man himself," because he "can become the object of manipulation directing his desires and needs and modifying his behavior and even his system of values" (39). Even if "all agree to build a new society at the service of men, it is still essential to know what sort of man is in question" (39). One must recall at this point that it was this Pope who termed the Church "an expert in humanity," and also a champion of a "true humanism."[11] We are permitted to conclude that only a perceived "great danger for societies of tomorrow and for man himself" would prompt a Roman Catholic pope, in the exercise of his magisterial position to involve himself in the methodology of the social sciences, including economics.[12]

It is unlikely that there will be no further continuation of social teachings by future popes in keeping with the tradition that was pioneered and securely established by Leo XIII well over a century ago. But even now, the present and immediate future generations already have sufficient guidelines to do what was the ultimate purpose of these social teachings: to put the principles into action in order to reorder our present post-Christian society into one more in conformity with Christian principles. What Pius XII said in 1952 may be even more valid in a certain sense now as we move onward into the new millennium.[13]

> This is not the moment to discuss, to search for new principles, to fix new aims and goals. Both the one and the other, already known and in substance recognized since they were given by Christ Himself, clearly taught by the Church down the ages, and adapted to immediate circumstances by the late Supreme Pontiffs, need nothing more now than concrete realization."

Notes

1. Etienne Gilson, ed., *The Church Speaks to the Modern World* (Garden City: Doubleday & Co., 1954), 29.

2. Pope John Paul II, *Sollicitudo Rei Socialis,* par. 1.

3. Ibid. par. 41.

4. John XXIII, *Mater et Magistra,* pars. 218, and 223. There has been at work a kind of reductionist trend within the Church since Vatican II, to limit the infallible teaching authority of the papacy to a few, rare, solemn proclamations which specifically invoke the infallible power recognized in the papacy and defined by the First Vatican Council. Indeed, Pius XII had already noted this fallacious tendency in his encyclical *Humani Generis* in 1950. Ignored almost entirely is what is called the *ordinary magisterium,* exercised far more frequently by popes than the *extraordinary magisterium.* Also, it is sometimes forgotten that papal authority applies to both faith *and* morals. Since papal social encyclicals involve mostly moral issues (justice, charity, etc.), they are also a part of that ordinary *magisterium*, as Blessed John XXIII made clear once and for all.

5. Of its nature, Church doctrine relating to faith and morals does not change, in the sense of reversing its direction. There is development, however, inasmuch as its teachings come to be applied in different ways to changing historical situations. In the storms of theological controversy which beset the Church, and which upset and confused many of the faithful especially following Vatican II, it was sometimes proposed that doctrines had changed precisely in the sense that they had been reversed, e.g., on contraception.

6. Pius XII, whose voluminous teachings are cited more than any other single human source in the Vatican II documents, never wrote an encyclical that was declared to be specifically a *social* one. This is not to say that he did not teach on social matters ranging from the family, to the economic and political order, also at the international level. Actually, Swiss Dominican scholars headed by the Arthur Utz published three large volumes containing his social teachings: Arthur-Fridolin Utz, O.P., and Joseph-Fulko Groner, O.P., *Soziale Summe Pius XII* (Freiburg (Switzerland): Paulus Verlag, 1954–1961. Probably the first encyclical of Pius XII's pontificate, *Summi Pontificatus* (1939), should be regarded as a social encyclical because of its content. His illustrious *Christmas Messages*, in particular, represent a compendium of his social teachings.

7. John XXIII, who succeeded Pius XII as pope, in his own first *Christmas Message* of December 23, 1958, stated that "Moreover, quite apart from any official declaration, which would be premature, the threefold title of Eminent Teacher (*Doctor Optimus*), Light of Holy Church, and Lover of the Divine Law well befits the blessed memory of him, the Pontiff of our favored age."

8. Cf. John XXIII, *Pacem in Terris,* par. 159.

9. Paul VI began using the expression, "solidarity," with great frequency in addresses and written proclamations throughout his pontificate. In *Octogesima Adveniens,* for example, it appears in the relevant sense no less than ten times. However, it is necessary to point out that this important concept was used also, for perhaps the first time, by Pius XII in the same sense that Pope John Paul II used when declaring it "a Christian virtue" in *Sollicitudo Rei Socialis.* In *Summi Pontificatus* (1939) we find reference to "that law of human solidarity and charity..." (30), and in his *Christmas Message* of 1952 on *The Rights of Man,* it emerged as a dominant theme.

10. It is worth recalling again that the terms "liberal" and "liberalism" are used in social encyclicals, as is still common in much of European discourse, to refer to the original economic liberalism, implying, free markets, free trade, free enterprise, free competition, etc., in other words as virtually the opposite of what that term has come to mean in current usage in the United States.

11. Cf. *Populorum Progressio*, pars. 13, 42.

12. Here, once again, Pius XII had already hinted at this problem and carried that theme through three successive *Christmas Messages* in 1953, 1954, and 1955. In 1953 he

indicated that "the living realities of the individual person and of society...cannot be analyzed into quantitative relationships." In 1954, he pointed out that "in relations between men, even merely economic relations, nothing is produced spontaneously—as does occur in nature, which is subject to necessary laws—but everything depends substantially on the spirit." And in the 1955 Message this idea recurred in the statement "that a quantitative method, however perfected, neither can, nor ought to, control the social and historical reality of human life." See Vincent A. Yzermans, ed., *The Major Addresses of Pope Pius XII* (St. Paul: North Central Publishing Co., 1961), 2: 177,191, 203.

Heinrich Pesch, S.J., who developed the outlines for an economic system based on the principle of solidarity, dealt extensively with this methodological problem from the perspective of a trained economist. He found the mathematical method to be wholly inadequate and inappropriate for economic analysis, among other reasons, because it was based on a positivistic approach to what is a social science. Cf. Heinrich Pesch, *Lehrbuch der Nationalökonomie* (Freiburg im Br.: Herder, 1924), vol. I: 561-563; also the English translation: *Lehrbuch der Nationalökonomie/Teaching Guide to Economics* (Lewiston, NY: Edwin Mellen Press, 2002), vol. I, bk.2: 364-366).

13. Pius XII, *Address* in St. Peter's Square on February 10, 1952. Cf. Yzermans, 1: 193.

Bibliography

Abbott, Walter M., General Editor. *The Documents of Vatican II.* New York: The Guild Press, 1966.

Andreae, Clemens-August. *Mensch und Wirtschaft.* Innsbruck: Tyrolia-Verlag, 1966.

Benedict XVI. Encyclical Letter *Caritas in Veritate.* Vatican City: Libreria Editrice Vaticana, 2009.

Bock, Edward C. *Wilhelm Von Ketteler, Bishop of Mainz: His Life, Times and Ideas.* Washington, D C: University Press of America,1977.

Bruehl, Charles P. *The Pope's Plan.* New York: The Devin Adair Co., 1939.

Carlen, Claudia IHM (ed.), *The Papal Encyclicals.* 5 vols. N.p.: McGrath, 1981.

Carrier, Hervé. *The Social Doctrine of the Church Revisited.* Vatican City: The Pontifical Council for Justice and Peace, 1990.

Charles, Rodger, S.J. *The Social Teaching of Vatican II.* San Francisco: Ignatius Press, 1982.

Chinigo, Michael, ed. *The Pope Speaks.* New York: Pantheon Books Inc., 1957.

———. *The Teachings of Pope John XXIII.* New York: Grosset & Dunlap, 1967.

The Church and Reconstruction of the Modern World: The Social Encyclicals of Pius XI. Edited, with an Introduction by Terence P. McLaughlin. C.S.B. Garden City, NY: Doubleday Image Books, 1957.

Clark, Colin. *Population Growth and Land Use.* New York: St Martin's Press,1968.

Compendium of the Social Doctrine of the Church. Washington, DC: United States Conference of Catholic Bishops, 2004.

Coughlin, Charles, E. *A Series of Lectures on Social Justice.* Royal Oak, MI: Radio League of the Little Flower, 1935.

Cronin, John, F., *Catholic Social Principles,* Milwaukee: Bruce, 1950.

Dempsey, Bernard W., S.J. *The Functional Economy.* Englewood Cliffs, NJ: Prentice-Hall, 1958.

Dirksen, Cletus, C.PP.S., *Catholic Social Principles.* St. Louis: Herder, 1961.

Doctrina Pontificia III (*Documentos Sociales*). Madrid: Biblioteca de Autores Cristianos, 1964.

Ederer, Rupert J. *The Evolution of Money.* Washington, DC: Public Affairs Press, 1964.

——. *Heinrich Pesch on Solidarist Economics.* Lanham, MD: University Press of America, 1998.

——. *The Social Teachings of Wilhelm Emmanuel von Ketteler.* Washington, DC: University Press of America, 1981.

Encyclicals and Other Messages of John XXIII. Washington, DC: The Pope Speaks Press, 1964.
Encyclopedia of Catholic Social Thought, Social Science, and Social Policy. 2 vols. Ed. Michael L. Coulter, Stephen Krason, Richard S. Myers, and Joseph Varacalli. Lanham, MD: Scarecrow Press, 2007.
Fahey, Denis C.S.Sp. *The Mystical Body of Christ and the Reorganization of Society.* Cork: The Forum Press, 1945.
Flannery, Austin, O.P. *Vatican II,* Vol. 1. Collegeville, MN: Liturgical Press, 1975.
Flannery, Austin, O.P. *Vatican II,* Vol. 2. Boston: St. Paul Editions, 1982.
Freemantle, Anne, Editor. *The Papal Encyclicals in their Historical Context.* New York: G.P. Putnam, 1956.
Gearty, Patrick W. *The Economic Thought of Msgr. John A. Ryan.* Washington. DC: Catholic University of America Press, 1953.
Gilson, Etienne. *The Church Speaks to the Modern World: The Social Teachings of Leo XIII.* Garden City, NY: Image Books, 1954.
Giordani, Igino. *The Social Message of Jesus.* Patterson, NJ: St. Anthony Guild Press, 1943.
Graham, John T. *Donoso Cortés.* Columbia, MO.: University of Missouri Press, 1974.
Guerry, Emil (Archbishop). *The Social Doctrine of the Catholic Church.* New York: Alba House, 1961.
Haas, Francis J. *Man & Society.* New York: Appleton-Century-Crofts, 1952.
Habsburg, Otto von. *The Social Order of Tomorrow.* Westminster, MD: Newman Press, 1959.
Herrera, Robert A. *Donoso Cortés.* Grand Rapids, MI: Eerdmans, 1995.
Höffner, Joseph (Cardinal). *Christian Social Teaching.* Bratislava: LC, 1983.
Husslein, Joseph, S.J. *Social Wellsprings.* 2 vols. Milwaukee: Bruce, 1940, 1942.
Institute of Social Order at St. Louis University. *Social Orientations.* Chicago: Loyola University Press, 1954.
John XXIII. *Mater et Magistra.* Trans. William J. Gibbons, S.J. In *Seven Great Encyclicals.* Glen Rock, NJ: Paulist Press, 1963, 217-274.
John Paul II. *Centesimus Annus.* Sherbrooke, Quebec: Éditions Paulines, 1991.
——. *Encyclical Letter On Human Work (Laborem Exercens).* Boston: St. Paul Editions, 1981.
——. *Encyclical Letter On Social Concern* (*Sollicitudo Rei Socialis*). Boston: St. Paul Editions, 1987.
Leo XIII. *Rerum Novarum.* In *Seven Great Encyclicals.* Glen Rock, NJ: Paulist Press, 1963, 1-36.
Marchione, Sister Margherita. *Papa Pio XII : An Anthology on the 70th Anniversary of His Coronation.* Vatican City: Libreria Editrice Vaticana, 2009.
——. *Pope Pius XII. History and Hagiography.* Vatican City: Libreria Editrice Vaticana, 2010.
Marx, Reinhard (Archbishop). *Das Kapital.* Munich: Pattloch Verlag, 2008.
Masse, Benjamin, S. J. *Justice for All.* Milwaukee: Bruce, 1964.
Messner, Johannes. *Social Ethics.* St. Louis: Herder, 1964.
——. *Das Gemeinwohl.* Osnabrück: Verlag A. Fromm, 1962.
——. *Dolfuss: An Austrian Patriot.* Norfolk, VA: IHS Press, 2004.
Miller, Raymond J. *Forty Years After: Pius XI and the Social Order.* St. Paul, MN: Radio Replies Press, 1947.
Mueller, Franz H. *The Church and the Social Question.* Washington: The American Enterprise Institute, 1984.
——. *Soziale Theorie des Betriebes.* Berlin: Duncker & Humblot, 1952.
——. *Heinrich Pesch: Sein Leben und seine Lehre.* Cologne: J.P. Bachem, 1980.

Naughton, Michael. *The Good Stewards*. Lanham, MD: University Press of America, 1992.

Nell-Breuning, Oswald von. *Reorganization of Social Economy*. Trans. Bernard W. Dempsey, S.J. Milwaukee: Bruce, 1936-37.

Paul VI. *The Coming Eightieth (Octogesima Adveniens)*. Boston: St. Paul Editions, 1971.

——. *On the Development of Peoples (Populorum Progressio)*. Washington, DC: United States Catholic Conference, 1967.

Pesch, Heinrich. *Lehrbuch der Nationalökonomie/Teaching Guide to Economics*. Trans. Rupert J. Ederer. 5 vols. In 10 Books. Lewiston, NY: Edwin Mellen Press, 2002-2003.

——. *Liberalism, Socialism, and Christian Social Order*. Trans. Rupert J. Ederer. 5 vols. Lewiston: Edwin Mellen Press, 2002-2006.

——. *Ethics and the National Economy*. Trans. Rupert J. Ederer. Norfolk, VA: IHS Press, 2004.

Peterson, David J. *Revoking the Moral Order*. Lanham, MD: Lexington Books, 1999.

Pius XI. *Quadragesimo Anno*. In *Seven Great Encyclicals*. Glen Rock, NJ: Paulist Press, 1963, 125-168.

Ryan, John A. *Distributive Justice*. New York: Macmillan, 1916.

_____. *The Living Wage: Its Ethical and Economic Aspects*. New York: Macmillan, 1906.

Schasching, Johann S.J. *Katholische Soziallehre und Moderne Apostolat*. Innsbruck: Tyrolia-Verlag, 1956.

——. *Die Soziale Botschaft der Kirche von Leo XIII bis Johannes XXIII*. Innsbruck: Tyrolia-Verlag, 1963.

Schumacher, E.F. *Small is Beautiful*. New York: Harper & Row, 1973.

Seven Great Encyclicals. Glen Rock, NJ: Paulist Press, 1963.

Utz, Arthur F., and Groner, Joseph F., *Die Soziale Summe Pius XII*. 3 vols. Freiburg (Switzerland): Paulusverlag, 1954-1961.

Yzermans, Vincent, A., ed. *The Major Addresses of Pope Pius XII*. 2 vols. St. Paul, MN: North Central Publishing Co., 1961.

Index

About the Author

Rupert J. Ederer is Professor of Economics *Emeritus* at the Buffalo State College branch of the State University of New York. He was born in Munich, Germany in 1923, and immigrated to the United States with the Ederer family in 1926. After serving in the U. S. Army during World War II, he earned his M.A. (1950) and Ph.D (1954) in economics at St. Louis University. He taught successively at St. Bonaventure University (N.Y.), Quincy College (Ill.), Canisius College (Buffalo, N.Y.), and Rosary Hill College (Amherst, N. Y.). Professor Ederer also served as Lecturer in the Extension Division of the Cornell University School of Industrial and Labor Relations, and for four years as Research Director for the Switchman's Union of North America. He has published widely in various journals, and there are also several books. These include: *The Evolution of Money* (1964); *The Social Teachings of Wilhelm Emmanuel von Ketteler* (1980); *Ethics and the National Economy* (1988, 2004); *Heinrich Pesch on Solidarist Economics* (1998). After retiring from teaching in 1985, Professor Ederer translated into English Heinrich Pesch's five volume *Lehrbuch der Nationalökonomie*, and his *Liberalismus, Sozialismus, und christliche Gesellschaftsordnung*. The former was published between 2002 and 2003 in ten volumes as the *Lehrbuch der Nationalökonomie/Teaching Guide to Economics.* The later appeared in five volumes as *Liberalism, Socialism and Christian Social Order* between 2000 and 2006. Both were published by the Edwin Mellen Press of Lewiston, N.Y.